BOTTOM
of the
POT

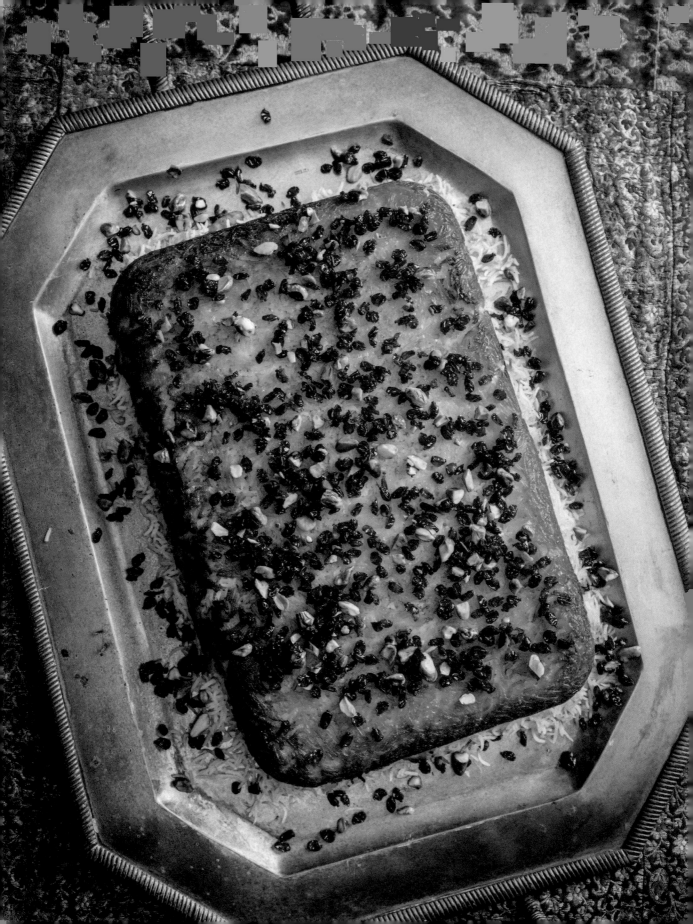

For Luna and Soleil,
who light up my nights and my days

Our fellow diners stopped to watch. They were displaced
people, just like us, and they understood all too well
these kinds of reunions, these moments when a piece of your
old house comes floating by in the river.

—ABRAHAM VERGHESE, *CUTTING FOR STONE*

CONTENTS

PROLOGUE
THE JOURNEY HOME

LOS ANGELES, 2016

It begins with rice. As it always has.

The unmistakable aroma of *chelo*—Persian steamed rice—greets me at the end of the long hallway in our Los Angeles apartment building. It's a nondescript labyrinth of a passageway, unable to will itself out of the 1970s. Walls coated in an unfortunate shade of pink merge into the worn industrial carpet. Every stain, crack in the wall, and fault in the ceiling is a constant reminder that the Big One—this is California, after all—is right around the corner. My entire family is visiting, and I know Maman, my mother, will have dinner prepared.

The path that leads to our apartment is divided every twenty feet by heavy metal doors intended to seal off smoke and flames, in case of an emergency. As I pause outside the very first door, I can't help noticing that these firewalls have done a pretty lousy job of containing the most important smell in my life.

Iranians have breached the system.

With rice.

The intoxicating scent carries a promise for all who encounter it. The very same promise that has traveled with me over three continents and three decades. The vibrant smells and flavors have shifted, changed, and adapted as they continually seek a home, a place to land. Longing to claim their rightful place over time, borders, cultures, and spice cupboards, much like my own journey. But they are always following the same promise—the promise of family and friends gathered around a table.

The stealthy trespasser encircles me, beckoning me forward, enticing and taunting me with the welcoming scene that I know lies ahead. A cramped kitchen table set with mismatched platters, big and small. There will be *sabzi khordan*—a platter of fresh green herbs whose curious presence tends to take the uninitiated by surprise—to balance out the meal and aid digestion. (Persians are forever obsessed with digestion.) There might be a small bowl of *aash*—a hearty Persian soup—to open up the appetite. A jar of *torshi*—sour pickles—will be passed around to liven up both meal and conversation with a tangy burst of flavor. A glorious bowl of *maast-o-khiar*—yogurt and cucumber—the ambassador of each and every meal, proudly embracing its role of cutting through the richness of any dish and, on occasion, cooling those impassioned Persian constitutions. Someone will ask for a piece of bread to make a *loghmeh* (the perfect bite) with a slice of briny *paneer* (cheese) and a couple of soaked walnuts. The fresh herbs will sneak their way in as well.

There will be congratulatory clapping, intricate finger-snapping, and Baba, my father, and my brother, Ramin, might even break out into song and dance as the *khoresh* is brought to the table. If there is rice, there is bound to be khoresh—a vibrant, flavorful stew. Maman will most certainly *tarof* by deflecting all compliments and wondering out loud if the khoresh simmered long enough, if the rice cooked too long, and if there is enough food to go around.

Between the folds of these warm promises, however, there hides a hint of bittersweet—a sense of longing and melancholy. Once again, the beat of nostalgia courses through my body. Memory tapping lightly at my door. Sometimes I grant it permission; sometimes I don't. It's a slippery slope—the unpaved road of memory.

But tonight, I am in a generous mood. So I welcome it in, both the bitter and the sweet, and I follow the scent of rice as I walk down the hallway.

As I fumble around my purse in search of keys, I can hear my stepmother, Kumi, sister-in-law, Teresa, and nephew, Jordan, usher everyone to take their places at the kitchen table. Mismatched chairs join the mismatched plates. It's not a quiet affair. After all, we don't hail from a quiet corner of the world. There will be lively discussion and passionate debate. To the unaccustomed ear it will sound much more serious than it really is. Joke-telling, philoso-phizing, poetry reciting, and politicizing. And at some point, everyone will attempt to make some grand proclamation about *che bayad kard*—what's to be done.

What's to be done about the state of the world, the state of the Middle East, the price of yogurt, the price of oil. What's to be done with the leftovers and tomorrow night's dinner. Talk of tomorrow's meals will dominate before tonight's dinner is even served. All the while, Maman will be fretting about one thing or another as she carefully adds a couple of tablespoons of water to sunset-hued saffron, magically releasing its scent, color, and thousands of years of history. No matter where the meal or how times have changed, there is always saffron, steeped in water. Though tastes, recipes, and preparations evolve, as they should, some traditions are set in stone.

The stealthy invader has lost its patience and snuck back through the crack under the door, as only it can. Time is of the essence when it comes to serving Iranian rice. Through the door and over the jangle of my keys, I hear my children, Luna and Soleil, gather around with bated breath and fingers crossed. And that can only mean one thing: it's time to flip the rice. The serving dish goes over the pot. The air turns thick with anticipation and hope.

There's always hope.

Hope for a successful and crunchy *tahdig*—the coveted crispy rice at the bottom of the pot. Hope for the price of yogurt to go down. Hope for fresh and new ideas to emerge for tomorrow night's dinner. Hope for the day when the embers that continually ignite and set ablaze the Middle East—that region that gave birth to civilization, yet has struggled so immensely to gently cradle it in its arms—finally crackle and burn off.

There's always hope.

I place a firm grip on the doorknob and swing the apartment door open, greeted by the exultant sound of success. The *swish* of the release as the rice drops from pot to dish. The reveal as the pot is pulled up and away. And there she presents herself in all her glory—golden and regal—the tahdig herself. I look over to Maman. Her hands don't hold the rice pot, as I was expecting. Instead, she has a gentle hand on my husband's shoulder. She stands behind him as he proudly holds the tahdig dish in front of him. To my surprise, it hasn't been Maman helming the kitchen, calling forth the beautiful storm of scents and memories that pulled me home, but rather my husband, Drew. He lets out a deep sigh of relief and flashes me a triumphant smile. Our children and the rest of the family break out into joyous cheers and thunderous applause. The rice, and tahdig-making torch, have been passed.

Welcome home.

INTRODUCTION

My family left Iran when I was eight years old. It was the height of the 1979 Iranian Revolution and hostage crisis. Those were chaotic and uncertain times, and my recollections of Iran flicker in and out of focus. Amid the murmurs of unrest on the streets of Tehran there were family trips to the Caspian Sea, to the lush landscapes and rice paddies of Shomal—the north, my father's birthplace. There, every day, you could find the freshest seafood, prepared simply, with plenty of crushed garlic, a hint of mint, and a squeeze of *narenj*—Seville orange.

There were summer vacations at my grandfather's house in Tabriz, my mother's birthplace, a traditional Persian home that has forever cemented itself in my memory as a majestic labyrinth. There, under a canopy of fruit trees, we'd lunch on gigantic meatballs stuffed with nuts and dried fruits that carried with them the scents of the colorful spice bazaars we strolled through. And in Tehran, my birthplace, there was always a home-cooked meal of *chelo khoresh*—rice and stew—to gather around at our modest apartment kitchen table. It was also at that very same table that the difficult decision was made to leave our home, without knowing that we would be leaving it for good. Leaving it without entrusting to memory the final meal eaten around that kitchen table.

Memory is an elusive seductress, hard to pin down. She teases with a hazy snapshot of what once was. The same picture shifts, seen through various filters, depending on who is doing the remembering. Who is doing the recounting. A newly opened bottle of rose water, the bitter tang of a dried lime. Sometimes that's all it takes to get lost in her grip.

The murmurs of unrest turned into demonstrations, which became a revolution, leading to blackouts, sirens, and bombs. We quickly said our good-byes to relatives, many of whom we would never see again, and overnight, life changed entirely as we departed for Italy. My parents had met in Rome, a decade earlier, as young students. My mother, a poet, immersing herself in Italian literature, and my father studying architecture. My older brother, Ramin, was born there. Rome was a home away from home, a safe haven for us. On Tuesday nights we gathered around a simple plate of fresh mozzarella, tomatoes, and basil with a sprinkle of salt and a drizzle of olive oil. Sunday nights consisted of homestyle *chelo kabab*—rice with pan-grilled kabab—while we watched an extravagant Italian variety show.

We spent a brief, but formative, few years in Rome before eventually immigrating to Canada. Always, with the scent of saffron and a perfectly steamed pot of rice trailing us across oceans and borders. It took a revolution, and thousands of miles between me and Iran, the land I once called home, to fully comprehend the effect a simple pot of rice would have on my life.

It was during those years in our new Canadian home that I became aware of the power of my mother's home-cooked Persian meals. Instead of spending time explaining to my new Canadian friends where Iran was on the map, and teaching them how to properly pro-nounce the name of the country (*I-ran. You ran where? It's Eee-raan. Persian, Iranian, Persia, Iran, they all refer to the same land and the same people.*) and trying to dispel the sensational-ized images of my homeland that would flash across the nightly news, all I had to do was implement my secret weapon: after-school playdates that drifted into dinner. There is not a kid in the world who does not fall for and love a crispy *tahdig*, the Trojan horse of Persian cooking. This was food that had the unique ability to break down barriers, introducing and connecting my newly made friends to my culture and to me.

Shortly after graduating from university, I left Vancouver for Los Angeles in search of sunny skies and in pursuit of an acting career. In Los Angeles I quickly found myself hungry. Not because of an actual lack of food, but because I was starved for a home-cooked Persian meal, for a taste of home. Notebook and pencil in hand, I called up my mother, and I frantically took notes to re-create my favorite Persian dishes.

The "recipes" Maman shared with me were nothing more than a bare-bones list of ingredients, always with the proviso to use whatever was available in the fridge or pantry.

"Make do with what you have" and "Cook with your eyes, touch, nose, and taste" were and still are her mottos. Amounts were specified in such terms as "as much as you like," "the tip of a knife," "just enough for its scent to dance around the kitchen, making your head spin and your heart thump," "as much as will make it tasty," and my favorite: "whatever it takes to bring it to life." This was cooking that relied on intuition, constant tasting, and a good dose of lemon juice. Extracting recipes from my mother and other family members and friends was not a straightforward process. It also meant patiently listening to the stories each dish or ingredient sparked. The road from a sprinkle of saffron to dancing the night away in the cafés of 1952 Tehran is short indeed.

A few years later, as I found my way around my kitchen and started cooking for my own family, those "recipes" took on a life of their own, simmering with their own stories at the bottom of the pot. The kitchen became a place where I could escape, relax, and reconnect with myself. The chopping board became my yoga mat, in true L.A. style.

This book is a collection of recipes and stories from the past and present. These are the home-cooked meals that I grew up eating and the everyday food that I now prepare for my own family. Traditional Persian food varies from region to region, neighborhood to neighborhood, and home to home. Everyone has very strong feelings about the food from their particular region. The same stew can differ slightly in taste and preparation depending on its geographical location. This is what I refer to as accented food. My cooking is naturally a reflection of most of my life lived outside Iran, and it simmers with its own multicultural accent. But at its core it's home cooking, and it's meant to be shared with family and friends—with plenty of storytelling sprinkled in.

My hope is that once you start cooking from this book, the recipes will pick up on your accent, and they will become a part of your story.

LIMOO OMANI (DRIED LIMES)

MUSIR (PERSIAN DRIED SHALLOTS)

ZERESHK (BARBERRIES)

MAKING IT DELICIOUS

Iranians hold very strong feelings about what traditional Persian food should taste like, smell like, and look like, but the spirit of Persian cooking itself is quite forgiving. If there is a spice or herb you don't like, omit it. If your taste buds tell you to use more of something, do so. And no matter what, always remember to "make it delicious." This is the phrase that has followed me from home to home and from kitchen to kitchen. There comes a moment in the cooking process where you have followed the recipe exactly as written, but it still needs that extra little something. This is what my mother calls the *hala khosh mazash kon*, the "now make it delicious" moment. This is when you, your hand, your taste buds, your current mood, and your instincts step in and add that extra little something to bring a dish to life, to give it character. This moment usually doesn't come at the very end of the cooking process but somewhere in the middle. Taste as you go. Taste for salt and acidity (see Pucker Up, page 10). Add water to thin out, or remove the lid to thicken, or simply allow the dish to simmer longer to "blossom, mature, and fall into place." On the following pages are a few of the ingredients in my Persian-inspired pantry, spice cupboard, fridge, and freezer that go into bringing a dish to life and making it delicious.

Some of the ingredients in my pantry might not be as familiar to you or might take a little bit of legwork to find. In each ingredient description I specify where you might be able to shop for it. Online sites are always a sure bet to find all of the ingredients mentioned here. I've also tried to incorporate the rare ingredients throughout the book, giving you plenty of opportunities to use them in dishes ranging from savory to sweets to drinks.

THE PERSIAN PALATE

Pucker Up

So, what does Persian food taste like? Fragrant, flavorful, fresh, elegant, cozy, unfussy, like a love poem, quietly assertive, certainly never shy. Always bright.

The quintessential taste that distinguishes Persian food from others is sour. Iranians have an intense love affair with all things tangy. Not an overwhelming, make-you-wince kind of tang, but the kind that wakes up your taste buds. A variety of acids are used to cut through the richness of stews, to brighten up a hearty pot of *aash*—Persian-style soups—and to "bring to life" and balance every bite.

Most of the souring ingredients used in this book, such as lemons, limes, yogurt, and pomegranate molasses, are common and easy to find. A few, such as dried limes or verjuice (the juice of unripe sour green grapes) might be less familiar, but they are definitely worth seeking out to add a distinct Persian tang to liven up any dish in your kitchen.

See page 349 for the Pucker Up ingredients list.

A Field of Greens—*Sabzi*—Fresh and Dried

On any given day, you'll find our kitchen table draped with kitchen towels topped with a veritable field of fresh green herbs. Iranian cooking depends on aromatic green herbs—called *sabzi*, deriving from the word *sabz*, which means "green"—in masses. Parsley, cilantro, dill, fenugreek, tarragon, mint, basil, along with alliums such as green onions, chives, and leeks, are cooked in any number of combinations in stews, aash, or *kookoos*—Iranian-style frittatas. And, of course, a meal wouldn't be complete or considered balanced without a side platter of fresh green herbs—Sabzi Khordan (page 32).

Washing and chopping bunches upon bunches of herbs takes time and patience, and that

is not always convenient and suited to our modern, busy lives. But the reward of a bright and vibrant stew like Morgh-e Torsh (page 167) for a Sunday night dinner or a soothing aash to chase the winter blues away makes it all well worth it. Here are some tips on how to simplify this process.

SHOPPING: When we first moved to Vancouver from Iran via Italy, we were equally confused and amused by the tiny packages of herbs you could on occasion find in the supermarkets. Iranian dishes call for herbs in abundant bunches, as opposed to cups, let alone herbs measured by the tablespoon. That is also how I have written quantities for greens in this book—by the bunches and handfuls. (Stuffing and packing herbs into measuring cups and spoons sucks out every ounce of joy in me and goes against any natural Persian cooking instinct. But, should you enjoy and require it, whenever possible I have also included rough measurements of herbs forced into measuring utensils.) Don't fret over how big or small your handful is; just skip the overpriced small packages, grab a loose bunch, and get cooking. Thankfully, these days you can find beautiful stacks of fresh green herbs at just about any local supermarket or farmers' market. Generally, one bunch of fresh herbs is about four ounces.

CLEANING: Whenever possible I try to have my green herbs prepped ahead of time (This also goes for most vegetables, salad greens, etc.) Taking a few minutes to do this not only alleviates unnecessary kitchen stress, but also makes cooking more of a pleasure and something to look forward to. When I get home from the market, I fill my kitchen sink or the bowl of my salad spinner (or any large bowl) with fresh water, and I submerge the greens. Give them time to relax and bathe for a few minutes, then gently lift them up and out of the water so you don't disturb all the dirt and sand that has settled at the bottom of the bowl. Place the greens in a colander and run fresh water over them. Dry them in a salad spinner. Spread kitchen towels over a table or counter and scatter the greens across in a single layer to fully dry. The secret to successfully chopping green herbs is making sure they are bone-dry. Once dry, you can start chopping. Or you can wrap them in a barely damp kitchen towel or paper towels, place them in a plastic bag, and store them in the fridge to be used later. The greens should keep fresh in the fridge for about three days.

SORTING: Going through and picking the leaves off bunches upon bunches of herbs is a daunting task, to say the least. You will need to put some time aside for it, but don't get too caught up with exactitude. Trim the tough longer stems, and save these for a fresh and flavorful stock. Use the leaves and more tender stems. This is where I enlist the help of others. It doesn't matter if you're family or a guest. If herbs need to be sorted through, you will be put to work. This is also a great way to get kids involved and introduce them to new smells and tastes. Scatter the herbs across the table, sit together, and pick off the tender stems and leaves. There is a meditative rhythm and ritual to it all. It's one of those rare times we are asked to slow down, and we are able to converse, to commiserate, to gossip, to air out grievances, to share secrets and dreams. Life happens in these spaces, amid a field of greens.

CHOPPING: I highly recommend using a food processor, if possible, to chop large quantities of herbs. If you don't have access to a food processor, a very sharp knife and a large cutting board will be useful. If you are using a food processor, pulse the herbs in bunches to get the desired-sized chop. You don't want to run the food processor so long that the herbs turn mushy.

PREPPING AHEAD AND STORAGE: If you don't have time to use the chopped herbs right away, you can store them for later use, cutting down on precious time when you prepare a dish. Place the chopped herbs in an airtight container lined and topped with a paper towel to absorb moisture. Store in the fridge for up to a day. Most stews require that you sauté the herbs first. I will often do this and then freeze the sautéed herbs in a container or plastic bag to be used later.

FRESH VERSUS DRIED: The general rule of thumb when substituting dried herbs for fresh is 1 bunch fresh roughly equals ¼ cup dried. It's fine to substitute dried for fresh for many of the aash and stew recipes, but it's best to use fresh or a mix of both whenever possible.

See page 353 for A Field of Greens ingredients list.

The Spice Cupboard—*Advieh*

It is often assumed that Persian food is spicy, which is not the case. Southern Iranian food does use heat as a main flavoring, but that is not true for the rest of the cuisine (unless it's to taste and personal preference). Rather than spicy, Persian food makes use of many heady spices—*advieh*. Turmeric, cinnamon, rose petals, cardamom, nutmeg, *golpar* (Persian hogweed; see page 357), and of course saffron. These spices and the jars that so humbly house them tell the stories of our lives.

Advieh means "spice", any spice. But it can also refer to a fragrant and flavorful spice mix. Various spice mixes can be used for stews, rice dishes, meat mixtures, seafood, and pickles. The spices used vary from region to region and from home to home. Common spices used in any combination can include turmeric, cinnamon, cardamom, nutmeg, rose petals, golpar, coriander, black pepper, and cumin. I use my advieh mix in stew, soup, and meat recipes throughout this book. Make a batch and use as needed. As with all good things, a little goes a long way.

Advieh

Spice Mix for Stews and Meats

MAKES ABOUT 4 TABLESPOONS

---

2 teaspoons ground cinnamon

2 teaspoons ground dried rose petals (see page 18)

1 teaspoon ground cumin

1 teaspoon ground cardamom

1 teaspoon ground nutmeg

½ teaspoon ground coriander

Place all the ingredients in a small bowl and combine. Store in a spice jar and use as needed.

SAFFRON—Z'AFARAN

Saffron is the most expensive spice in the world, and it is the golden flag bearer of Iran and the Persian kitchen. Persian food is synonymous with saffron, ubiquitous in savory dishes, drinks, and desserts. There really isn't a substitute for saffron's intoxicating scent, flavor, and deep sunset hue. Saffron is expensive, and that is for good reason. At harvest, each stigma at the center of the crocus flower is individually picked and dried. But Iranian home cooks have figured out a way to stretch and use saffron economically. Very little saffron is needed to stain and flavor a dish; in fact, too much saffron can turn a dish bitter.

TO PREPARE SAFFRON THE PERSIAN WAY

Make sure to purchase good-quality saffron strands rather than ground saffron or bottled saffron water, both of which are most likely mixed with other spices or dyed with food coloring. Grind the saffron threads to a fine powder with a mortar and pestle, or use a dedicated spice grinder (make sure there is no residual flavor or scent of any other herb or spice lingering). This will take a few minutes. If the threads are not dry enough and not grinding you can add a small pinch of sugar or salt to help the process, but I've never had any issues with excess humidity with Iranian saffron.

Carefully transfer the saffron powder to a jar (tiny jam jars are perfect); you don't want to lose a single speck. Store the ground saffron in a cool, dark cabinet. When ready to use, bring a small amount of water to a boil, turn the kettle off, and let it sit for a couple of minutes. Sprinkle the specified amount of saffron in a small glass or bowl, and add the required amount of hot water (not boiling water, which is said to kill saffron's soul). Stir, cover, and steep for 5 to 10 minutes. This process releases the flavor, color, and medicinal properties of the saffron. This is your saffron water, and it can be added to the dish as indicated.

Before you wash out the glass the saffron was steeping in, make sure there isn't a single speck of this liquid gold clinging to its sides. This is precious stuff. Drizzle in a little more hot water, and either add it to the dish or knock it back yourself. Saffron is said to be a natural antidepressant and aphrodisiac. But *too* much saffron is said to bring about "excessive laughter and delirium." (Source: generations of Persian mothers and grandmothers.) All good things in moderation.

One more note on saffron: Because of its price tag and precious reputation, it often becomes like the prized dress or the good china that gets stashed away for that very special occasion that never comes. And before you know it, a whole year has gone by since you last used two strands of saffron for that one recipe you once came across. The rest of your precious saffron is still waiting in vain in the back of the cupboard, or it's sharing long-lost-love stories with that hunk of Parmesan rind you had stashed away in the freezer. Don't wait for that special occasion. Today, tomorrow, and every day are special occasions. Use your saffron. She's worth it, and you're worth it.

Saffron can be purchased from most well-stocked grocery stores and from Iranian, Middle Eastern, and Mediterranean markets. It is also available online. Another sure way to score some good-quality saffron is to make Iranian friends and profess your love of Persian food. Not only will you be invited over for a tasty dinner, but chances are at some point you will be gifted a beautiful package of saffron.

DRIED DAMASK ROSE PETALS—*GOL MOHAMADI*

One thing is clear: perfume plays an important role in Persian food, which is why ground dried rose petals are so commonly used to perfume and flavor dishes. Dried damask rose petals are not sweet in flavor. They are savory, and they are used in stews, dips, and sauces. (They are particularly tasty dusted on yogurt.) Although dried whole rose petals make for a beautiful garnish, they cannot be eaten, as they are tough, chewy, and slightly bitter.

TO USE DRIED DAMASK ROSE PETALS

Purchase packaged culinary-grade dried damask rose petals from Iranian or Middle Eastern markets or online. When the package is opened you should instantly be hit with a distinct, deeply satisfying aroma. Separate the fragrant petals from the tough woody stems. Set aside some petals, if you like, for beauty and garnish. Place the rest of the petals in a spice grinder or mini food processor and grind to a fine powder. Place the ground petals in a jar and use as needed. Rose petals symbolize love and friendship.

SALT

My salt cellar keeps me company through thick and thin, and it sits patiently and observantly right by the stove at my beck and call. How much salt to add to food is very personal and intuitive. At our house we hardly ever salt at the table, unless, once in a blue moon, it's a fancy finishing sea salt. Salt from a saltshaker sprinkled on a finished dish often tastes, well, salty. Instead, I like to salt as I cook, in layers, to draw out the natural flavors of each ingredient. Taste and salt as you go. A pinch here, a "tip of a knife" there. All the recipes in this book call for kosher salt (I use Diamond Crystal), which is readily available and economical.

Keep in mind that it's best if a box of salt only has salt in its ingredients list. Additives can make the food taste metallic and sharp. The kosher salt called for in this book is significantly less salty than regular table salt, and it is a little less salty than fine-grain sea salt. Adjust the salt amounts according to what kind you use and to your taste.

See page 355 for more Spice Cupboard ingredients.

The Art of Big-Batch Cooking and the Gift of Leftovers

Iranians, typically, like to prepare a plethora of food, be it one dish or several. It's ingrained in our DNA to be prepared to feed anyone who might walk through the door. The biggest worry of an Iranian home cook is not having enough food to serve at the table, lest someone show up unexpectedly. This need for abundance extends beyond socioeconomic means. It can simply be a large pot of rice and lentils—Adas Polo (page 123). The most symbolic dish that can stretch to a feed a crowd is Aabgoosht (page 92). Simple, humble, unfussy, yet deeply satisfying peasant food that you can always famously keep adding more water or a few extra potatoes to, or toss pieces of bread in to fill it out and extend it should someone walk through that proverbial door.

While researching this book and conversing with family and friends, it became very clear that the older the recipe and the person I spoke to, the larger the required quantities in the recipe. My mother's *barbari* bread recipe begins with 20 kilograms of flour. This also speaks to the resourcefulness of the Iranian kitchen and the frugality (in the best sense of the word) of the Persian home cook. Food is considered a sacred gift. So even if it's just a nub of onion that has been sadly fading in the crisper, it gets tossed in an aash or mixed into a kookoo. Almost-stale and dry pieces of bread are dunked into a soup, or they are mixed with feta cheese and get a new lease on life as a tasty snack. It's in this same spirit that I approach big-batch cooking.

With our busy, modern-day lives of balancing work, parenthood, and multitudes of daily commitments, it's impossible to commit to hours of lovingly simmering and bringing to life a tantalizing pot of *khoresh* on any given night. What I like to do is set aside time on the weekend and make a big batch of our favorite stew. While I'm at it, I chop bunches of herbs and bloom saffron. I might make two stews (not quite big enough to feed an army, but still) and enjoy one that night with family and anyone else who might walk through the door. I set aside a portion for the next day's school and work lunches, and store the rest in containers in the freezer to be devoured on a busy weeknight. Nothing hits the spot more than to come home on a Wednesday night to the comforts of a pot of aash or a fragrant eggplant stew, all prepared weeks before for a Sunday-night dinner. Having a container of frozen Khoresh Fesenjan (page 157) accidentally tumble out of the freezer is hitting the freezer jackpot!

Throughout this book, recipes will have an "Ahead" section with tips on how to prep the dish ahead of time and indicating which dishes make great freezer-food candidates. When I first moved out on my own, whenever my mom visited she would fill my freezer with individual containers of various stews, kookoo, aash, and rice dishes (cooked rice freezes really well). These days, when I visit my mom, I try to fill her freezer with some of these same favorites. The cycle always comes full circle. Hopefully with a packed freezer ready to serve, feed, and comfort.

LITTLE WHISPERS

The essence of Persian home cooking relies on the age-old tradition of using fresh ingredients first and foremost, wasting as little as possible by using the ingredients we already have on hand, repurposing leftovers, and of course sprinkling in a good dose of kitchen folklore and wisdom throughout the process. According to ancient Persian medicine, the effect of food on the body, both positive and negative, cannot be overlooked. Dating back to the Zoroastrians, food falls into two categories: *garmi* (hot/warming) and *sardi* (cold/cooling). This does not refer to the actual temperature or spiciness of the food, but the effect of a particular ingredient on the body. If there are too many ingredients or spices in a dish from one category, then balance in the body is thrown off and illness may result. Hence, most dishes and meals naturally cater to creating balance between garmi and sardi ingredients.

This theory also extends to each person's temperament. If you're the type of person who burns hot (emotionally and otherwise), you might consider consuming more cooling foods, such as yogurt; if you're more temperate in nature, you might consider more warming foods, such as walnuts and dates, to warm your blood. Perhaps my inherent love and need for yogurt best explains my inner nature. Growing up it seemed like all Iranians naturally knew which foods fell into which category, and meals were subconsciously, or at times consciously, due to illness or the weather, designed around this hot and cold concept. Out of respect to the scientists and doctors in our family I will say that none of this is based on hard science, but even the doctors in the family agree that if it brings comfort (like a warm bowl of chicken soup), then that is all the more reason to embrace it.

The Persian kitchen is also rich in symbolism. Heedful words, the likes of: always steep ground saffron in hot water, but never boiling. Boiled water kills saffron's soul, which will kill the dish, and in turn destroy thousands of years of history and culture, which will inevitably sour our experience of the meal, thus affecting our digestion and ultimately our overall well-being. No pressure! These old wives' tales are what I refer to as the "little whispers" that will forever echo in my ear. Like a parent's love and words of advice, they are unconditional and constant, always there for me to call on—when and if needed.

The Perfect Bite at the Sofreh

In keeping with the concept of garmi and sardi foods, a Persian meal is all about creating the perfect, balanced bite. As a result, all dishes are brought to the *sofreh* at the same time. The sofreh refers to the tablecloth on which the food is served. A typical Persian meal at our house will consist of rice, khoresh, a side of *sabzi khordan*, a small bowl of *torshi* (pickles), and either plain yogurt or *maast-o khiar*—yogurt and cucumber. All of these dishes are served simultaneously in service of creating the perfect balanced bite.

On the days when we need instant comfort and warmth, we'll make a big pot of aash. Or we might have a small bowl to start our meal. If we have company, we might include a couple of extra dips and another stew or a fish, meat, or vegetable dish. A kettle of tea is always at a simmer, and fresh fruit and a handful of nuts are essential everyday snacks. Dessert is typically just a little something sweet, like a couple of dates or a few dried mulberries, or the occasional slice of Baghlava Cake (page 316) to sweeten the post-dinner tea.

And Finally—Throw It All Away

Back in my acting school days, we were required to do as much homework and research as possible on the background and life of the characters we were playing. Build a backstory. Gather as much information as possible. But we were told that when the lights went up on the stage or "action" was called, we were to throw it all away. Forget about all the homework and research, trust that it will all have seeped in and marinated. All that is required is to simply be in the moment, open and ready to play.

I think this applies to cooking as well. If you're new to Persian food, you will come across some new information here. You'll be introduced to new spices, stories, herbs, and aromas. Read through the stories. Read through the recipes, and gather as many of the ingredients as you can. The first time around, follow the recipe as closely as you can. Treat it like a rehearsal of sorts. But at the end of that first time (or the second or third time you make the dish or a dish similar to it), relax, throw it all away, play, and make it your own. Trust that it will be okay, and you'll know what to do to "make it delicious" for you and your family at your sofreh.

MAZEH

Appetizers
&
Accompaniments

SABZI KHORDAN . . . 32
Fresh Herb Platter

KASHKI BADEMJAN . . . 35
Eggplant Dip with Kashk

NOON-O PANEER-O GERDOO . . . 39
Cheese and Walnut Wrap

ZEYTOON PARVARDEH . . . 40
Pomegranate Marinated Olives

MAAST-O KHIAR . . . 43
Yogurt Cucumber

MAAST-O MUSIR . . . 44
Persian Shallot Dip

BORANI-YEH KADOO . . . 45
Summer Squash Yogurt Dip

BORANI-YEH LABOO . . . 49
Yogurt Beet Dip

ADASI . . . 50
Lentil Dip

TOMATO CUCUMBER SALAD . . . 53

ARUGULA ORANGE FENNEL SALAD . . . 54

CABBAGE SALAD . . . 56

NAZKHATOUN . . . 57
Smoky Eggplant Pomegranate Dip

DALAAR . . . 60
Green Herb Salt

SEERABEH . . . 63
Walnut Verjuice Dip

CHAGHALEH BADAM VA GOJEH SABZ . . . 65
Raw Green Almonds and Sour Green Plums

SOUR CHERRY AND FETA CROSTINI . . . 66

TORSHI LITEH . . . 68
Eggplant and Herb Pickles

MUSIC & POETRY

The deep, cushy, cream-colored love seat in our apartment back in Tehran was nicknamed "the American"—expansive, comfortable, without a care in the world. I was four, maybe five years old, and notorious for giving my parents a hard time about going to bed at a decent hour. Many late nights were thus spent curled up on the American, eyes heavy with sleep, desperately trying to keep awake, not to miss a single moment, and eventually lulled into a sweet slumber by the entrancing sounds of the *santur, tar* (traditional Persian instruments similar to a sitar), *tonbak* (a traditional handheld drum), violin, and the magical rhymes and rhythms of poetry. My childhood lullaby.

My parents love to entertain, and they graciously embrace the art of Persian hospitality. It was very much the norm to have our house filled with musicians, singers, poets, and lovers of all of the above. These were my poet mother's mentors, peers, collaborators, and friends. There is a deep-seated respect for music and poetry among Persians of all walks and stripes. Traditional, classical Persian music may sound as if out of a dream, otherworldly to the unaccustomed ear. Much like the layering of the heady spices and scents of the cuisine, the music is nuanced and complex, challenging our senses, pushing our comfort levels, yet always welcoming and hospitable to everyone.

Inevitably, our dinner parties would end up with everyone sitting in the round and participating in something like a jam session, inspiration leading the way. Baba, my father, always the life of the party and never short of a joke, made sure everyone was comfortable with a drink in one hand and a *mazeh*—a taste—to complement the beverage of choice in the other. Instruments were tuned, voices were warmed, and a tray of little bites was passed around to see the night through and welcome dawn. With me and my American soaking it all in.

On those nights that I didn't doze off to the haunting melodies, somewhere in between the longing call of the santur and the warm, honeyed response of the vocals, I would quietly crawl my way to the mazeh platter and sneak little bites—*loghmeh*—of warm flatbreads dipped in cool savory-spiced yogurt or filled with *paneer*, fresh basil, and walnuts that had soaked all day in water and salt to remove their bitterness. As everyone applauded the intricate love affair of music and verse, I quickly wound my way back to the comforts of the American. Once in a while, in between a lilt of a song or a strum of the tar, someone would, much to my delight, conspiratorially pass me five garlicky, tangy, pomegranate-marinated olives—*zeytoon parvardeh*. One for each finger. One by one, I would take my time, sucking the olive of all its tangy juices. Hoping the longer it took me to finish, the longer the music would last, and the longer I could be a part of it all. Hoping finally, I would discover all the mysteries and secrets of the night, and boast about it to my brother the next morning.

I don't know what became of the American. We parted ways in abrupt fashion. No proper good-byes, no closure. I hope that whoever inherited it still curls up in its cushy armrest and, somewhere within the warm folds of its fabric, can still hear the rhythmic beats of the tonbak and the enchanted giggles of a little girl thrilled to have shared in a little mazeh on a magical night. Tangy olive lips smacking and sticky fingers snapping.

Think of the Persian table as a vibrant, colorful mosaic. Persian food isn't served one course at a time, but rather all the main dishes and accompaniments land on the *sofreh* simultaneously, family style. Colorful yogurt dips, a platter of fresh herbs, and small bowls of sour pickles all play an essential role in the rich symphony that makes up a Persian meal. These sides harmonize beautifully, accompanying the main rice and stew dishes, hitting all the right notes in service of creating the perfect, balanced bite. But don't feel like you have to set out every single side all the time to enjoy a Persian meal—we don't. A simple side of plain yogurt, a small bowl of Tomato Cucumber Salad (page 53), olives, or any bits of fresh herbs lingering in the fridge are perfectly acceptable and encouraged.

This chapter includes our go-to side dishes, which can also transfer to a mazeh platter as an appetizer spread. I've also thrown in a couple of snack ideas that are perfect for nibbling on at any time of day.

Sabzi Khordan

Fresh Herb Platter

Munching on fresh green herbs with almost every meal is about as Iranian as it gets. We are a culture obsessed with digestion, and fresh herbs, such as mint, basil, and parsley, make an appearance at our table not only to brighten and lighten every bite, but to aid in the digestion of the richer main dishes. Sabzi Khordan is the one dish at our table that our friends are always most intrigued by, and understandably so. After all, what does one do when presented with a heaping platter of fragrant, fresh green herbs, a few radishes, and raw green onions? (Traditionally, chunks of raw onion are also included, touted to be antibacterial and beneficial for overall health.) Sabzi Khordan translates to "herbs for eating," so . . . you just eat it. As the Sabzi Khordan platter is passed around, grab a few sprigs of your preferred herbs, a couple of radishes, and a slice of green onion. Place the herbs on the side of your plate. Scoop up some rice and stew, and as you start chewing, add a basil leaf, or parsley, mint, etc., to the bite already in your mouth. Instantly you will be amazed at how all the flavors and textures pop and come to life. Then quickly repeat to affirm your findings. By the third and fourth perfectly balanced bite, you will forget that consuming a meal without Sabzi Khordan was even an option.

If I'm hosting a dinner party and am feeling inspired I'll put together a more elaborate platter of Sabzi Khordan, boasting a variety of brilliant green herbs, a thick slice of sharp feta cheese, walnuts (soaked to remove their bitterness), and pieces of just-warmed-through flatbread. But on most nights, what you will most likely find at our family table is a small plate of Sabzi Khordan strewn together with any odds and ends of forgotten herbs lingering in the back of the crisper. Not every meal needs to be a complete philharmonic—most nights a simple pickup band hits just the right notes.

The following are some suggestions for the kinds of herbs and alliums that can be included for a platter of Sabzi Khordan. Mix and match as you like, and use whatever is winking at you from the back of the crisper.

Persian basil (look for lemon basil, see page 353)

Mint, stems trimmed

Parsley, stems trimmed

Cilantro, stems trimmed

Dill sprigs, stems trimmed

Green onions, trimmed and cut into about 3-inch pieces

Tarragon

Chives

Radishes, ends trimmed, halved or quartered

Watermelon radishes, sliced

Baby Japanese turnips, quartered

Walnuts, soaked in cold water and a pinch of salt for at least 4 hours or overnight

Feta cheese, cubed

Dried mint, as a garnish for the feta (optional)

Ground dried rose petals, as a garnish for the feta (optional; see page 18)

Olive oil for drizzling on the feta (optional)

(continued)

Sabzi Khordan *(continued)*

Place handfuls of any combination of the ingredients on a small plate or a large platter. I like to keep the herbs bunched separately, rather than mixing them together in one big bunch, so people can pick and choose to their liking. Enjoy at the table with just about any meal, or serve with bread as an appetizer.

PREP AHEAD: The most time-consuming part of assembling a platter of Sabzi Khordan is washing, drying, and trimming the herbs. See page 12 for herb prepping. Up to 3 hours in advance, arrange all the (trimmed, washed, and dried) herbs, radishes, and alliums on a platter. Cover with a slightly damp paper towel, and place the platter in the fridge. If the paper towel dries, sprinkle a little water over it to keep the greens fresh. If any greens are leftover, they can be tossed in a sandwich, stew, kookoo, or aash.

Kashki Bademjan

Eggplant Dip with Kashk

Kashki Bademjan is the quintessential Iranian dip that seduces even the most ardent egg-plant doubters. Firm, thin eggplant (like the Japanese or Chinese varieties) is first fried or roasted (I roast here) and then cooked through in a little water with a hint of earthy turmeric until fleshy and luscious. But what really lifts this dish and gives it its name is the final stirring in of kashk (page 349), bringing it to life with a bold kick of umami and deliv-ering the requisite Persian tang and acidity to the more demure eggplant.

Made from cooked-down and concentrated sour yogurt, kashk has an extremely rich flavor similar to a pungent aged cheese like Parmesan. Be mindful that kashk is quite salty, so taste for salt after you add kashk. But fret not, if you can't get your hands on any kashk, this crowd-pleaser of a dip can also be made with Greek yogurt, crème fraîche, or sour cream. And don't overlook the Piaz Daagh–Seer Daagh–Na'na Daagh—fried onion-garlic-mint topping—which brings out the full flavor of the dip. Serve Kashki Bademjan as an appetizer with a side of warm sangak or lavash bread for scooping. Or, for a less tradi-tional presentation, spread it on individual slices of toasted crusty bread. We also like it with a side of plain rice for a quick, light lunch or dinner.

SERVES 8 AS AN APPETIZER

1½ pounds Japanese or Chinese eggplant (about 5 Japanese or 3 Chinese), tops trimmed, halved lengthwise

¼ cup plus 2 tablespoons olive oil, divided (plus more as needed)

Kosher salt

1 medium yellow onion, diced

3 cloves garlic, roughly chopped

¼ teaspoon ground turmeric

Piaz Daagh–Seer Daagh–Na'na Daagh (fried onion-garlic-mint topping, page 38)

Kashk, Greek yogurt, crème fraîche, or sour cream

A few walnuts, roughly chopped

Lavash or sangak bread for serving

Ground black pepper

Heat the oven to 450°F with the rack set in the upper-third position. Line a large baking sheet with parchment paper.

Place the eggplant halves flesh-side up on the baking sheet and carefully score the eggplant in a crosshatch pattern, taking care not to pierce through the skin. Brush the eggplant with about ¼ cup of the olive oil. Use more if necessary, as eggplant absorbs a lot of oil. Liberally sprinkle each half with salt and roast the eggplant for about 18 min-utes, until slightly browned and softened but not completely cooked through. Set aside.

(continued)

Meanwhile, in a large pan, heat the remaining 2 tablespoons olive oil over medium heat. Add the onion and cook, stirring occasionally, until softened and golden, about 10 minutes. Sprinkle with salt, reduce the heat to medium-low, add the garlic, and cook until the garlic softens, about 5 minutes.

Add the roasted eggplant to the onion-garlic mixture. Add enough water to cover the eggplant halfway, about ¾ cup. Start with less water and add more if necessary. Sprinkle in the turmeric and ¼ teaspoon pepper, and stir to combine. Increase the heat to medium and bring to a gentle boil. Reduce the heat to medium-low, cover, and simmer, stirring occasionally, until the eggplant has completely softened and cooked through and the water has been absorbed, 12 to 15 minutes. Add a little more water if the eggplant needs longer to cook. Or remove the lid to cook off the liquid. While the eggplant cooks, prepare the fried onion-garlic-mint topping.

Turn off the heat and mash the eggplant with the back of a spoon or fork, or use a potato masher. You can also pulse it a few times in the food processor. Mash until the mixture is well combined, the eggplant skin blends in, and no big chunks remain. Stir in the kashk. Start with 3 tablespoons and keep adding as needed. Stir, taste, stir, taste. More kashk? More salt? More pepper? Keep tasting and adding until your taste buds sing.

Transfer to a serving platter and top with about 2 tablespoons of the fried onion-garlic-mint. Garnish with chopped walnuts and a drizzle of extra kashk or yogurt. Serve warm or at room temperature, with lavash or sangak bread for scooping.

MAKE AHEAD: The entire dip can be made 3 days in advance. Gently heat through on the stove or in the oven when ready to serve.

PREP AHEAD: The eggplant can be roasted and stored in the fridge for up to 3 days or in the freezer for up to 3 months.

PLAN AHEAD: Freeze for up to 3 months. This is a great dip to have on hand in the freezer for a last-minute party. Simply thaw and gently heat through on the stove or in the oven before serving.

Kashki Bademjan *(continued)*

Piaz Daagh–Seer Daagh–Na'na Daagh
Fried onion-garlic-mint topping

This makes about ½ cup of topping. You won't be using it all in this recipe. Use as much as needed. Store the rest in the fridge or in the freezer and use to top any dips, soups, aash, or even burgers.

¼ cup olive oil (plus more as needed)

1 large yellow onion, diced

5 large cloves garlic, diced

¼ teaspoon kosher salt

1 teaspoon ground turmeric

1 tablespoon dried mint

In a medium pan, heat the oil over medium-high heat. Make sure the oil is nice and hot, but not smoking. Add the onion and cook, stirring frequently, until golden brown, 8 to 10 minutes. Reduce the heat to medium-low. Add the garlic and salt, and keep cooking, stirring as you go, for about 5 minutes. If the pan gets too dry, drizzle in more oil as needed. Stir in the turmeric and cook until fragrant, about 2 minutes. Remove from the heat and add the dried mint, quickly mixing it in. Set aside and use as needed.

MAKE AHEAD: The fried onion-garlic-mint can be made ahead of time and stored in the fridge for up to 1 week or in the freezer for up to 3 months.

Noon-o Paneer-o Gerdoo

Cheese and Walnut Wrap

Loghmeh *roughly translates to "the perfect-sized, little bite to pop in your mouth." A loghmeh is lovingly scooped up by a mother, grandmother, aunt, father, uncle, or grandfather, and handed over to a child. A piece of bread to sop up the last of the rice and stew lingering on the plate. For Iranians young and old, the most satisfying loghmeh is the most humble. Bread, cheese, walnuts, and a few fresh herbs—Noon-o Paneer-o Gerdoo. This is the bite that was handed to us as children to tide us over between meals. It can be a quick lunch or dinner when you're bone-tired, when the fridge has run out of its typical offerings, when nothing else will quite do. Noon-o Paneer-o Gerdoo is the bite I reach for on those days when I'm stumbling out of the house in a mad rush. But if I happen to have a few extra minutes to steal away, I'll enjoy my Noon-o Paneer-o Gerdoo loghmeh with a cup of tea and a couple of dates for energy.*

Barbari, sangak, or lavash bread

Feta cheese or white farmer's cheese

A few walnuts, soaked in water if you have time

Fresh herbs of choice: Persian basil, cilantro, parsley, mint, anything left over from the previous day's Sabzi Khordan (page 32)

A couple of slices of crisp Persian cucumber (optional)

Spread the cheese over the bread, top with walnuts, herbs, and cucumber, if desired. Wrap, or scoop up into a loghmeh.

MAKE AHEAD: Prepare the wrap and store it in a sandwich bag. Stash in your purse, and enjoy it on the road.

Zeytoon Parvardeh

Pomegranate Marinated Olives

Taste and memory is how I go about preparing these addictive pomegranate-marinated olives. Zeytoon Parvardeh hails from Gilan Province in the northern region of Iran. Start with your favorite green olives, nothing too salty or briny to compete with the marinade. I'm partial to Castelvetrano olives, which are readily available at most grocery stores. These crisp and bright Sicilian olives hold their own beautifully against the sharp, sweet-and-sour tang of the pomegranate molasses and the heft of the walnuts. In keeping with tradition, I have included, and love, the bright hint of golpar—Persian hogweed (page 357). It may be an unfamiliar tone, with its sharp scent and hints of citrus, but it is worth seeking out and including in your repertoire. Zeytoon Parvardeh is best prepared a couple of days in advance to allow the flavors to fully meld. Serve as an appetizer (it's a bright addition to a cheese board), or alongside a rice and stew meal.

SERVES 6

1 cup pitted Castelvetrano olives or any other tasty green olives of choice (about 6 ounces), sliced in half if large

½ cup walnuts, very finely ground almost to a paste

2 cloves garlic, crushed to a paste

¼ cup pomegranate molasses (plus more as needed)

1½ teaspoons dried mint (plus more as needed)

¾ teaspoon golpar (Persian hogweed), plus more for sprinkling (optional)

Pomegranate seeds (optional)

Place the olives in a bowl. Add the rest of the ingredients except for the pomegranate seeds. Stir well to combine. Taste and add more pomegranate molasses and dried mint, if necessary. Cover and marinate in the fridge for 24 to 72 hours. The flavors improve and intensify the longer it marinates. Bring to room temperature 30 minutes before serving to remove the chill. Garnish with pomegranate seeds (if using) and an extra sprinkling of golpar and serve.

MAKE AHEAD: Prepare up to 3 days in advance and store covered in the fridge.

Maast-o Khiar

Yogurt Cucumber

If it's not a container of plain yogurt ever-present at our dinner table, then it's a cooling bowl of Maast-o Khiar. This beloved dip can be garnished and adorned any which way you like. In its simplest form it's nothing more than regular plain yogurt and either grated or chopped cucumber, with a sprinkling of salt. If the cucumber is too juicy just add some strained Greek yogurt to thicken it up. I don't like to get rid of the cucumber juice because all the flavor is in the juice. We love adding dried mint and ground dried rose petals for perfume, beauty, and a boost of flavor.

If I am serving Maast-o Khiar as part of an appetizer platter, I prefer to use thicker Greek yogurt to make it easier to scoop up with bread, potato chips, or crisp veggies. If I am serving it at the table alongside a typical rice and stew meal, I use regular plain yogurt. A little bit of rice, a little bit of stew, a few fresh herbs, and a little bit of Maast-o Khiar.

SERVES 6 AS A SIDE DISH OR DIP

2 cups plain, full-fat yogurt or Greek yogurt (or a combination)

1¼ cups chopped or grated cucumber with juices; from 2 or 3 Persian cucumbers or ½ English cucumber

1 teaspoon kosher salt

1 tablespoon dried mint

¼ teaspoon ground dried rose petals (plus more for garnish, optional; see page 18)

Small pinch of black pepper

ADDITIONAL INGREDIENTS MAY INCLUDE:

Fresh mint leaves

Fresh or dried dill

Raisins

Walnuts, chopped

1 small clove garlic, crushed to a paste

Fresh chives, chopped

In a medium bowl, combine the yogurt, cucumber, salt, and dried mint (rubbed between your palms to release fragrance and flavor). Add the rose petals and black pepper. If the cucumber is especially juicy, add some Greek yogurt to thicken it. Now begin the tasting dance. This is where everyone gets involved. A little taste, a little more salt, another lick, another sprinkle of dried mint. Garnish with an extra sprinkling of dried mint and ground rose petals. It's a canvas open to your taste and creativity. Go simple, or big and bold.

MAKE AHEAD: Prepare up to 3 days in advance. If the yogurt weeps stir it and add a little more yogurt to thicken. The fragrance and flavor of the mint and rose petals will dissipate over time.

Maast-o Musir
Persian Shallot Dip

There is no substitute for the sharp flavor and scent of musir *(moo-seer)—Persian shallots. Musir is more delicate in flavor than garlic, and smokier in scent and taste than what we consider a typical shallot. It is an allium native to Iran and Central Asia, and touted for its antibacterial and medicinal qualities. Musir is dried and sold in packets in Iranian markets and online. I've tried making this dip with regular shallots, but it just doesn't deliver the same flavor punch. I highly encourage you to seek out the dried packets and indulge in this creamy, thick, smoky yogurt dip.*

Maast-o Musir always conjures up memories of our arrival in Vancouver and my introduction to the ubiquitous North American party staple: French onion dip, usually served out of a tub picked up straight from the corner convenience store. In return, I always enjoyed introducing my school friends to its Eastern cousin: Maast-o Musir. And regardless of whether you looked East or West, we always met in the middle with plenty of chips on hand ready to dip in. Serve as a dip for chips, bread, or crisp veggies, or as a side dish alongside any of the rice dishes.

SERVES 6

2½ tablespoons musir (Persian dried shallots)

1 cup Greek yogurt

1 sprig tarragon, finely chopped, about 2 teaspoons (optional)

½ teaspoon kosher salt

Olive oil for drizzling (optional)

Place the musir in a small bowl and cover with just-boiled water. Soak for 30 minutes, until softened, but still with a bite. Drain and finely dice, discarding any that are too tough. In a medium bowl, combine the chopped musir, yogurt, tarragon, and salt. Cover and chill in the fridge for a couple of hours for the flavors to meld. Drizzle with olive oil if you like, and serve.

MAKE AHEAD: Maast-o Musir can be made up to 3 days in advance and stored in the fridge. If the yogurt weeps, stir it and add a little more yogurt to thicken it.

Borani-yeh Kadoo

Summer Squash Yogurt Dip

Borani *is a yogurt-based dish typically served as a side alongside a meal or with bread as an appetizer or a quick lunch or snack. As Margaret Shaida recounts in her wonderful book* The Legendary Cuisine of Persia, *the origin of the word* borani *stems from the Sassanian dynasty, circa AD 626, and Queen Pourandokht, who ruled over Iran at the time. The queen was apparently enamored of yogurt, and all the yogurt dishes that were inspired by and created for her by the royal chefs became known as* poorani, *named after the queen herself. However, after the Arab conquests of Iran, the names of these dishes changed to* borani *because the letter "p" does not exist in the Arabic alphabet.*

Borani-yeh Kadoo is a welcome dish for those few weeks in late summer when it seems like there will never be a shortage of zucchini or summer squash. You can first fry the yellow squash halves in a pan on the stove, but I prefer to roast them all in one go in a hot oven. Then finish cooking them off in a rich and juicy tomato sauce, with piaz daagh—*fried onion. Spread over garlicky Greek yogurt, and give thanks to Queen Pourandokht for inspiring so many of these delectable yogurt-based dishes. Any which way you spell it.*

SERVES 6

2 medium zucchini plus 2 medium yellow squash or any combination (about 2 pounds total), stems trimmed, sliced into ¼-inch-thick rounds

2 tablespoons plus ¼ cup olive oil, divided (plus more as needed)

Kosher salt

Ground black pepper

1 medium yellow onion, sliced into ¼-inch-thick half-moons

1 cup cherry tomatoes, quartered

2 tablespoons tomato paste

½ teaspoon ground dried oregano

1 cup Greek yogurt

1 large clove garlic, crushed to a paste

A few fresh basil or oregano leaves (optional)

Preheat the oven to 425°F with the rack set in the upper-third position. Line a baking sheet with parchment paper and set aside.

Bring a kettle of water to a boil and keep it at a simmer.

In a medium bowl, toss the zucchini with 2 tablespoons of the olive oil, and season with salt and pepper. Spread out in a single layer on the prepared baking sheet. (Use two sheets, if necessary, so the squash doesn't steam.) Roast until softened but not completely cooked through (the squash will finish cooking in the sauce), about 15 minutes. Set aside.

Meanwhile, in a large pan, heat the remaining ¼ cup oil over medium-high heat, until the oil is hot but not smoking. Add the onion and cook, stirring frequently, until golden brown, about 8 to 10 minutes. Reduce the heat to medium and keep cooking, stirring often, until fried and crispy in bits and pieces, about 5 minutes. If the pan gets too dry, drizzle in more oil. Play with the heat if need be. You don't want the onion to burn but you don't want it soft and mushy either. Set aside a heaping tablespoon of the fried onion on a paper towel to use as garnish when serving.

Add the cherry tomatoes, tomato paste, and dried oregano to the pan. Mix well and cook for 3 to 5 minutes. Add 1 cup of the just-boiled water and 1 teaspoon salt, stir, and bring to a quick boil. Add the roasted squash slices. Simmer, stirring occasionally, until the mixture has thickened and fallen into place and most of the squash slices have broken down and collapsed into the sauce, about 20 minutes. Taste, and add more salt and pepper if needed. Remove from the heat and set aside to cool for a few minutes.

In a small bowl, combine the yogurt, garlic, and a pinch of salt. Spread the yogurt on a serving dish and top with the squash mixture. You can also drizzle or dollop the top with a little bit of the garlicky yogurt if you like. Garnish with the reserved onions, and a few torn basil or oregano leaves for extra beauty.

MAKE AHEAD: The squash-tomato mix can be cooked up to 3 days in advance and stored in the fridge. Add the yogurt when serving.

PREP AHEAD: The squash can be roasted in advance and stored in the fridge up to 3 days.

Borani-yeh Laboo

Yogurt Beet Dip

Nothing brightens up a meal and everyone's moods more than a bowl of this fuchsia Borani-yeh Laboo. The tang from the vinegar and yogurt balances and cuts through the earthy sweetness of the beets, and the tarragon adds a fresh bite. You can cook the beets by steaming them on the stovetop or in the oven. Or you can simply use store-bought cooked beets. Scoop up with warm lavash bread, or spread on crisp endive leaves for a striking mazeh.

SERVES 6

1 medium beet, cooked and peeled

1 cup Greek yogurt

3 tablespoons red wine vinegar

¼ teaspoon kosher salt

1 teaspoon dried mint

1 teaspoon finely chopped fresh tarragon (optional)

Olive oil for drizzling

Into a medium bowl, grate the beet on the large holes of a box grater. Add the rest of the ingredients, except the olive oil, and mix to completely combine. Taste to make it delicious, keeping in mind that the flavors will develop and deepen as the dip rests. Cover and place in the fridge for at least 1 hour for the flavors to develop before serving. Stir, drizzle with olive oil if you like, and serve.

MAKE AHEAD: Prepare up to 3 days in advance and store in the fridge in an airtight container. If the yogurt weeps, simply stir to incorporate again. Drizzle with olive oil before serving.

Adasi
Lentil Dip

Traditionally Adasi is made with varying consistencies and flavors. Some prefer it more soup-like; some prefer to mash the lentils. I like to prepare Adasi with earthy Puy lentils (also known as French green lentils) so they better hold their shape. But brown and regular green lentils will work fine too, if that's what you have on hand. Keep in mind brown lentils take less time to cook. Be generous with the final drizzle of olive oil and the bite of the vinegar. Taste as you go, and keep drizzling and splashing until you hit your perfect note. Serve Adasi as an appetizer or lunch with crusty bread or folded into warm flat bread, and an accompanying glass of wine.

SERVES 6

2 tablespoons olive oil (plus more for drizzling)

1 medium yellow onion, diced

Kosher salt

3 large cloves garlic, finely chopped

¾ teaspoon ground cumin

½ teaspoon ground allspice

Ground black pepper

1 cup Puy (French) green lentils, picked through and rinsed

¼ cup dry white wine

2½ cups water (plus more as needed)

1 tablespoon red wine vinegar (plus more as needed)

Small handful of fresh basil, chopped

Small handful of fresh parsley, tough stems trimmed, chopped

½ teaspoon golpar (Persian hogweed; see page 357; optional)

In a medium saucepan, heat the oil over medium-high heat. Add the onion and cook, stirring frequently, until golden brown, about 12 minutes. Sprinkle with salt, and reduce the heat to medium. Add the garlic, cumin, allspice, and black pepper to taste, and cook for 2 minutes, stirring so the garlic doesn't burn. Add the lentils, stir, and add the wine. Cook until the wine is absorbed, about 3 minutes. Add the water and 1½ teaspoons salt. Bring to a boil over high heat, partially cover, reduce the heat to medium-low, and simmer until the water has been absorbed and the lentils are tender but still hold their shape, 30 to 45 minutes. Add more water if necessary for the lentils to cook through.

Transfer to a serving dish and cool for a few minutes. Add the vinegar, fresh herbs, and golpar, and drizzle generously with olive oil. Now make it delicious. Vinegar, salt, pepper, golpar? One more glug of oil?

MAKE AHEAD: Prepare up to 3 days in advance. Serve at room temperature; add vinegar and oil as needed.

Tomato Cucumber Salad

Growing up, at the end of every meal, my brother and I would fix our gaze on two bowls on the table: the Maast-o Khiar (page 43) bowl and the salad bowl. We'd ready ourselves to pounce, to lick and slurp either bowl clean before the other got to it. The best part of the salad as far as we were concerned was the sauce, the dressing, left shimmering in the bowl. Sour, salty, with remnants of tomato juice swirling with olive oil. Whoever moved fastest got the prize of tipping the big bowl right back and selfishly indulging in the sauce.

Salads are still a simple affair in our house: a good sprinkling of salt, pepper, a drizzle of olive oil, a splash of something tangy. Taste, toss, and repeat until your taste buds burst with joy. Tomato Cucumber Salad is like a well-loved family member, a reliable and constant companion to all of our meals. Finely chop the ingredients for a closer interpretation of the classic Iranian Shirazi salad. Or slice any which way you like with any and all varieties and shades of tomatoes, cucumber, and herbs.

These days I have a new salad adversary at the table, my daughter Luna. She puts on her game face, fixes her gaze on the salad as if it's a bowl of ice cream, and in her most intimidating voice asks, "Ready for a salad war, Mama?" as we both pounce.

SERVES 4 TO 6

2 Persian cucumbers, chopped or sliced

2 cups cherry tomatoes, sliced in half

2 green onions, sliced

Large handful of fresh green herbs (any combination of parsley, mint, basil, or cilantro), tough stems trimmed, roughly chopped

½ teaspoon kosher salt

2 tablespoons olive oil

2 teaspoons red wine vinegar, apple cider vinegar, white wine vinegar, verjuice, or lemon juice

Ground black pepper

Place the cucumbers, tomatoes, green onions, and herbs in a large bowl. Sprinkle with the salt (remember, tomatoes like salt), and drizzle the top with the olive oil. Splash on the vinegar, or squeeze half a lemon. Sprinkle a little pepper and toss, toss, toss. Next comes the best part: taste and sprinkle, drizzle, and splash until you are ready to pounce.

Arugula Orange Fennel Salad

Arugula Orange Fennel Salad covers both salad and dessert cravings. This may not be a traditional Iranian salad, but it wholeheartedly embraces the Persian obsession with proper digestion, with a nod to the fruit and dates typically served after a meal. Peppery, bitter arugula and cool, crisp, anise-y fennel are touted as digestive wonders, while orange slices and dates lightly perfumed in orange blossom water seduce any post-meal sweet tooth. Top with a handful of toasted pumpkin seeds and pomegranate seeds for crunch, if you like. This salad is best tossed and served right away. The arugula wilts and gets sad very quickly when dressed. If possible look for the sturdier, large-leafed arugula found at farmers' markets. It holds its shape better and has more of a bite than the packaged kind sold at grocery stores.

SERVES 6

2 teaspoons unsalted pumpkin seeds or any nuts or seeds of choice

2 medium oranges

5 Medjool dates, chopped

⅛ teaspoon orange blossom water

4 ounces arugula (about 5 cups)

1 large fennel bulb, thinly sliced

2 tablespoons olive oil (plus more as needed)

1 tablespoon fresh lemon juice or red wine vinegar (plus more as needed)

Kosher salt

Ground black pepper

Pomegranate seeds (optional)

Golpar (Persian hogweed, see page 357; optional)

In a small pan, lightly toast the pumpkin seeds over medium heat, stirring frequently so they don't burn, until fragrant, about 5 minutes. Set aside to cool.

Cut off the ends of the oranges. Place an orange on your cutting board and cut around the skin and white pith, following the natural curve of the fruit. Slice in rounds and place the orange slices and dates in a shallow bowl. Repeat with the remaining orange. Drizzle the orange blossom water over the oranges and dates, and place in the fridge for 10 minutes, but not any longer as they'll release too much juice.

In a mixing bowl, toss the arugula and fennel with the oil, lemon juice or vinegar, ½ teaspoon salt, and pepper to taste. Taste and toss to your liking. Place the arugula and fennel on a platter, and top with the orange slices (and any juices) and dates. Scatter the pumpkin seeds and pomegranate seeds on top. Sprinkle with a little golpar (if using), and serve right away.

Cabbage Salad

As a child my favorite way of eating cabbage was sliced and drizzled with plenty of vinegar or lemon juice and served as a super-tangy salad alongside the heartier dishes. Don't be shy with the vinegar and lemon juice here, you need it to stand up to and soften the sharp, bossy bite of the cabbage. I also like to add a splash of fresh orange juice to lighten it up if I have an orange hanging around. Red cabbage adds a beautiful hue to this salad, but green cabbage works just as well, or use a combination of both. And if you happen to brush against some raw green almonds (see page 65) in those brief couple of weeks in early spring, slice them up and add them here for an extra pop of color and an unexpected added crunch. This salad does well prepared ahead. Pack it up for a picnic and serve with Kookoo Sibzamini (page 207) or Kotlet (pages 275–279).

SERVES 6

1 small head red or green cabbage (about 1¼ pounds), thinly sliced

1 large carrot, shredded or grated

2 green onions, sliced

½ bunch parsley, tough stems removed, chopped

Kosher salt

Ground black pepper

¼ cup olive oil (plus more as needed)

¼ cup red wine vinegar (plus more as needed)

3 tablespoons fresh lemon juice (plus more as needed)

2 tablespoons fresh orange juice (optional)

Place the cabbage, carrots, green onions, and parsley in a large bowl. Make sure you have enough room to toss everything well. Sprinkle generously with salt and pepper to taste, drizzle with the olive oil, and splash in the vinegar, lemon juice, and orange juice (if using). Toss madly. Taste, and taste some more, and add more of anything as needed. This salad should be tangy so add more vinegar and/or lemon juice until you get there.

MAKE AHEAD: Make this salad up to 2 days in advance and store it in the fridge in an airtight container.

PREP AHEAD: The cabbage can be sliced up to 3 days in advance and stored in the fridge in a resealable bag. Don't shred the carrots in advance as they can turn brown. The parsley can be chopped 1 day in advance and stored in the fridge (see fresh herb prep, page 12).

Nazkhatoun

Smoky Eggplant Pomegranate Dip

The marriage of eggplant, sweet tomatoes, and garlic is a classic combination spanning the rice paddies of Gilan Province to the shores of the Mediterranean. The addition of tangy pomegranate molasses, bright mint, and whole eggplant roasted until smoky and burned to a crisp makes Nazkhatoun distinctly Middle Eastern, and more specifically northern Iranian. Naz loosely translates to sweet, delicate, or cute. Khatoun is synonymous with the more commonly used word khanoom, meaning "lady." But there is nothing cute about this dish. This Nazkhatoun confidently asserts herself, bursting with flavor. This is a great make-ahead dish as the flavors enhance as they sit and marinate. Serve with bread as an appetizer or with some rice as a light lunch or dinner.

SERVES 6

2 large eggplants (about 2 pounds), or 2 pounds Japanese or Chinese eggplant

4 medium tomatoes (about 1 pound)

3 tablespoons olive oil (plus more for drizzling)

2 large cloves garlic, crushed to a paste

1½ teaspoons kosher salt

1 to 2 tablespoons pomegranate molasses (plus more as needed)

1 teaspoon golpar (Persian hogweed; see page 357)

½ teaspoon ground black pepper

1 tablespoon dried mint

Small handful of fresh cilantro, stems trimmed, chopped

Fresh mint

Pomegranate seeds

Heat a grill until very hot (500°F). Prick the skin of the eggplant in a few spots with a fork. Place the eggplant on the grill and roast for 40 to 60 minutes, turning occasionally, until the skin is charred and crisp all over, and the flesh collapses and is soft and sinking into itself. If a grill is not an option, put the pricked eggplant on a baking sheet and roast in a 450°F oven for about 45 minutes. Alternatively, if you have a gas stove you can also place the eggplant directly on the burner, rotating it every so often. Make sure you line the burner with foil to catch the eggplant drippings.

Meanwhile, prepare the tomatoes. Fill a small pot with enough water to cover the tomatoes, about 4 cups, and bring to a boil. Score the tops of the tomatoes with an X, and have a large bowl of ice water ready. Place the tomatoes in the boiling water for 1 minute. Drain and immediately dunk the tomatoes in the ice bath, like jumping into a

cold pool right out of the hot tub. Stick your hands in the bowl and easily peel the tomatoes. Cut the tomatoes in half, scoop out the seeds, chop the tomatoes, and set aside.

Once the eggplant is ready, set it over a colander for the juices to drip until it's cool enough to handle. Peel the eggplant and scoop out the flesh. Discard the peel and any clumps of seeds (the seeds make the dish bitter).

Put the oil and garlic in a medium pan and set it over medium-low heat. Cook the garlic until golden and fragrant, stirring often so it doesn't burn, about 5 minutes. Raise the heat to medium and add the chopped tomatoes. Marvel at the scent of tomatoes, garlic, and olive oil. Sprinkle the tomatoes with salt and cook until most of their juices have been absorbed, 5 to 8 minutes.

Add the eggplant, pomegranate molasses, golpar, 1½ teaspoons salt, and pepper. Cook, uncovered, until all the flavors meld, about 10 minutes. Crush the dried mint between your fingertips to release its fragrance and flavor. Add it to the pan, give a quick stir, and remove from the heat. Stir and taste. It should be pleasingly tart. Add more salt, dried mint, golpar, and pomegranate molasses as desired.

Transfer to a serving bowl. Stir in the cilantro, and garnish with fresh mint, pomegranate seeds, and a drizzle of olive oil, if you like. Serve warm or at room temperature.

MAKE AHEAD: The flavors in Nazkhatoun deepen and enhance as it rests and marinates. Prepare it up to 3 days in advance, cover, and store in the fridge.

PREP AHEAD: The tomatoes can be peeled, seeded, and cooked up to 3 days in advance. Store in the fridge until ready to use.

PLAN AHEAD: Freeze (up to 3 months), thaw, bring to room temperature, and serve when in need of a quick, last-minute dip.

Dalaar

Green Herb Salt

Dalaar, also pronounced dalal *or* darar, *depending on which town you hail from, is a bright, fresh, and flavorful salty herb mix, often used as a salt replacement. It is a specialty from the northern Iranian provinces of Gilan and Mazandran. Dalaar's distinct flavor shines from the use of a handful of green herbs native only to the northern region of Iran, such as* khalvash, choochan, *and* choochakh *(herbs in the mint family). A small amount is combined with cilantro, mint, and plenty of salt, and pounded to form a paste. In my efforts to make my own Dalaar as authentically as possible using the herbs at my disposal in Southern California, I reached out to the wonderful young Iranian chef Hanif Sadr in Berkeley, who serves up northern Iranian cuisine at his pop-up dinners called Komaaj. Hanif shared that in order to re-create the scent and flavors of the impossible-to-find northern Iranian herbs, we can look to our own surroundings and seek what is native to our own landscape. Combine cilantro and mint, with a small touch of a bitter herb, such as sharp summer savory, sorrel, arugula, basil, or tarragon. I use savory here, but feel free to experiment with what is available to you.*

Soleil has become our official Dalaar maker lately, pounding and bashing the herbs and salt in a mortar and pestle, releasing their aroma and magic, as Luna and I happily spread it on crisp Persian cucumbers and create our own Dalaar memories—California-style. Serve Dalaar with sliced Persian cucumbers as a cool summer snack or as a salad. It can also be served as a spread alongside sour green plums and raw green almonds (see page 65), crisp lettuce, orange slices, and tart green apples, or stirred into yogurt and salad dressings.

MAKES ABOUT ⅓ CUP

1 bunch cilantro, stems removed

½ bunch mint, stems removed

1¼ teaspoons kosher salt, or to taste

2 teaspoons fresh savory, or 1 teaspoon dried

Roughly run your knife through the cilantro and mint leaves once or twice. Place all the ingredients in a mortar and pestle and grind and bash into a thick paste, until well combined and dizzyingly fragrant. Taste and see if it needs anything. Alternatively, you can place all the ingredients in a food processor and pulse into a paste, taking care not to turn the herbs into mush.

(continued)

Dalaar *(continued)*

    Keep in mind that Dalaar is a salt replacement, and only a little is used at a time, so it should be pleasantly salty. You can use Dalaar right away, but for optimal taste, transfer it to a container and place in the fridge for 24 hours for the flavors to marry.

MAKE AHEAD: Dalaar will keep in the fridge for well over a week.

PREP AHEAD: See page 12 for fresh herb prep.

Seerabeh

Walnut Verjuice Dip

Seerabeh is a tangy walnut and verjuice–based northern Iranian sauce typically served with fish. I also like to thicken it slightly and serve it as a dip with crisp veggies and flatbread. Verjuice (page 352) is the star acid used here and worth seeking out to subtly brighten and tame the fervor of the walnuts. But you can also try substituting lemon juice. Just start with less and add more as desired. Make this dip a couple of days ahead; the flavors settle and really come to life after a good rest in the fridge.

SERVES 6

1 cup walnuts, finely ground to a paste

3 cloves garlic, crushed to a paste

¾ cup verjuice (plus more as needed)

½ teaspoon kosher salt

⅛ teaspoon ground turmeric

⅛ teaspoon ground black pepper

Handful of fresh cilantro, tough stems trimmed, finely chopped

Fresh mint

Place the walnut paste in a medium pan. Gently toast over medium heat, stirring often, until fragrant, about 5 minutes. Take care not to burn it. Add the garlic, verjuice, salt, turmeric, and pepper. Be careful: the verjuice will spit as soon as it hits the hot pan. Reduce the heat to medium-low and simmer the sauce until it slightly thickens (it will thicken more as it sits), about 10 minutes. Transfer the sauce to a bowl. Stir in the cilantro and set aside to cool for a few minutes. Taste and add another splash of verjuice, and some salt and pepper, if needed. It will most likely need it. Cover and let rest in the fridge for a day or two before serving.

MAKE AHEAD: Prepare up to 3 days in advance and store in the fridge.

Chaghaleh Badam va Gojeh Sabz

Raw Green Almonds and Sour Green Plums

Persians have an affinity for a variety of unripe, crunchy, sour fruits and nuts. Such is the case for our love of raw green almonds and sour green plums. A giddy feeling takes over our house when these early springtime snacks start popping at the market. It used to be that you could find them only at Iranian or other Middle Eastern markets, but in the past few years they've been appearing at farmers' markets. The simplest and most pleasurable way to snack on both of these delights is to sprinkle them with a little salt and munch away. The almonds are eaten whole but, as all Persian mothers will warn, go easy on both the almonds and plums. Eating too many will not make for a happy digestive system. Both chaghaleh badam *and* gojeh sabz *can also be pickled or used in stews or* aash. *You can also slice up the fuzzy green almonds and add them to a salad, like Cabbage Salad (page 56). The season for both these treats is short, between late March and early May.*

Large handful of raw green almonds

Large handful of sour green plums

Kosher salt for sprinkling

Dalaar (page 60), for dipping (optional)

Golpar (Persian hogweed; see page 357), for sprinkling (optional)

Rinse the fuzzy green almonds and the sour green plums in cold water. If you have time, soak the almonds in ice-cold water for about 10 minutes and drain them. Serve both with salt for sprinkling, or a small dish of Dalaar for dipping.

Another fun way to serve sour green plums is to drape a kitchen towel that you don't mind staining over a cutting board, place the plums on half of the towel, and fold the other half over the plums, covering them. Then whack and bash the plums to your heart's content with a rolling pin or the back of a pan, until they just break up. Scoop up the plums and place them in a bowl, sprinkle with salt and a little golpar, or alternatively with Dalaar. Cover the bowl with the kitchen towel and shake and shimmy the bowl hard, back and forth, like a crazed tambourine player, until the sour green plums and their juices soak up the salt or Dalaar. Dig in with your hands.

Sour Cherry and Feta Crostini

This Sour Cherry and Feta Crostini is inspired by my childhood breakfasts of tea, feta cheese, and floral jams. I love serving it as an appetizer, maybe with a cool glass of rosé, or as part of a brunch spread. It's the first thing to go flying off the table. If sour cherries are not in season, or you are simply in no mood to make your own preserves, you can purchase sour cherry preserves from Middle Eastern or Mediterranean markets, and online. But keep in mind that they will most likely be much sweeter. These crostini also shine topped with poached quince (page 325) or roasted rhubarb (page 319).

Sour Cherry Preserves

MAKES ABOUT 1½ CUPS

1 pound sour cherries, pitted

1 cup sugar

1 tablespoon fresh lime juice

1 tablespoon rose water (optional)

Place the sour cherries in a medium bowl. Add the sugar and mix. Partially cover and set aside to macerate for 3 hours or overnight.

Place the macerated cherries and their juices in a heavy-bottomed medium pan, and add the lime juice. Bring to a quick boil over medium-high heat (this won't take long, so keep a close eye on it). Reduce the heat to medium-low and simmer, stirring often, until the cherries soften and the mixture slightly thickens, 20 to 25 minutes. Transfer the cherries to a glass jar. The cherries will release a lot of juice; you can keep reducing the juices for another 5 minutes, but keep in mind that the preserves will thicken considerably as they sit. Pour the syrup over the cherries and add the rose water (if using). Stir, and set aside to cool to room temperature. Cover and store in the fridge. These will keep in the fridge for well over a month, if they don't get eaten before then.

Crostini

Baguette, sliced

Olive oil for drizzling

Feta cheese

Sour Cherry Preserves

Crushed pistachios

Fresh mint leaves

Toast the bread in the oven or on a grill until nice and crisp. Lightly drizzle with a fragrant olive oil. Spread the feta cheese on the baguette slices. Top with sour cherry preserves, crushed pistachios, and a couple of mint leaves, and serve.

Torshi Liteh

Eggplant and Herb Pickles

The great symphony of a Persian meal would be incomplete without the presence of torshi—*a variety of pickled vegetables and fruits.* Torshi *is derived from the word* torsh, *meaning "sour." In keeping with satisfying the Persian palate for all things sour, torshi is served like a relish alongside the main dishes. There are endless combinations and preparations of torshi. Here I've chosen our favorite. Torshi Liteh makes a regular appearance at our table and it's one that the kids enjoy as much as the adults.* Liteh *is typically a mix of eggplant, herbs, and spices. The spice mix—Advieh Torshi—will strike you as a long list. But many of the spices are common and most likely in your spice cupboard already. Use as many of the recommended spices as you can. Nigella seeds (*siah daneh*) and golpar in particular lend this torshi its distinct taste. You can also purchase packaged spice mixes for torshi from Persian markets and online.*

Note: It is imperative that all the vegetables and herbs used in torshi be completely dry after washing. Otherwise the moisture and condensation will make the torshi go bad. Also, take care to use a clean spoon to scoop out the torshi, avoiding any cross contamination, and avoid the addition of any oils to the torshi. If these precautions are taken, torshi can keep in the fridge for months.

MAKES ABOUT 2 QUARTS

1½ pounds Chinese or Japanese eggplant (about 5 Japanese or 3 large Chinese), tops and ends trimmed, sliced into ½-inch-thick rounds

1 quart plus ½ cup good-quality white wine vinegar, divided (plus more as needed)

1 bunch parsley, stems trimmed

1 bunch cilantro, stems trimmed, finely chopped

½ bunch mint, stems trimmed, finely chopped

½ bunch tarragon, leaves picked off the stems, finely chopped

1 large carrot, grated on the large holes of a box grater

4 cloves garlic, finely chopped

ADVIEH TORSHI
(TORSHI SPICE MIX)

4 whole black peppercorns

2 allspice berries

1 bay leaf, crumbled

1 teaspoon siah daneh (nigella seeds; see page 355)

1 teaspoon kosher salt

½ teaspoon coriander seeds

¼ teaspoon golpar (Persian hogweed; see page 357)

¼ teaspoon ground cinnamon

¼ teaspoon ground cardamom

¼ teaspoon ground dried rose petals (see page 18)

⅛ teaspoon cumin seeds

⅛ teaspoon mustard seeds

Place the sliced eggplant in a large pot and cover with white wine vinegar, about 1 quart. Raise the heat to high and bring to a boil. Reduce the heat to medium and cook, uncovered, stirring occasionally, until the eggplant has completely softened and cooked through, about 10 minutes. Strain the eggplant in a large fine-mesh strainer. Set aside to strain and cool completely.

Meanwhile, combine all the torshi spice mix ingredients in a small bowl and set aside. Once cooled, set the eggplant in a large bowl and mash with the back of a fork. Add the parsley, cilantro, mint, tarragon, grated carrot, garlic, spice mix, and ½ cup white wine vinegar. Mix well. Transfer the mixture to a sterilized glass jar with a tight-fitting lid. Start adding enough vinegar to cover the mixture by ½ inch at the top. The top of the torshi should always be covered with ½ inch of vinegar. Seal the jar and set aside in a cool dark spot for 48 hours. Move the torshi to the fridge and leave to pickle for at least 3 to 4 weeks before digging in. The torshi will keep in the fridge for many months. Top off with vinegar as needed.

PREP AHEAD: See page 12 for prepping fresh green herbs.

HEART

In our home growing up, a pot of *aash* was always at a simmer and a container of yogurt was omnipresent at the table to restore order and balance not only to the meal, but to the body and the world at large. A slightly tangy, creamy, wobbly, cooling side of *maast* to cut through a rich, warm stew or aash. Aash, a nourishing variety of hearty soups brimming with fresh green herbs, legumes, and grains, is the foundation of the Persian kitchen, and plain yogurt its heart.

When we first moved to Vancouver, circa the early 1980s, a tub of plain, full-fat yogurt proved an unforeseen challenge to come by. Single-serving containers of sweetened, cavity-inducing yogurt were the closest thing to be found. Or a special trip was required to a far-flung health food store, where you could possibly find a slightly larger container of overpriced yogurt, and a variety of edible goods resembling cardboard and hay.

In our house there was no talk of probiotics or gut health in relation to brain health, and nobody counted numbers of active, inactive, or proactive cultures. We just consumed plain or savory-flavored (rarely sweetened, unless with a drizzle of honey) yogurt by the bowlful because it was said to be a healer and a unifier. Digestion, indigestion, skin, cuts, scrapes, burns, hair, marriage, divorce, memory loss, and a broken heart. Name the ailment, and yogurt was the cure. To this day nothing satisfies a mid-afternoon or late-night craving more than a big bowl of plain yogurt with a large handful, or two, of salty chips on the side.

In the midst of the Iranian Revolution, uncertainty and long food lines dominated our kitchen table talks as we sought comfort in a pot of aash topped with a big dollop of maast. The strength of the economy, and in turn the stability of the country, was determined by the price of oil and the price of yogurt. The longer the yogurt line, the pricier the yogurt, the more unstable the country. None of which boded well for the future of the average citizen. In our new peaceful hometown of Vancouver, British Columbia, yogurt lines were of no concern, because there just wasn't any to be found.

My mother, Maman, never one to settle for a pot of aash without a swirl of yogurt, fully embraced and committed to her new role as resourceful immigrant mama. She determined the only way to survive was to make big batches of homemade yogurt in our tiny apartment kitchen. Milk, culture, a pot, a pinky finger, and a good night's rest wrapped up in a cozy blanket were all that was needed.

Slowly and gently the milk was brought up to temperature, just shy of a boil. Next the heat was turned off and the pot of milk was left alone to its own devices to cool. At some point Maman would take the temperature of the milk much in the same way that she would check my temperature when I didn't feel well, tenderly laying a hand on my forehead, or holding my wrist in her hand. Always a finger on my pulse. Her mother's intuition carried over to the welfare of the milk as well, as she immersed her pinky finger in the hot pot. If she was able to keep her finger in there comfortably for five seconds without scalding it, it meant the milk's fever had broken, and it was ready to be cultured, and who better to culture it than a university-professor-turned-resourceful-immigrant mama? A few dollops of plain yogurt, either from the previous week's batch or from a small container purchased from some far-flung location, were scooped out and plopped into the milk. Then the pot was covered and readied for its midnight slumber.

Once a week, on yogurt-making nights, I offered up my childhood blanket to keep the pot of soon-to-be luscious yogurt warm. The very same blanket that had been left behind in Iran, unaware that I would never return to it. The same blanket that was covertly retrieved by Maman and brought back to me in Rome. The same blanket that now occupies a small corner of my closet in Los Angeles, tucked away but always present, ready to serve.

As we said our good nights, Maman would first wrap the pot of newly cultured milk in a soft sheet, just in case any errant fuzz balls from my blanket were to find their way into the firmly covered pot. Then she would gently lay my blanket over it and tuck in the yogurt. The familiar, comforting sour scent of fermentation rocking us to sleep. Overnight, the pot of what was once plain milk wondrously transformed into a pot of fresh, thick maast. As far as I was concerned the night held inexplicable magical powers, and my blanket was privy to all its secrets.

During our kitchen table yogurt talks, I had overheard incredulous tales of how years ago, Russian or Greek immigrants cultured their batches of homemade yogurt with culture they had managed to sneak in from the homeland. Dollops of yogurt that miraculously survived treacherous sea travel. Which made me surmise that despite my mother's best efforts to fortify and secure the maast pot against any errant invaders, a little piece of Iran always somehow managed to seep through the fibers of my well-traveled blanket and make its way into the yogurt, dolloped into the aash pot and into our hearts.

What sets aash apart from a typical brothy soup is consistency—aash is richer and thicker. Aash is so integral to Iranian cuisine that the word for "cook" is *aash paz*—the maker of aash. The word for "kitchen" is *aash paz khaneh*—the house or room where aash is prepared. You can serve a small bowl of aash at the start of a meal to open up the appetite and fortify the stomach for the ensuing meal, or it can be served as a meal all unto itself. Aash tastes even better made ahead of time, allowing the flavors to deepen and come to life. This chapter includes a mix of traditional aash along with a few of our favorite soups.

A starchy rice is typically used to thicken and flavor the aash. If you don't have time to use dried beans you can always use canned beans, in which case you might need less water, and remember to adjust the seasoning accordingly. The same goes for the bunches of herbs. It's okay to substitute one bunch here and there for ¼ cup of dried. But I recommend using as many fresh herbs as you can.

How you accessorize your aash is key. Be it a dollop of thick, creamy yogurt, a swirl of umami-rich *kashk*, fried onion-garlic-mint (page 38), an extra drizzle of olive oil or vinegar, chopped fresh herbs, or simply a squeeze of lemon.

Much like the kitchen itself, aash also serves as the symbolic and culinary call to nourish, cure, celebrate, and unite. If there is a special occasion, there is a corresponding aash to commemorate it. If there is an ailment, there is an aash to cure it. And if there is a need for the neighborhood, the community to unite and join hands to celebrate or to aid and comfort one another in times of sorrow, it is done over a big pot of aash. Taking turns, slowly stirring in wishes and hopes for a healthier, brighter future.

Aash-e Dogha
Yogurt Soup

Agha joon and Mamani, my paternal grandparents, spent the early years of their marriage in Baku, the capital of the Republic of Azerbaijan. Agha joon was a merchant and at the time exported Iranian rice to Baku. There are many variations and iterations of this simple and beloved yogurt-based soup, also known as dovga, *Azerbaijani wedding soup, and* aash-e doogh *in Iran. This is Mamani's version, which has traveled from Baku to Gilan Province in Iran and was shared with me by my cousin Laleh in Paris. Like a game of telephone, the recipe has been whispered and passed along over time and oceans. Use a full-fat sour yogurt, sometimes called European style, for this aash.*

The most important note in preparing Aash-e Dogha is to stir, stir, and stir this aash, always in one direction, so the yogurt doesn't split, boil over, or stick to the bottom of the pot. Good time to pull up a stool and get the kids involved, or pour yourself a glass of wine to keep the hand that is not doing the stirring occupied. I find the constant stirring imperative in the first fifteen minutes, as the aash comes up to a boil. But then you can ease up on it a little (easing up on the wine is optional) and tend to other matters, as long as you are close by to keep an eye on it and give a stir every couple of minutes. No one seems to know why the aash has to be stirred in one direction, and no one wants to risk finding out why. Mamani's recipe uses only meatballs, but you can easily trade in the meatballs for cooked chickpeas for a vegetarian meal, or use a combination of the two. The same goes for the herbs: use any fragrant herbs you like. Baby spinach also works well. Like all other aash, Aash-e Dogha is even better the next day. Just remember to stir in one direction—as the world turns.

SERVES 6

1 recipe Everyday Meatballs
(page 260)

3 tablespoons unbleached,
all-purpose flour

4 cups (one 32-ounce container)
plain, full-fat sour yogurt

½ medium yellow onion, grated
on the small holes of a box
grater (or use a food processor
and blitz it to a pulp)

2 tablespoons jasmine rice,
rinsed

2 tablespoons butter

2¾ teaspoons kosher salt (plus
more as needed)

¼ teaspoon ground black
pepper (plus more as needed)

Handful of dill and/or mint,
tough stems trimmed, roughly
chopped (optional)

½ bunch cilantro, tough stems
trimmed, roughly chopped

(continued)

Form the meatballs into small rounds (about 2 teaspoons of mix per meatball, about 34 meatballs total). Set aside until ready to use.

In a small bowl, combine the flour with 3 tablespoons water until smooth. Set aside. Prep, measure out, and have all the other ingredients within reach before you start on the aash.

Off the heat, briskly whisk the yogurt and 4 cups water in a large heavy-bottomed pot until fully combined and frothy. Give the flour mixture a quick stir, making sure there are no lumps, and add it to the pot along with the onion. Stir to combine, place on the stove, and bring to a boil over medium-high heat, stirring constantly—in one direction! It will take 10 to 12 minutes to bring to a boil. Keep at a gentle boil, stirring constantly, for 5 minutes.

Reduce the heat to medium, and add the rice and butter. Simmer, stirring frequently, until the rice is tender, about 10 minutes. You can tend to the dirty dishes in the sink or help out with math homework at this point, but don't go far away. Keep the one-way stirring going; you just don't have to be stuck to the pot and wooden spoon.

Add the meatballs, salt, and pepper, and simmer until the meatballs have cooked through and all the flavors have melded, about 20 minutes. Taste and add more salt and pepper as you like. Remove from the heat, stir in the herbs to just wilt through, and serve.

MAKE AHEAD: Prepare up to 3 days in advance. Aash-e Dogha tastes even better made ahead of time. Reheat gently on the stovetop and add water as needed to thin out, then taste and adjust the seasoning.

PREP AHEAD: The meatballs can be made up to 3 hours in advance and stored in the fridge. Bring to room temperature before adding to the aash.

PLAN AHEAD: This aash does not freeze well.

Aash-e Miveh

Fruit Soup

Aash-e Miveh is a ghazal—*a love poem—celebrating the bounty of summer fruits during the dreary, colder winter months. Drying sweet summer fruits whole, or into* lavashak— *fruit leathers—is a very common form of preservation in Iran. Dried fruits are used abundantly in savory dishes, such as aash and stews, and for stuffing meatballs, chicken, or fish. If you happen to come across* ghooreh *(sour green grapes; see page 351—fresh ones are in season from late May to mid-June) you can throw some in here along with the vinegar to cut through and balance the sweetness of the fruit. Use any combination of dried fruits you like. Serve this Aash-e Miveh when you need a reminder of warm summer nights. It also makes for a soothing and lovely dish at a holiday table.*

SERVES 6

¼ cup olive oil

1 medium yellow onion, diced

2 cloves garlic, chopped

⅓ cup jasmine rice, rinsed

½ teaspoon ground turmeric

Kosher salt

¼ cup red kidney beans, picked through and soaked for at least 6 hours

¼ cup chickpeas, picked through and soaked for at least 6 hours

Piaz Daagh–Seer Daagh–Na'na Daagh (fried onion-garlic-mint; page 38)

½ cup yellow split peas, picked through and rinsed

Ground black pepper

1 bunch parsley, tough stems trimmed, finely chopped

1 bunch cilantro, tough stems trimmed, finely chopped

½ bunch green onions, finely chopped

¼ bunch mint, stems trimmed, finely chopped, or 1 tablespoon dried

6 dried apricots, chopped

6 dried prunes, chopped

¼ cup dried cranberries

¼ cup dark or golden raisins

½ bunch beet greens or spinach, finely chopped

2 tablespoons ghooreh (sour green grapes; see page 351), rinsed well if in brine (optional)

¼ cup red wine vinegar (plus more as needed)

In a large pot, heat the oil over medium-high heat. Add the onion and cook, stirring frequently, until golden brown, about 8 minutes. Reduce the heat to medium, and add the garlic, rice, turmeric, and a pinch of salt. Cook until fragrant, about 2 minutes. Add the red kidney beans and chickpeas, give a stir, and add 9 cups water. Partially cover, raise the heat to high, and bring to a boil. Reduce the heat to medium, and briskly simmer for 25 minutes.

Meanwhile, prepare the Piaz Daagh–Seer Daagh–Na'na Daagh and set aside, if you don't have some stashed in the fridge or freezer.

Add the yellow split peas, 1 tablespoon salt, and ¼ teaspoon pepper to the aash. Give a quick stir, bring back up to a quick boil, reduce the heat to medium, and briskly simmer, partially covered, for 10 minutes. Add

Aash-e Miveh *(continued)*

the parsley, cilantro, green onions, and mint, bring back up to a gentle boil, reduce the heat to medium-low, partially cover, and simmer, stirring occasionally, for 30 minutes.

Add the dried fruits, beet greens, and ghooreh (if using). Bring back up to a quick boil, reduce the heat to low, cover with the lid slightly ajar, and simmer until the beans have cooked through and all the flavors shine, 20 to 30 minutes. Taste as you go and add more water as needed, the aash will thicken substantially. Add the vinegar just before serving. Keep in mind the vinegar will dissipate over time. Top each bowl with some Piaz Daagh–Seer Daagh–Na'na Daagh and serve.

MAKE AHEAD: This aash really falls into place as it sits. Make it up to 3 days in advance, store it in the fridge, add water to thin it (it will really thicken as it sits), and adjust seasoning when reheating.

PREP AHEAD: See page 12 for fresh herb prep and storage. Remember to chop up the mint right before cooking, not earlier, as it will turn bitter.

PLAN AHEAD: Store for up to 3 months in the freezer. Thaw and reheat, adding more water as needed.

Aash-e Gojeh Farangi

Tomato Soup

Aash-e Gojeh Farangi found its way to us from Roohy jan, my step-grandmother's, kitchen in Tabriz. It's the kind of homemade pot of comfort you daydream of on a busy and hectic day. The only liberty I've taken is adding a couple of cloves of garlic to complement the tomatoes. The black-eyed peas are parcooked separately here so their murky broth doesn't muddy the color of the aash, an extra little step in the name of beauty. I sometimes swap out the bulgur wheat for farro, and if you cannot eat wheat you can also omit it and add more rice. Verjuice adds the zing to this aash, but depending on the richness of your tomato paste and tomatoes you might not need any extra acidity at all. Be sure to pick ripe but firm tomatoes to make the grating easier. If tomatoes are not in season a can of good-quality crushed tomatoes can be used.

SERVES 6

½ cup black-eyed peas, picked through and soaked for 6 hours, and drained

Kosher salt

¼ cup olive oil

1 medium yellow onion, diced

2 cloves garlic, chopped

⅓ cup coarse (#3) bulgur, rinsed

⅓ cup jasmine rice, rinsed

4 cups chicken stock or vegetable stock

6 beefsteak tomatoes

1 bunch parsley, tough stems trimmed, finely chopped

1 bunch cilantro, tough stems trimmed, finely chopped

1 bunch green onions, finely chopped

1 tablespoon dried mint

2 tablespoons tomato paste

Verjuice or lemon juice

Ground black pepper

Na'na daagh (mint oil) (optional)

NA'NA DAAGH

3 tablespoons cup olive oil

2 tablespoons cup dried mint

Place the black-eyed peas in a small pot. Cover with 1¼ cups water and add ½ teaspoon salt. Partially cover and bring to a gentle boil, turn down the heat to medium-low, and simmer until the beans have slightly softened but not completely cooked through, 10 to 15 minutes. They will finish cooking through in the aash. Drain and set aside.

In a large pot, heat the oil over medium heat. Add the onion and cook, stirring occasionally, until soft and golden, about 8 minutes. Add the garlic, bulgur, rice, and a pinch of salt. Stir and cook for a couple of minutes. Add the chicken stock and 2 cups water, raise the heat to high, and bring to a boil. Reduce the heat to medium, cover with the lid slightly ajar, and simmer for 10 minutes.

Meanwhile, prepare the tomatoes. Chop one tomato and set aside. Cut the rest of the tomatoes in half across the equator and grate the tomatoes on the large holes of a box grater. Hold your fingers flat against the tomato while you grate. Discard the tomato skin and set aside the tomato pulp (you should have about 3 cups).

Add the parsley, cilantro, green onions, dried mint, 1 tablespoon salt, and ¼ teaspoon pepper to the pot, bring back up to a gentle boil, reduce the heat to medium-low, cover with the lid slightly ajar, and simmer for 15 minutes. Add the tomato paste, tomato pulp, and black-eyed peas, bring back up to a rapid simmer, cover with the lid slightly ajar, reduce the heat to low, and simmer for 30 minutes, until the aash falls into place and comes to life. The longer it simmers, the tastier it becomes. Five minutes before serving add the chopped tomatoes and verjuice to taste if desired. Taste as you go, adding more salt or pepper as you like.

Prepare the na'na daagh while the aash simmers. In a small saucepan, heat the oil over medium heat. Add the mint to the hot oil, give a quick stir, and immediately remove from the heat. Mint burns very quickly.

Garnish the aash with a little na'na daagh and serve.

MAKE AHEAD: Prepare up to 3 days in advance. Add water and more verjuice and seasoning as needed. The na'na daagh will keep in the fridge for up to 1 week.

PREP AHEAD: See page 12 for fresh herb prep. The tomatoes can be grated up to 1 day in advance and stored in the fridge.

PLAN AHEAD: Store for up to 3 months in the freezer. The na'na daagh can also be frozen up to 3 months.

Soup-e Jo ba Adas

Barley and Lentil Soup

Barley and Lentil Soup is the one-pot meal I turn to when I can't bear thinking of what to make for dinner. It's not a traditional Persian aash or soup, but more a combination of the more common Persian barley soup and lentil soup. I stumbled on this family favorite by digging out bits and pieces from the fridge, pantry, and freezer, where I keep flattened squares of tomato paste sealed in baggies stashed in every nook and cranny. The limoo Omani—*dried limes—brighten up the hearty mix of barley and lentils, while the tomato paste adds color and depth. I encourage you to seek out the dried limes as they are the stars of this soup and add a very distinct flavor. If you're unable to find any, a splash of lemon juice, vinegar, or verjuice added at the end gets the job done. Feel free to use any fresh greens you have on hand: spinach, kale, and beet greens (you can also use a few beet stems as you would the chard stems) are all excellent candidates.*

SERVES 6

¼ cup olive oil (plus more for drizzling)

1 medium yellow onion, diced

3 carrots, diced

3 celery stalks, diced

4 large rainbow chard leaves, stems diced, greens finely chopped

2 bay leaves

4 large cloves garlic, chopped

Kosher salt

2 tablespoons tomato paste

½ cup pearled barley

3 medium limoo Omani, pierced (dried limes; see page 349)

Ground black pepper

¾ cup green or brown lentils, picked through and rinsed

Handful of fresh parsley, tough stems trimmed, chopped

4 green onions, sliced

Plain yogurt for serving (optional)

In a large pot, heat the oil over medium heat. Add the onion, carrots, celery, chard stems (set the chard greens aside to add later), bay leaves, garlic, and a good pinch of salt. Cook, stirring occasionally, until the vegetables soften and are fragrant, about 10 minutes.

Stir in the tomato paste and the barley, and cook for 2 minutes, taking care not to burn the tomato paste. Add 10 cups water, turn the heat up to high, and bring to a boil. Add the dried limes, 1 tablespoon salt, and ¼ teaspoon pepper. Reduce the heat to medium-low, cover with the lid slightly ajar, and simmer for 20 minutes. Once or twice, very gently squeeze the dried limes against the side of the pot with a spoon to release their juice. You don't want to squeeze so hard that the limes burst, but as they soften you just want to encourage them to spit out their juices.

Add the lentils and the chard greens, and turn the heat up to bring the soup back to a gentle boil. Reduce the heat to medium-low, cover with the lid slightly ajar, and simmer until the lentils have cooked through, 20 to 30 minutes. Taste as you go and add more salt, pepper, and water to thin out as needed. Stir in the parsley in the final minutes to wilt.

Put the green onions in a small bowl for everyone to garnish their soup as they like. Sometimes I like to top off my bowl with a small (or not so small) dollop of thick, creamy yogurt. Sometimes it's a drizzle of olive oil. Sometimes it's both.

MAKE AHEAD: Prepare up to 3 days in advance. You'll need to adjust the water and seasoning when reheating as it will really thicken up.

PREP AHEAD: If you have 15 minutes in the morning or the night before, chop and prep all the vegetables, except for the garlic. Garlic can be peeled ahead but not chopped. Store all chopped vegetables in an airtight container in the fridge.

PLAN AHEAD: Leftovers of Barley and Lentil Soup make a fabulous school or work lunch. Or freeze the leftovers and enjoy in a few weeks' time on a busy weeknight.

Aash-e Shooli

Lentil and Beet Soup

Steaming-hot, sweet, sticky beets served whole on cold winter days are a mainstay of Iranian street food. Like many ingredients in the Persian kitchen, beets are touted for their healing properties, and are enjoyed hot, cold (beet juice another popular street offering), as a dip (Borani-yeh Laboo, page 49), and in soups. Aash-e Shooli is a Yazdi specialty said to be a "cure" for colds. Hearty enough from the addition of the lentils, this aash really hits the spot on those gray winter days when you need a bright pick-me-up. You can use everyday, utilitarian brown or green lentils. I prefer using green lentils whenever possible as brown lentils can turn the color of the aash a little muddy. If you are unable to find beets by the bunch with the beet greens attached, use spinach instead. The syrupy, sweet-and-sour hint of the balsamic vinegar gives a jolt to the grounded, earthy flavors of the lentils and beets, but feel free to use red wine vinegar or apple cider vinegar. I suggest running the beets through the grating disk of the food processor to keep from staining your fingers magenta. But that, too, can be healing in lifting the spirits.

SERVES 6

¼ cup olive oil (plus more for drizzling)

1 medium red onion, diced

2 tablespoons unsalted butter

4 cloves garlic, chopped

1 leek, white and light green parts only, chopped

Kosher salt

¼ cup jasmine rice, rinsed and drained

½ teaspoon ground turmeric

½ teaspoon ground cumin

½ teaspoon ground coriander

¾ cup green or brown lentils, picked through and rinsed

2 medium beets (about ¾ pound), peeled and grated on the large holes of a box grater (save the greens)

7 cups chicken broth, vegetable broth, or water (or a combination of broth and water)

Ground black pepper

5 beet greens, stems removed, finely chopped

1 bunch dill (save a few sprigs for topping), stems removed, finely chopped

2 tablespoons balsamic vinegar (plus more as needed)

Yogurt for topping (optional)

In a large pot, heat the oil over medium-high heat. Add the onion and cook, stirring frequently, until golden brown, about 8 minutes. Reduce the heat to medium-low, add the butter, garlic, leek, and a good pinch of salt and cook until softened, about 5 minutes. Add the rice, turmeric, cumin, and coriander, and stir for a couple of minutes, until fragrant.

Add the lentils, beets, broth, 2 teaspoons salt, and ¼ teaspoon pepper. Turn up the heat, and bring to a boil. Reduce the heat to medium-low, cover with the lid slightly ajar, and simmer for 30 minutes, stirring once in a while.

Add the beet greens and dill. Cover and simmer until the lentils have cooked through but are not mushy, and all the flavors have happily melded, about 15 minutes. Add more water if needed to thin out. Turn off the heat and stir in the balsamic vinegar. Serve with a drizzle of olive oil and/or a swirl of yogurt, and a few dill fronds. Place the vinegar on the table and let everyone drizzle more as they like.

MAKE AHEAD: Prepare up to 3 days ahead. Add water as needed when reheating, as the lentils and beets will suck up a significant amount of broth. Taste and adjust the seasoning as needed.

PREP AHEAD: The beets can be grated up to 1 day in advance and stored in an airtight container in the fridge.

PLAN AHEAD: Portion off in containers and freeze for up to 3 months. Thaw and reheat at the first sign of the sniffles.

Butternut Squash Soup

This silky-smooth soup makes an appearance on our dinner table once a week during the fall months. Butternut squash always sounds so luscious, but I find it often needs a little something extra to give it a boost of flavor. For this soup I like to combine the squash with a sweet potato and fragrant, warming spices that I have on hand in my spice cupboard, such as cumin and cinnamon. Sometimes, if the mood and inspiration strike, I also drizzle in the smallest amount of maple syrup and/or orange blossom water when blending the soup. The sweetness from the syrup and the fragrance from the flower water should be a faint curiosity lingering in the back, a note you can't quite put your finger on. A final sprinkling of crimson red sumac looks beautiful against the deep orange of the soup and adds a tangy accent, an exclamation mark, to its slight sweetness. Serve with your favorite crusty bread for everyone to tear off at the table and dip into their bowls.

SERVES 6

3 tablespoons olive oil

1 red onion, chopped

2 cloves garlic, chopped

Kosher salt

1 medium butternut squash (about 2¾ pounds), peeled, seeded, and chopped

1 sweet potato (about 8 ounces), peeled and chopped

½ teaspoon ground cinnamon

¾ teaspoon ground cumin

¼ teaspoon ground coriander

Ground black pepper

⅛ to ¼ teaspoon ground saffron (optional)

Drizzle of maple syrup (optional)

A few drops of orange blossom water (optional)

Sumac for serving

In a large pot, heat the oil over medium heat. Add the onion and cook until soft and translucent, about 8 minutes. Add the garlic and a pinch of salt and cook for another 2 minutes. Add the squash, sweet potato, cinnamon, cumin, coriander, 2½ teaspoons salt, and ¼ teaspoon pepper. Stir to combine and cook, stirring occasionally, until fragrant, about 5 minutes.

Add 3½ cups water, turn the heat up to high, and bring to a boil. Reduce the heat to medium-low and add the saffron, if using. Stir to combine, cover, and simmer until the squash and sweet potatoes are soft and cooked through, about 25 minutes. Taste the broth for seasoning.

(continued)

Butternut Squash Soup *(continued)*

Blend the soup in a blender until smooth. Give a taste. If you like, drizzle with the tiniest bit of maple syrup and/or orange blossom water, and blitz again to combine. Serve and brighten up each bowl and palette with a sprinkling of sumac.

MAKE AHEAD: Prepare up to 3 days in advance. Thin out with water when reheating, if necessary.

PREP AHEAD: The vegetables (except for the garlic) can all be chopped 1 day ahead and stored in the refrigerator in a sealed container.

PLAN AHEAD: Freeze this soup tonight and enjoy it the next time you're about to call for take-out. Add a little water if necessary when reheating.

Aabgoosht

Aabgoosht is neither soup nor aash. It's a combination of part aromatic soup and part rich and flavorful stew. It means "meat (goosht) broth/water (aab)" and it's the embodiment of Persian "poor person's food." In recent years it has also become a darling of those just discovering Iranian food. Pieces of beef, lamb, or veal shank are slowly simmered in a rich tomato-based broth. Beans and potatoes are added for bulk and to enrich the broth with starchy goodness. Humble ingredients and a few key spices magically transform a meager meal into a celebrated one. If a family does not have the means to afford meat, then they rely on the bones and the marrow to flavor the broth and provide nourishment. This is a meal that famously can stretch and feed unexpected visitors. Simply add more water to the broth, or drop in a couple more potatoes, or add a handful more beans.

You can serve Aabgoosht as is after it has slowly and gently simmered away. But for a more traditional and fun presentation the broth is served separately with pieces of torn sangak *bread plopped in. The meat, beans, and potatoes are then pounded to a chunky paste—*goosht koobideh—*with a flat-surfaced meat pounder and served with sangak or lavash bread, Torshi Liteh (page 68), and plenty of Sabzi Khordan (page 32) for a bright and fresh lift.*

SERVES 6

¼ cup olive oil

1 yellow onion, diced

2½ to 3 pounds beef, lamb, or veal shank on the bone, fat trimmed, cut into large (about 2-inch) pieces with the bone attached

1 teaspoon ground turmeric

2 tablespoons tomato paste

Kosher salt

½ cup chickpeas, soaked for at least 6 hours

½ cup red kidney beans, soaked for at least 6 hours

2 large Yukon Gold potatoes (about 1 pound), peeled and quartered

4 medium limoo Omani, pierced (dried limes; see page 349)

1 teaspoon Advieh (page 15)

Ground black pepper

1 to 2 lemons

Sangak bread for serving

In a large pot, heat the oil over medium-high heat. Add the onion and cook, stirring frequently, until golden brown, about 8 minutes. Add the meat, turmeric, tomato paste, and a good pinch of salt and cook for 5 minutes for the meat to take on color, taking care not to burn the tomato paste. Add 6 cups water, raise the heat to high, and bring to a boil. Cover, reduce the heat to low, and simmer until the meat is tender, about 1½ hours.

Add the chickpeas and red kidney beans, bring back up to a gentle boil, reduce the heat to medium-low, and simmer with the lid slightly ajar for 45 minutes. Add the potatoes, dried limes, 1 tablespoon salt. Advieh, and ¼ teaspoon pepper. Bring back up to a rapid simmer, reduce the heat to low, cover with the lid slightly ajar, and simmer until the meat, beans, and potatoes are tender, about 1 hour.

As the stew simmers and the flavors come to life remember to gently squeeze the dried limes against the side of the pot with a wooden spoon a couple of times to release their juice. Taste, and add a squeeze or two of lemon as needed. Fish out the bone and tap it to release the marrow and stir the marrow to combine if it hasn't already melted into the broth. Discard the bone and the dried limes, and remove from the heat.

Abgoosht can be served in bowls as is. Alternatively, strain the broth and divide it into individual serving bowls. Transfer the meat, potatoes, and beans mixture to a large bowl and pound with a meat pounder (or any large flat-surfaced mortar; you can also use a fork or a potato masher) into a well combined chunky paste—goosht koobideh—similar to the texture of refried beans. Season with salt and pepper, a drizzle of the broth, and a squeeze of lemon juice, as needed. Taste and make it delicious.

Serve the broth bowls with lemon wedges and pieces of toasted sangak bread to tear and plop in. Place the goosht koobideh in the middle of the table for everyone to scoop up with more warmed-through sangak bread.

MAKE AHEAD: Prepare up to 3 days in advance and store in the fridge. Adjust the water and seasoning when reheating.

PLAN AHEAD: Any leftovers can be frozen for up to 3 months.

AABGOOSHT

Aash-e Nazri

Wish Soup

To make a nazr *means to make a pledge or a wish. If a person or a family is going through a hardship, like an illness, or awaiting news of some kind, they make a wish and prepare this aash. Extended family, friends, and neighbors contribute to the aash, donating a portion of the ingredients, in hopes of the wish coming true. The aash is then shared with the community. If the wish comes true a pledge is made to prepare the aash annually and share it with those in need.*

Aash-e Nazri, also known as aash-e sholeh ghalamkar, *captures not only the true essence of aash but also speaks directly to the heart and spirit of the Persian kitchen, in both use of ingredients and the dish's symbolism. The sentiment behind this aash speaks to the generosity of the human spirit, coming together in times of strife and in times of celebration.*

With that generosity of the heart and the pantry in mind, pretty much any combination of beans, grains, and greens can work here. Swap out the mung beans for lentils, the farro (not typically an Iranian ingredient but one of my favorite wheat grains) for bulgur or more rice, leek greens for the green onion. Try black-eyed peas, fancy heirloom beans (I wouldn't use black beans, though, as their flavor and color would overwhelm this aash). Call up your friends, have them show up early to help you sort through the herbs. Make a big batch of this aash together. Set the pot in the middle of the table. Set some aside to share with your neighbors, and dig in. And if you have a wish, make sure to stir that in as well.

SERVES 6

¼ cup olive oil

1 large yellow onion, diced

Kosher salt

4 cloves garlic, chopped

5 beet stems (green leaves saved), chopped (optional)

½ teaspoon ground turmeric

⅓ cup jasmine rice, rinsed

¼ cup farro

⅓ cup chickpeas, picked through and soaked for at least 6 hours

⅓ cup cannellini beans, picked through and soaked for at least 6 hours

⅓ cup red kidney beans, picked through and soaked for at least 6 hours

⅓ cup mung beans, picked through and soaked for at least 3 hours

1 bunch parsley, tough stems trimmed, finely chopped

1 bunch cilantro, tough stems trimmed, finely chopped

1 bunch dill, tough stems trimmed, finely chopped

1 bunch green onions, finely chopped

½ bunch beet greens or spinach, finely chopped

2 tablespoons Piaz Daagh–Seer Daagh–Na'na Daagh (fried onion-garlic-mint, page 38, plus more as garnish)

Ground black pepper

3 tablespoons kashk or Greek yogurt or sour cream or crème fraîche (plus more as garnish)

In a large pot, heat the oil over medium-high heat. Add the onion and cook, stirring frequently, until golden brown, 8 minutes. Sprinkle with a little salt. Reduce the heat to medium, add the garlic, beet stems, and a good pinch of salt, and cook until slightly softened, about 5 minutes.

Add the turmeric, rice, and farro, and cook, stirring, until fragrant, about 2 minutes. Add the chickpeas, cannellini beans, red kidney beans, and 12 cups water. Raise the heat to high and bring to a boil. Reduce the heat to medium, cover with the lid slightly ajar, and simmer for 35 to 40 minutes.

Meanwhile, you can prepare the Piaz Daagh–Seer Daagh–Na'na Daagh, if you don't have some stashed in the fridge or freezer.

Add the mung beans. Bring back up to a gentle boil and reduce the heat to medium, cover with the lid slightly ajar, and simmer until the beans have slightly softened, 10 to 15 minutes. Add all the herbs, chopped green onions, beet greens, 2 tablespoons of Piaz Daagh–Seer Daagh–Na'na Daagh, 1 tablespoon salt, and ¼ teaspoon pepper. Cover with the lid slightly ajar and simmer for 30 to 40 minutes, until all the flavors and fragrances fall into place and blossom. Stir occasionally, making sure nothing sticks to the bottom of the pot. Add more water if the aash gets too thick. Taste as you go, and add more salt and pepper as you like. Keep in mind that the kashk is salty.

Turn off the heat and stir in the kashk or yogurt. Taste and add more to your liking. Garnish with extra kashk or yogurt and Piaz Daagh–Seer Daagh–Na'na Daagh, serve, and tuck in.

MAKE AHEAD: Prepare up to 3 days in advance. Aash-e Nazri simply gets better prepared ahead of time, as the flavors come together, intensify, and really fall into place. Gently reheat on the stovetop, and add water to thin out and adjust the seasoning as needed.

PREP AHEAD: The fresh herbs can be prepped (page 12) 1 day ahead and stored in airtight containers in the fridge. Make a batch of Piaz Daagh–Seer Daagh–Na'na Daagh and always have some on hand in the freezer or fridge.

PLAN AHEAD: Store up to 3 months in the freezer. Portion off and grab on a harried weeknight. Reheat, soothe, and make a wish.

Rice,
Tahdig &
Grains

JEWELS

Maman, my mother, sits at her dedicated spot at our Los Angeles kitchen table. She speaks to me of Hafez, Khayyam, Rumi, and Sa'adi. The jewels of Persian literature, the weavers of truth, love, and light. I do my best to listen patiently to the stories I have heard countless times, as I eye the *tick-tock* of the clock and consider dinner options. I remind myself that these days and these conversations are fleeting. I am fully aware of the preciousness of time. Time is insolent, it knows no do-overs, it is a dictator that can never be overthrown. No revolution and no hunger strike can ever change its course.

As she breaks down a verse—*tee, tak, tak, tee, tak, tak*—I heave a twenty-pound sack of rice off the pantry floor and watch as each grain clanks into the bowl: *tee, tak, tak, tee, tak, tak*. I rinse the rice a few times, washing off the starch, swirling it around with my finger, just as she taught me.

Luna and Soleil, my daughters, my shadows, burst into the kitchen, abruptly breaking the rhythm of Khayyam's *Rubaiyat*. In a frenzy they orbit around me and their grandmother. Spinning and spinning, they ask the inevitable question: What's for dinner? *Chelo khoresh*, rice with stew, I respond. With *tahdig*, they implore as they run out. Of course there will be tahdig, their grandmother calls after them. No matter what, there will always be tahdig. It's who we are. It's where we come from.

I bring a pot of water to a boil as Maman slowly makes her way to the stove. Frail and ravaged knees now dictate her every move, but her focus is laser sharp and beamed on the rice pot. She's concerned I haven't added enough water and salt to the pot. Reminding me that the rice needs plenty of room to stretch its legs, preparing itself for its grand pas de deux, and because it leaps around in there for a very short time it's our only chance to salt it. A most familiar conversation.

I add the rice to the well-salted water, and there we pause. Mother and daughter at the rice pot. Tradition, culture, and the meaning of life contained in this one critical moment. Exactly when to drain the rice?

We take turns breaking a grain between our fingers and place a few more in our mouths. Each grain should soften on the outside but still have a bite to it on the inside. Where only moments ago the poetry of Hafez and Sa'adi and the giggles and squeals of children reverberated, the house is now filled with silence. For a brief moment time surrenders and stands still as we bite a single grain of rice.

"Now! Now! Turn it off! Drain it, drain it! Now! Now!"

Maman's commands shatter the silence. I frantically search for the kitchen mitts because every second is critical and everything is critical. It's just a pot of rice, I want to remind us, it'll all be okay. But I don't, because it's more than a pot of rice.

I gently nudge Maman out of the way and grab the pot. While the rice drains I melt the butter and she sprinkles the saffron, for color, for warmth, for a sunrise and a sunset. She scatters some grains over the bottom of the pot, the tahdig layer, as I add the rest and make small vent holes for the steam to escape. She covers the pot and turns up the heat. And once again we both take our places at the rice pot. As soon as the steam slips out of the sides of the lid, Maman gives her finger a little lick and quickly taps the side of the pot. It sizzles. Confirming that the tahdig is setting, the rice is steaming, and the heat can be turned down. We wrap the lid in its shawl, a *damkoni*—dishtowel—to catch any condensation dripping back into the pot. Because every grain of rice should be separate, long, fluffy, and shine on its own. Each grain of rice a jewel scattered across the platter.

When the rice is ready, Maman lifts the lid off the pot as Luna and Soleil find their way back inside. I set the platter next to Maman. But she moves aside and makes room for me.

If it all goes as planned, the fruits of our labor will be met with high-fives, high jumps, and quasi-cartwheels all around. If it all falls apart (quite literally), shoulders will slump, and slight groans will replace the cheers. But everyone will do their best to make me feel better. Next time, they'll say. Because when it comes to tahdig, time is quite forgiving. As many do-overs as you please. After all, it's just a pot of rice.

I place the serving dish over the pot. Inhale. Hold my breath. Tighten up my abs, chant a little mantra, and flip the pot over. A slight exhale slips out at the first sign of success: the *swoosh* sound of the rice dropping from pot to platter. Gently, I pull the pot up and away and there she is: the bottom of the pot—tahdig. A golden sun burning bright in the embrace of a full moon, crispy grains of rice encrusted in perfect formation. It's magic every time. I fully exhale as little hands reach in to break off pieces.

I lift the platter and instinctively extend an arm out to Maman. She balances herself and gives her weight over to me. My other arm reaches for Luna and Soleil as the four of us and a platter of rice make the slow, short walk from stove to kitchen table. Mothers, daughters, and a pot of rice. It's who we are. It's where we come from.

Rice is the crown jewel of Persian cuisine. A platter of fragrant rice is almost always present at the table, the perfect companion to the many flavorful stews, *kookoo*, and kabab, as well as other meat, fish, and vegetable dishes. As a child, there was nothing more comforting to me than a plate of rice with a side of plain yogurt. My version of plain buttered pasta.

To make rice the Persian way, it's essential that you begin with a fragrant long-grain rice, such as basmati. *Chelo*-style (see page 104)—the traditional two-step method of rice preparation—is a little more involved and might not be as familiar, but once you get the hang of the concept, and with some practice, it moves along fairly quickly.

Folklore and mystery shroud the preparation of tahdig (*tah-deeg*), the prized golden, crispy rice, potatoes, or bread encrusted at the bottom of the pot. *Tah* translates to "bottom" and *dig* means "pot." Keep in mind, tahdig-making is not a science but an art form. No one turns out a beautiful tahdig every single time, but when you do it's worthy of a celebration. And on those occasions that it doesn't turn out and your efforts stick to the bottom of the pot, there's nothing more delectable than everyone gathering around one pot, digging in with a wooden spoon and scraping out the crispy grains.

New to rice making? Start with *kateh*-style (the more familiar absorption method), or invest in a Persian rice cooker (see page 114), which takes the guessing out of tahdig-making.

Polo refers to mixed-rice dishes, where you prepare a mix of vegetables, herbs, fruits, legumes, and/or meats, and then layer the mix in with parcooked rice and finish cooking them together. You can prepare the mixed rice dishes with both chelo-style rice or kateh-style rice. In this chapter you will find recipes for both.

Chelo ba Tahdig
Steamed Persian Rice with Tahdig

Chelo is Iran's culinary gift to rice lovers worldwide. This is the traditional two-step method of rice preparation—parboil the rice and drain, add enough oil to the bottom of the pot to turn out (fingers crossed) a crispy, crunchy tahdig, add the rice back to the pot and steam. The result has the tell-tale signs of lovingly prepared Persian rice: long, individual, fragrant, saffron-stained grains of rice, scattered like jewels across a platter with pieces of golden, crispy tahdig shining alongside. I save this method of rice preparation for the weekend and when entertaining.

SERVES 6

---

3 cups white basmati rice

Kosher salt

4 tablespoons clarified butter or unsalted butter, divided (plus more as needed)

1 tablespoon olive oil (plus more as needed)

¼ teaspoon ground saffron, steeped in ¼ cup hot water (see page 17)

1. Place the rice in a medium bowl, and fill it with cold water. Gently wash the rice by swishing it around with your finger, then drain. Repeat until the water runs clear, about 5 rinses. Cover the rice with cold water (about 2 cups), add 2 tablespoons salt, and give a gentle stir. Soak the rice for at least 30 minutes and up to 8 hours, depending on the quality of your rice.

2. Fill a large pot with plenty of water, about 12 cups, bring to a boil, and add a big heaping ¼ cup salt. Drain the rice (but don't rinse) and add it to the pot. Stir once gently and don't go anywhere, as the water can boil over very easily. Scoop off any foam that rises to the top. Taste the water for salt. It should be salty like the sea. Add more salt, if necessary. As soon as you see the first of the rice grains pop up, set your timer for 4 minutes. Start testing the rice at 4 minutes. What you're looking for is a grain that is tender on the outside but still with a bite to it on the inside. This can take anywhere between

5 to 7 minutes, depending on the type of rice. As soon as you think the rice is ready, drain it in a colander and give it a very quick rinse with lukewarm water (use the spray option on your faucet if available; if not, place your hand under the tap and create a spray with your fingers). Test the rice; if it's too salty give it another quick rinse. Set aside to drain completely. Wash and dry the pot, if using the same pot.

3. Place the colander beside you by the stove. Set the rice pot over medium heat. Add 2 tablespoons of the butter, olive oil, and 1 tablespoon of the saffron water, and melt the butter. Swirl the oil around so it evenly covers the bottom of the pot and a little up the sides, adding more butter and/or oil if needed. Work quickly now. As soon as the oil starts sizzling, with a spatula, add enough rice to fully cover the bottom of the pot in a thin layer. Pack down the rice with the back of a spatula. This your tahdig layer.

4. Gently scatter the rest of the rice over the tahdig layer in a pyramid shape, making sure the tahdig layer is covered with more rice. With the handle of a wooden spoon poke a few holes in the rice without hitting the tahdig layer, to allow the steam to escape. Turn up the heat to medium-high, cover, and cook for 10 to 12 minutes for the tahdig to set. You can also try the tahdig test: wet your finger and quickly tap or sprinkle a little water on the side of the pot. If the pot sizzles and the water quickly evaporates, it's time to turn down the heat.

While the tahdig sets, in a small saucepan or microwave melt the remaining 2 tablespoons butter and add it to the remaining saffron water.

5. Lift the lid (without dripping the condensation trapped under the lid back into the pot) and drizzle the butter-saffron mixture over the rice. Wrap the lid in a kitchen towel or a couple of layers of paper towel to catch the condensation. Make sure the kitchen towel or paper towels are secured up top so they don't catch fire! Place the lid firmly back on the pot. Reduce the heat to medium and cook for 10 minutes, until steam escapes from the sides of the pot. Then reduce the heat to medium-low or low (depending on your element), and place a heat diffuser under the pot, if you have one. Cook for 30 to 40 minutes, rotating the pot a few times for even crisping, until the rice is tender and fluffy and the tahdig is crispy and golden.

(continued)

6. To help release the tahdig, fill the sink with about 1 inch of cold water, and set the rice pot in the water quickly. Alternatively, you can wet a kitchen towel and set the pot on the wet towel. To serve, you can scatter the rice, like jewels, across a platter. Gently remove the tahdig whole or in pieces, and serve it on the side. Or, for a more dramatic and applause-worthy presentation, place an appropriate-sized platter over the pot, take a deep breath, and quickly and confidently flip the pot over. There should be a *swish* sound of the release of the tahdig. If your tahdig turns out golden, crispy, and regal, pour yourself, and family and friends, something celebratory, do a little dance, and dig in. If the tahdig doesn't quite turn out as expected—do the very same. It's just a pot of rice, after all. And there's always the promise of next time. As many tahdig do-overs as you like.

*To make the mixed rice dishes Loobia Polo (page 117), Sheveed Polo (page 125), and Adas Polo (page 123) in this manner, begin by making the tahdig layer in step 3. In step 4, add a layer of rice, then a layer of mix. Repeat the layers until all the mix and rice have been used up. End with a rice layer and carry on as usual.

A FEW TIPS AND REMINDERS

❖ Use the best-quality, fragrant, long-grain white rice, such as basmati. Visit an Iranian market if you can and ask them to point you to their favorite brand. Be prepared for a 20-minute diatribe on rice. Iranians love to talk about rice.

❖ Consider the kind of pot you are going to use. These rice recipes are for a 5- or 6-quart, 8- to 10-inch diameter nonstick pot. You can also use an equivalent pan with a tight-fitting lid. When parboiling the rice, a large enough pot is needed to allow the grains to expand and elongate without getting clumpy. If your pot is wider than 10 inches, add more butter or oil accordingly. Generally, you want the surface of the pot or pan to be covered with about ⅛ inch of oil.

❖ For the most fail-safe chance of turning out a successful crispy tahdig, use a nonstick pot. A well-seasoned cast-iron pan or pot can work as well, but you may need to increase the butter-oil amounts. Also make sure your cast-iron pan has plenty of room for the rice and that it has a tight-fitting lid. Many cast-iron pans have a pouring spout which makes it impossible to completely seal with a lid. It also takes some muscle to flip a cast-iron pan. A cast enamel Dutch oven can be moodier in turning out a successful tahdig. Increase the butter-oil amounts and hope for the best. And finally, I raise my glass to those who can turn out a fantastic tahdig in a stainless steel pot, but I don't recommend it. The chances of the tahdig sticking and burning are high, and you might ruin your pot in the process.

❖ I prefer using clarified butter or butter and olive oil to set the tahdig. I don't use vegetable oil out of personal preference, but if you do, go ahead and replace the full amount indicated with vegetable oil or a combination of butter and oil. Drizzle the top of the rice with butter or olive oil, though, since it's tastier.

❖ Get to know your heat source. It might take a couple of tries to figure out how hot your element burns. If your tahdig burned at medium-high for 10 minutes, decrease the heat and/or time for next time. If it didn't crisp up enough, increase the heat and/or time for next time.

❖ A heat diffuser works as extra insurance so the tahdig doesn't stick, and the heat is distributed evenly. It comes in quite handy especially if you use a gas stove.

❖ Don't be alarmed by the amount of salt. The rice boils in the salted water for a very short period of time (just like pasta), and this is your chance to flavor the rice. You can also wash off some of the salt when draining the rice.

CHOOSE YOUR TAHDIG

Yogurt tahdig

The fat from a few tablespoons of yogurt mixed with the rice helps prevent the tahdig from sticking to the pot. It also adds a pleasant tanginess to the tahdig. Yogurt tahdig won't be as crispy as a regular rice tahdig, but it's quite tasty and easy to turn out. Follow the chelo (page 104) directions up to the end of step 2. In a medium bowl, mix 3 tablespoons of Greek yogurt with 3 cups of parboiled rice and ½ teaspoon of saffron water. Melt the butter and oil over medium heat (don't add extra saffron water to the bottom of the pot). Spread the yogurt-rice mixture evenly across the bottom of the pot. Pick up at step 4 in the chelo directions and carry on. Keep in mind that yogurt tahdig sets for the first 10 minutes on medium heat (not medium-high), and it is then reduced to medium-low to low for 35 minutes.

Bread tahdig

Bread tahdig, typically made from lavash bread, is one of my favorite treats. It's like a crisped-up lavash chip. Use a thicker lavash to prevent burning. You can also use sliced-open pita bread or a tortilla. I like to use bread tahdig as a barrier when preparing mixed rice dishes that can burn easily, like the tomato paste in Loobia Polo (page 117), which can quickly burn. Cut out a piece of bread to fit the surface of the pot. Alternatively, you can cut the bread into pieces and patch the bottom of the pot with it in a single layer. Follow the chelo (page 104) directions up to the end of step 2. Melt the butter and oil over medium heat, add 1 tablespoon of saffron water, and place the lavash bread on the bottom of the pot. Pick up at step 4 of the chelo directions and carry on. Keep in mind that bread tahdig sets for the first 10 minutes on medium heat (not medium-high), and it is then reduced to medium-low to low for 35 minutes.

Potato tahdig

Crispy, salty, saffron-tinged potatoes layered on top of fluffy basmati rice is the stuff of dreams for kids and adults alike. The trick is to slice the potatoes just thin enough so they don't burn and not too thick so they cook through. You can use Yukon Gold or russet potatoes. Typically, one large potato is enough to cover the bottom of a 10-inch pan or pot. Slice the potato into ¼-inch-thick rounds and toss with a tiny pinch of ground saffron. Only prepare 1 tablespoon of saffron water to drizzle on top of the rice. Follow the chelo (page 104) directions up to the end of step 2. Melt the butter and oil over medium-high heat, and sprinkle with a small pinch of salt. Place the potato rounds in the pot or pan in a tight single layer, and sprinkle the potatoes with a little salt. Fry the potatoes uncovered for 5 minutes; the potatoes should be golden—reduce the heat slightly if they start to burn. Reduce the heat to medium, add the rice, and pick up at step 5 of the chelo recipe. If you have extra potato slices you can fry them separately in a pan and serve them with the rice.

Individual tahdig or tahdig to feed a crowd

A couple of years ago, Luna asked me to prepare tahdig for the Thanksgiving cultural feast at her school—about fifty kids and a few adults. Any sane person would have promptly turned down the request. But I was so thrilled that she wanted to share this treat with her classmates that I agreed to take on the challenge. With the encouragement and tips from all the lovely people in the Instagram community, I filled every pot I own with rice, sprinkled copious amounts of saffron, and used all four burners to turn out tahdig to feed a crowd.

Just before flipping the pots, I laced up my running shoes and had everything ready to go. I knew this would be a race against the clock. Flip the pot, break the tahdig into pieces, and get to the school as quickly as possible without the tahdig losing its crunch and without me breaking any traffic laws. Of course, by the time I made it to school they were running behind and the tahdig sat longer, softening. Losing its pizzazz. I tried, but the lesson was what I instinctively knew and chose to ignore in the name of sharing and culture: Tahdig does not travel well. It should be eaten right away, crispy and hot. What I also learned is that you can cheat a little and make tahdig with leftover rice without preparing a whole pot of rice. Individual tahdig for one or enough for a few people to snack on. This is also a great way to use up any leftover rice.

Individual Tahdig

I use my small 6-inch nonstick skillet or a cast-iron pan for this. You'll need a tight-fitting lid. Borrow a lid from a saucepan.

For 1 to 2 people (if you're willing to share)

1 heaping cup cooked basmati rice

1 tablespoon Greek yogurt

Tiny sprinkle of ground saffron (optional)

1 tablespoon clarified butter, unsalted butter, or olive oil

Kosher salt

For 4 to 6 people (prepared in a 10-inch pan)

3 cups cooked basmati rice

2 tablespoons Greek yogurt

Tiny sprinkle of ground saffron (optional)

2 tablespoons clarified butter or unsalted butter

1 tablespoon olive oil

Kosher salt

In a small bowl, combine the cooked rice and yogurt. Sprinkle with the tiniest pinch of saffron, if you like. Melt the butter in a skillet over medium heat. As soon as the butter sizzles, sprinkle on a little salt. Spread the rice mixture evenly across the bottom of the pot, packing it down. Wrap the lid in a small kitchen towel or a couple of layers of paper towel to catch the condensation. Cover and cook for 10 minutes. Reduce the heat to medium-low to low, and cook for 15 to 25 minutes. The longer you cook it, the more the tahdig will set. Check at 15 minutes. If it's not as crisp as you like, cook it longer, checking every 5 minutes.

Kateh

Everyday Persian Rice

Where chelo-style rice is the more elegant, company-worthy rice dish, kateh-style rice is for our everyday family pot of rice. Kateh is rice cooked in the more familiar absorption method. Every grain of rice won't be as individual as chelo-style, but it is quicker in preparation, equally fragrant and comforting. Kateh can be prepared in any type of pot if you don't want a tahdig to set. If you'd like to make tahdig with Kateh, then I highly recommend using a nonstick pot. As children, whenever we had a stomachache we were always served a bowl of kateh ba maast—plain Kateh with plain yogurt. Like magic, it soothed us every single time. This is what my children crave now when feeling under the weather with a bellyache.

SERVES 6

KATEH WITH WHITE RICE

2 cups white basmati rice, rinsed and drained

2 heaping teaspoons kosher salt

2 tablespoons unsalted butter or olive oil (or a combination)

Place the rice, 3½ cups water, salt, and butter in a medium pot. Bring to a boil over high heat. Give a stir, reduce the heat to low, cover, and cook just until all the water has been absorbed, about 12 minutes. It's okay to lift the lid to check, if you don't have a glass lid. Wrap the lid in a kitchen towel or a couple of layers of paper towel to catch the condensation. Make sure the kitchen towel or paper towels are secured up top so they don't catch fire! Place the lid firmly back on the pot. Cook until the rice is cooked through and fluffy, about 15 minutes. Gently fluff with a spoon and serve.

If you'd like to make tahdig and you're using a nonstick pot, cook the rice for an additional 20 to 25 minutes until a crust (tahdig) forms.

KATEH WITH BROWN RICE

2 cups brown basmati rice, rinsed and drained

2 heaping teaspoons kosher salt

2 to 3 tablespoons butter or olive oil (or a combination)

Place the rice, 3½ cups water, salt, and butter in a medium pot. Bring to a boil over high heat. Give a stir, reduce the heat to low, cover, and cook just until the water has been absorbed, about 30 minutes. It's okay to lift the lid to check, if you don't have a glass lid. Wrap the lid in a kitchen towel or a couple of layers of paper towel to catch the condensation. Make sure the kitchen towel or paper towels are secured up top so they don't catch fire! Place the lid firmly back on the pot. Cook until the rice is cooked through and fluffy, 15 to 20 minutes. Gently fluff with a spoon and serve.

If you'd like to make tahdig and you're using a nonstick pot, cook the rice for an additional 15 to 25 minutes until a crust (tahdig) forms.

Persian Rice Cooker Rice

Allow me to introduce you to every Iranian home cook's secret weapon: the Persian rice cooker, or what I affectionately refer to as my "cheat pot." Just about every Iranian home cook I know relies on this appliance on a weekly basis. The beauty of this rice cooker is that it takes the guessing game, and anxiety, out of turning out the crunchiest, golden tahdig. However, this method is only possible specifically in an Iranian rice cooker. Please don't try this with any other type of rice cooker. Each model will have different settings, generally it takes about an hour to turn out a crunchy white rice tahdig. Brown rice takes slightly longer. You can also prepare mixed rice dishes or various types of tahdig in this rice cooker. Slightly less rice to water ratios will be needed for the mixed rice dishes. Use the recipe below as a guide; it might take a couple tries to get acquainted with your rice cooker.

These measurements are for a standard measuring cup, not for the measuring cup included in the rice cooker. Each rice cooker will have a minimum amount of rice that will need to be used. These measurements are for a 6-cup or larger rice cooker. We're also very careful with washing and storing the bowl insert of the rice cooker, as it is nonstick and can scratch easily. Always use a soft sponge to wash it, never use a metal serving utensil, and line the bottom of the bowl with paper towels before storing it away. If anything happens to the bowl insert you can purchase a new insert without having to buy a whole new rice cooker. You can purchase Iranian rice cookers, which are relatively inexpensive, online or at Iranian markets.

SERVES 6

White rice

3 cups white basmati rice, rinsed and drained

1 tablespoon kosher salt

¼ cup plus 1 tablespoon olive oil

Place the rice in the bowl of the rice cooker. Cover with 4¼ cups water, and add the salt and oil. Give a gentle stir with a wooden spoon, cover, and turn on to max/1 hr. When the rice is done, wearing oven mitts, place an appropriate-sized platter (one larger than the bowl) over the rice cooker bowl insert, lift the bowl out, and quickly and confidently flip like a cake. Serve immediately. Tahdig loses its crunch if it sits too long, so dig in right away.

Brown rice

3 cups brown basmati
rice, rinsed and drained

1 tablespoon kosher salt

¼ cup plus 1 tablespoon
olive oil

Place the rice in the bowl of the rice cooker. Cover with 5½ cups water, and add the salt and oil. Give a gentle stir with a wooden spoon, cover, and turn on to max/1 hr. When all the water has been absorbed, after about 40 minutes, turn the knob and add an extra 15 minutes. When the rice is done, wearing oven mitts, place an appropriate-sized platter (one larger than the bowl) over the rice cooker bowl insert, lift the bowl out, and quickly and confidently flip like a cake. Serve immediately. Tahdig loses its crunch if it sits too long, so dig in right away.

Mixed rice cooker dishes

WHITE RICE

2½ cups white basmati
rice, rinsed and drained

3½ cups water

2½ teaspoons kosher salt

¼ cup plus 1 tablespoon
olive oil

Rice mix

BROWN RICE

2½ cups brown basmati
rice, rinsed and drained

5 cups water

2½ teaspoons kosher salt

¼ cup plus 1 tablespoon
olive oil

Rice mix

Once all the water has been absorbed, around the 30-minute mark for white rice and the 45-minute mark for brown rice, scoop out most of the rice into a large platter or bowl, leaving behind the bottom tahdig layer. Gently fold in the mix and return everything back into the pot. Reset the knob to the 30-minute mark, cover, and continue cooking. You can also gently fold in the mix with the rice in the pot and carry on as usual. I prefer transferring to a platter first for ease of mixing without breaking the rice grains.

Loobia Polo

Green Bean Rice

Loobia Polo is our equivalent to mac and cheese. It is the ultimate comfort food that captures everyone's heart, Persian and non-Persian. I'm not sure what came first, Drew's love for me or his love for this dish, or his love for me sparked by his love for this dish. Loobia Polo is the dish our kids ask for at the end of a long school week, when all they want to do is tuck in with a good movie and a plate of green beans and chicken simmered in a fragrant tomato sauce, layered in between cinnamon-scented grains of rice. Traditionally, Loobia Polo is made with red meat, but we love the lighter mix of chicken against the warmth of the spices and rich tomato sauce. It goes without saying that leftovers make a superb school/work lunch. Serve with a side of plain yogurt or Maast-o Khiar (page 43), Tomato Cucumber Salad (page 53), a hit of Torshi Liteh (page 68), pick a good movie, and call it a night.

Loobia Polo can also be layered with chelo-style rice with tahdig (page 104). I particularly like lavash or potato tahdig with Loobia Polo because the tomato sauce in the mix can burn the rice tahdig. We often make this dish in our Iranian rice cooker with either white or brown rice (page 114).

SERVES 6

FOR THE MIX

¼ cup olive oil (plus more as needed)

1 yellow onion, diced

Kosher salt

1 pound green beans, trimmed and cut into ¼-inch pieces

2 skinless, boneless chicken breasts (about 1 pound), or 4 skinless, boneless chicken thighs (about 1 pound) (or a combination), cut into ¼-inch pieces

1 teaspoon ground turmeric

¾ teaspoon ground cinnamon

Finely ground black pepper

3 tablespoons tomato paste, diluted in ⅔ cup hot water

Scant ¼ teaspoon ground saffron, steeped in 2 tablespoons hot water (see page 17)

3 tablespoons fresh lemon juice (plus more as needed)

FOR THE RICE

2 cups white basmati rice, rinsed and drained

2 teaspoons Kosher salt

2 tablespoons butter or olive oil

First prepare the mix. In a large pan, heat the olive oil over medium heat. Add the onion, sprinkle with a pinch of salt, and cook, stirring occasionally, until soft and golden, about 8 minutes. Add the green beans and 1½ teaspoons salt, and cook, stirring often, for 8 to 10 minutes. If the pan gets too dry add more olive oil. Take care not to burn the green beans, but also take care that the beans maintain their shape and do not turn soft and mushy.

Add the chicken, turmeric, cinnamon, 1½ teaspoons salt, and ¼ teaspoon pepper. Cook, stirring occasionally, drizzling a little more oil as needed, until the chicken takes on a little color, about 3 minutes. Add the diluted tomato paste, saffron water, and lemon juice. Stir to combine. Reduce the heat to medium-low and cook at a gentle simmer, uncovered, for 15 to 20 minutes, until the chicken cooks through and all the flavors come to life. Taste as you go to make it delicious. Does it need a little more salt, more lemon juice? Taste and adjust. The mix should be juicy but not too runny, because it will get combined with the rice.

While the mix simmers prepare the rice kateh-style. Place the rice, 3½ cups water, salt, and butter in a large pot and bring to a boil over high heat. Give a stir, reduce the heat to low, cover, and cook just until all the water has been absorbed, 12 to 15 minutes. It's okay to lift the lid to check, if you don't have a glass lid. As soon as all the water absorbs, gently combine the green beans–chicken mix with the rice in the pot, or turn off the heat, tip the rice out onto a large platter or bowl, gently fold in the mix, return everything back into the pot, and turn up the heat to low. Wrap the lid in a kitchen towel or a couple of layers of paper towel to catch the condensation. Make sure the kitchen towel or paper towels are secured up top so they don't catch fire! Place the lid firmly back on the pot. Cook until the rice is cooked through and fluffy, and all the flavors have melded, 25 to 30 minutes. Gently fluff with a spoon and serve.

MAKE AHEAD: The green bean mix can be made up to 3 days in advance and stored in the fridge, or in the freezer for up to 3 months. Gently reheat before mixing with the rice.

PREP AHEAD: If you have green beans that are about to go bad, you can simply cook them with the onion and store them in the fridge (up to 3 days) or in the freezer (up to 3 months) and add the rest of the ingredients later.

PLAN AHEAD: This dish is tailor-made for a thermos school lunch. You can also freeze any leftovers (up to 3 months), thaw, and reheat. Add a little water when reheating to bring the rice back to life.

Tahcheen-e Morgh

Baked Saffron Yogurt Rice with Chicken

Tahcheen *means "arranged on the bottom," and it is a beauty of a dish. Juicy pieces of saffron chicken are arranged on a thick yogurt-and-egg tahdig and topped with basmati rice. Tahcheen can be made on the stovetop or in the oven. I prefer baking it in the oven because it can all be assembled ahead of time and then simply slipped into the oven. Use an oven-safe 9 x 13 x 2-inch clear glass casserole dish if possible. The glass dish allows you to spy on the tahdig and check on its progress. If you don't have a glass dish any appropriate-sized baking dish will work. Tahcheen is equally spectacular to entertain with or enjoy with family on a quiet and cozy evening. Serve with a side of yogurt and Sabzi Khordan (page 32).*

SERVES 8

3 cups white basmati rice

3 tablespoons olive oil

1 large yellow onion, sliced into ¼-inch-thick half-moons

Kosher salt

4 cloves garlic, chopped

10 skinless, boneless chicken thighs, cut in half

¼ teaspoon ground black pepper

¼ cup fresh lemon juice (plus more as needed)

¼ teaspoon ground saffron, steeped in 2 tablespoons hot water (see page 17)

1 cup Greek yogurt

1 large egg

Ground saffron for sprinkling

5 tablespoons butter, divided

TOPPING

1 tablespoon butter

½ cup barberries (see page 358), picked through and soaked for 15 minutes, drained

1 teaspoon sugar

Handful of raw pistachios, roughly chopped (optional)

Parboil the rice chelo-style (page 104) up to the end of step 2. Set aside to drain.

In a large pan, heat the oil over medium heat. Add the onion, sprinkle with a little salt, and cook, stirring occasionally, until soft and golden, about 8 minutes. Add the garlic and cook for 2 minutes. Add the chicken, 2¾ teaspoons salt, and the pepper, and cook until the chicken takes on a little color, about 3 minutes on each side. Add the lemon juice and the saffron water, turn the chicken pieces well in the bright orange sauce to coat all sides, and reduce the heat to medium-low. Partially cover and simmer, turning once in a while, until the chicken is tender and just cooked through, about 25 to 30 minutes. Taste and add more salt and lemon juice, if needed. Cut the chicken into ½-inch-long pieces and set aside in its juices.

Preheat the oven to 400°F with the rack set in the lowest position.

(continued)

Tahcheen-e Morgh *(continued)*

In a medium bowl, combine the yogurt, egg, and a tiny sprinkle of ground saffron. Fold in half of the parboiled rice, and set aside.

Place 3 tablespoons of the butter in the baking dish and place in the oven to melt, about 3 minutes. Swirl or brush the melted butter all over and up the sides of the dish. Spread the yogurt-rice mixture evenly on the bottom of the dish, pressing it down firmly. Add a layer of the chicken pieces evenly over the rice, top with a layer of the plain rice, drizzle with 2 tablespoons of chicken juices, smooth the top, and dot with the remaining 2 tablespoons butter. Cover tightly with foil and bake for about 1 hour 20 minutes. Check the bottom of the dish (if using a glass dish) to see if it is golden and crisp. Bake for an extra 5 to 10 minutes if necessary, but take care not to burn it. Take the tahcheen out of the oven, and let it rest for 5 minutes.

While the tahcheen rests prepare the barberry topping. In a small pan, melt the butter over medium heat. Add the barberries, sugar, and pistachios, give a quick stir to plump up the barberries, and cook for about 2 minutes. Take off the heat. Run a knife along the sides of the tahcheen to help release it. Place a large rectangular serving platter, baking tray, or cutting board over the tahcheen, take a deep breath, and flip. Garnish with the barberry topping, pour yourself something tasty for a job well done, and gather around the table with friends and family. Cut the tahcheen in 8 or more pieces and dig in.

MAKE AHEAD: The entire dish can be assembled a few hours in advance and stored in the fridge, covered. Bring to room temperature before placing in the oven.

PREP AHEAD: The rice can be parboiled, drained, and set aside a few hours in advance until ready to use.

Adas Polo

Lentil Rice

Lentils and rice are stalwart Persian pantry staples and the combination of the two gives us a humble dish that epitomizes the comforts of home. Adas Polo is the Persian cousin of the other beloved lentil and rice dish enjoyed across the Middle East—mujadara. The addition of golden brown onions, dates, and raisins sautéed with a drizzle of sweet saffron not only adds texture and color here but are a reflection of everything worth celebrating in the Persian pantry. Adas Polo has become a festive side dish at many Iranian-American Thanksgiving tables, with the warm spices and dried fruits giving it a festive autumnal appeal. You can also try a combination of raisins and dried cranberries. Prepare Adas Polo either chelo-style with tahdig (lavash and potato tahdig are best to act as a barrier against the dried fruits—see page 110, or kateh-style as I have here with white or nutty brown rice (page 115), or in an Iranian rice cooker (page 114). No matter how you serve it, this is a satisfying but unassuming dish. We like to tuck into Adas Polo simply with a side of plain yogurt, Tomato Cucumber Salad (page 53), and maybe a soft-boiled egg. But you can also serve it with Everyday Turmeric Chicken (page 220) or Saffron Chicken (page 223).

SERVES 6

1 cup green or brown lentils, picked through and rinsed

3 teaspoons kosher salt (plus more for seasoning)

2 cups white basmati rice, rinsed and drained

3½ cups chicken stock or water (or a combination)

4 tablespoons clarified butter or unsalted butter, divided

1 medium yellow onion, diced

6 Medjool dates, pitted and quartered

1 cup brown or golden raisins

½ teaspoon ground cinnamon

¼ teaspoon ground saffron, steeped in 3 tablespoons hot water (see page 17)

2 teaspoons ground cumin

Place the lentils in a medium saucepan. Cover with 1¾ cups water and add 1 teaspoon of the salt. Partially cover and bring to a boil over high heat. Reduce the heat to medium-low and cook until all the water has evaporated and the lentils are softened but not completely cooked through, about 20 minutes. If the lentils are ready but there's still water in the pot, drain the lentils. If the water is absorbed but the lentils aren't ready yet, add a little more water and cook longer. You just don't want mushy lentils. Set aside.

Meanwhile, place the rice, stock, and 2 tablespoons butter in a large pot and bring to a boil over high heat. Add the remaining

2 teaspoons salt, and give a stir. Cover, reduce the heat to low, and cook just until the stock has been absorbed, about 12 minutes. It's okay to lift the lid to check, if you don't have a glass lid.

Meanwhile, prepare the dried fruit mixture. Melt the remaining 2 tablespoons of butter over medium-high heat, and add the onion. Cook, stirring frequently, until golden brown, about 12 minutes. Play with the heat, turn it down a little if you need to. Reduce the heat to medium-low. Add the dates, raisins, cinnamon, and saffron water (careful, the saffron water will hiss as it hits the hot pan), and a sprinkle of salt. Stir and cook until the dried fruits just soften, about 3 minutes. Remove from the heat and partially cover so it doesn't dry out. You can also set aside about a tablespoon of the fruit mixture to use as topping when serving if you like.

As soon as the rice has absorbed all the water, sprinkle in the cumin in between the rice grains, gently mixing as you go. Fold in the lentils and the dried fruit mixture in the pot. Or tip the rice out onto a platter or bowl, gently fold in the lentils and dried fruit, and return everything back into the pot. Wrap the lid in a kitchen towel or a couple of layers of paper towels to catch the condensation. Make sure the kitchen towels or paper towels are secured up top so they don't catch fire! Place the lid firmly back on the pot. Cook on low until the lentils and rice are cooked through and fluffy, and all the flavors have melded, about 30 minutes. Gently fluff with a spoon, scatter the reserved dried fruit mixture on top, and serve.

MAKE AHEAD: The lentils can be parboiled a few hours in advance and set aside until ready to use. Don't prepare the fruit mixture in advance as it can dry out.

PLAN AHEAD: Adas Polo can be stored in the fridge (up to 3 days) and in the freezer (up to 3 months). Drizzle with water when reheating to plump up the rice and lentils again.

Sheveed Polo

Dill Rice

Sheveed Polo is a simple way to make use of a whole bunch of dill and transform an ordinary pot of plain rice. I like to use a mix of fresh and dried dill. The dried dill enhances the fragrance and it also draws out the humidity from the fresh dill so the rice doesn't turn mushy when steaming. You can also stir in the dill mix with chelo-style rice (page 104) or Persian rice cooker rice (page 114). This dish is often served with seafood or chicken. Serve with Everyday Turmeric Chicken (page 220), Saffron Chicken (page 223), Roasted Dill Salmon (page 245), Joojeh Kabab (page 237), or Stuffed Branzino (page 230), accompanied with a side of Torshi Liteh (page 68) or pickles of choice.

SERVES 6

1 large bunch dill, stems trimmed, finely chopped

3 tablespoons dried dill

2 cups white basmati rice, rinsed and drained

2 teaspoons kosher salt

2 tablespoons unsalted butter or olive oil

Set aside ¼ cup of the fresh dill. In a bowl, combine the rest of the fresh dill with the dried dill. Set aside.

Place the rice, 3½ cups water, salt, and butter in a medium pot. Bring to a boil over high heat. Give a stir, reduce the heat to low, cover, and cook just until the water has been absorbed, about 12 minutes. It's okay to lift the lid to check, if you don't have a glass lid.

Fold in the dill mixture with the rice. Wrap the lid in a kitchen towel or a couple of layers of paper towel to catch the condensation. Make sure the kitchen towel or paper towels are secured up top so they don't catch fire! Place the lid firmly back on the pot. Cook until the rice is cooked through and fluffy, about 15 minutes. Gently fluff with a spoon, then transfer to a serving platter as you scatter the reserved fresh dill in between.

PREP AHEAD: The dill can be washed and chopped up to 1 day in advance, and stored in a container lined and covered on top with a paper towel to absorb any moisture.

PLAN AHEAD: Leftovers can be stored in the fridge (up to 3 days) or in the freezer (up to 3 months). Add a little water when reheating to bring the rice back to life.

Sheeved Polo ba Tahdig-e Mahi
Dill Rice with Fish Tahdig

This is an absolute stunner of a dish. I reached out to Chef Hoss Zare, former owner and chef at the San Francisco restaurant The Fly Trap, for guidance on turning out a successful fish tahdig. Inspired by Chef Zare's enthusiasm for food, cooking, and life, I headed straight to the kitchen and started playing around with fish tahdig and came up with this version. The challenge here is to simultaneously crisp up the fish skin and cook the rice without drying out the fish while steaming the rice. A larger sized branzino works well here, but trout or a similar-sized fish is too delicate and will dry out. Sheveed Polo is a natural fit for rice with fish, but you can also prepare a plain saffron rice. You'll need a wide 12-inch or preferably 14-inch pan with a tight-fitting lid to accommodate the fish. Make sure you purchase very fresh fish and ask your fishmonger to butterfly the fish for you. I like to keep the head and tail on for a dramatic presentation (if it fits in the pan) but you can also have them removed.

SERVES 6

3 cups white basmati rice

1 large bunch dill, stems trimmed, finely chopped (set aside about 1 tablespoon to stuff the fish)

3 tablespoons dried dill

2 large branzino, butterflied, fins trimmed, head and tail on (if you like)

Olive oil

Kosher salt

Ground black pepper

Zest and juice of 1 lemon

2 large cloves garlic, very thinly sliced

7 tablespoons clarified butter or unsalted butter, divided

¼ teaspoon ground saffron steeped in ¼ cup hot water (see page 17)

Parboil the rice chelo-style (page 104) up to the end of step 2. Set aside to drain.

In a medium bowl, set aside 2 cups of the plain rice. Gently fold the fresh and dried dill into the rest of the rice in the colander. Set aside.

Drizzle the entire fish, inside and out, with olive oil, and season the fish generously, inside and out, with salt and pepper. Open the fish up like a book and stuff with the lemon zest, garlic slices, and reserved 1 tablespoon fresh dill, and drizzle with a little fresh lemon juice. Close the fish back up.

Set up your work station. Have all the ingredients close by, ready to go. In a large 12- to 14-inch-wide pan, melt 5 tablespoons of the butter with 3 tablespoons olive oil and 2 tablespoons of the saffron water over

medium-high heat. Be careful, it might spit and splatter. As soon as the butter melts and sizzles, place both fish in the pan. The fish should sizzle as soon as it hits the hot oil. Fry the fish until the skin starts to crisp, about 5 minutes. Now move quickly. Scatter the reserved plain rice over the fish, gently patting it down around the sides, for a tahdig layer. Top with the dill rice. With the handle of a wooden spoon poke a few holes in the rice, without hitting the fish layer. Cover and cook on medium-high for 8 minutes.

Meanwhile, in a small saucepan or microwave, melt the remaining 2 tablespoons butter and add it to the remaining saffron water.

Lift the lid and drizzle the butter-saffron mixture over the rice. Wrap the lid in a kitchen towel or a couple of layers of paper towel to catch the condensation. Make sure the kitchen towel or paper towels are secured up top so they don't catch fire! Place the lid firmly back on the pot. Reduce the heat to medium and cook for 10 minutes, until steam escapes from the sides of the pot. Then reduce the heat to medium-low or low, and place a heat diffuser under the pot, if you have one. Cook for 30 minutes, rotating the pot a few times for even crisping.

To help release the tahdig, fill the sink with about 1 inch of cold water, and set the rice pot in the water. Alternatively, you can wet a kitchen towel and set the pot on the wet towel. To serve, take a deep breath, place an appropriate-sized platter over the pot, and quickly and confidently flip the pot over. There should be a *swish* sound of the release of the fish tahdig. Take a bow for a job well done.

Baghali Polo

Fava Bean Rice

Baghali Polo is considered the king of mixed Persian rice dishes. But don't be intimidated by its royal reputation. It is a straightforward mix of rice, nutty favas, and dill. If fresh favas are in season, use them here. They can be a chore to pod and peel but with a little help the job gets done, or put on a movie and sit yourself and your bag of favas in front if it and mindlessly pod away. Frozen, peeled favas can be found at Iranian and Mediterranean markets, and some well-stocked grocery stores. Set aside a handful of fresh dill and favas to add to the rice when serving for a fresh hit of fragrance and color. This rice dish is also a good candidate for bread tahdig (page 110) or potato tahdig (page 111). Baghali Polo is traditionally served with celebratory Braised Lamb Shanks (page 225) or serve with Roasted Dill Salmon (page 245), Joojeh Kabab (page 237), Everyday Turmeric Chicken (page 220), or Saffron Chicken (page 223).

SERVES 6

---

3 cups white basmati rice

3 pounds fresh podded favas, or 3 cups frozen peeled favas, thawed

1 large bunch fresh dill, stems trimmed, finely chopped

3 tablespoons dried dill

3 tablespoons clarified butter or unsalted butter (plus more as needed)

1 tablespoon olive oil (plus more as needed)

¼ teaspoon ground saffron, steeped in 2 tablespoons hot water (see page 17)

Kosher salt

Parboil the rice chelo-style (page 104) up to the end of step 2. Set aside to drain.

If using fresh favas, bring a pot of water to a boil, and have an ice bath ready. Place the podded beans in the boiling water for a quick minute, drain, and dunk in the ice bath for another quick minute. Drain and easily pop the skin off. Set aside.

Set aside ¼ cup of the fresh dill and ½ cup of the fresh favas (if using fresh). Gently combine the rest of the fresh and dried dill and the rest of the favas with the rice in the colander, taking care not to break the grains of rice.

Place the colander beside you by the stove. Set the rice pot over medium heat. Add 2 tablespoons of the butter, the olive oil, and 1 tablespoon of the saffron water, and melt the butter. Swirl the oil around so it evenly covers the bottom of the pot and a

Baghali Polo *(continued)*

little up the sides; add more butter and/or oil if needed. Work quickly now. As soon as the oil starts sizzling, with a spatula add enough rice-fava mixture to fully cover the bottom of the pot in a thin layer. Pack down the rice with the back of a spatula. This is your tahdig layer.

Gently scatter the rest of the rice over the tahdig layer in a pyramid shape, making sure the tahdig layer is covered with more rice. With the handle of a wooden spoon poke a few holes in the rice without hitting the tahdig layer, to allow the steam to escape. Turn up the heat to medium-high, cover, and cook for 10 to 12 minutes for the tahdig to set. You can also try the tahdig test: Wet your finger and quickly tap or sprinkle a little water on the side of the pot. If the pot sizzles and the water quickly evaporates it's time to turn down the heat.

While the tahdig sets, in a small saucepan or microwave, melt the remaining 2 tablespoons butter and add it to the remaining saffron water.

Lift the lid (without dripping the condensation trapped under the lid back into the pot) and drizzle the butter-saffron mixture over the rice. Wrap the lid in a kitchen towel or a couple of layers of paper towel to catch the condensation. Make sure the kitchen towel or paper towels are secured up top so they don't catch fire! Place the lid firmly back on the pot. Reduce the heat to medium and cook for 10 minutes, until steam escapes from the sides of the pot. Then reduce the heat to medium-low or low (depending on your element), and place a heat diffuser under the pot, if you have one. Cook for 30 to 35 minutes, rotating the pot a few times for even crisping, until the rice is tender and fluffy and the tahdig is crispy and golden.

To help release the tahdig, fill the sink with about 1 inch of cold water, and set the rice pot in the water. Alternatively, you can wet a kitchen towel and set the pot on the wet towel. Serve the rice on a platter, and scatter the reserved fresh dill and favas in between. Gently remove the tahdig whole or in pieces and serve on the side.

PREP AHEAD: Fresh fava beans can be podded and frozen until ready to use.

PLAN AHEAD: Baghali Polo can be stored in the fridge (up to 3 days) and in the freezer (up to 3 months); drizzle with water when reheating to plump up the rice again.

Cabbage Farro

Roasting cabbage, flecked with earthy and warm cumin, is a tasty, quick, and efficient way to make use of an entire head of cabbage, as the cabbage sweetens and softens in bits and crisps in other pieces. Roasted cabbage on its own makes for a fine side dish, and it is one that we pick at hot, right out of the oven. But mixed with a hearty bowl of turmeric-and-cinnamon-dusted farro, topped with sweet golden raisins, and you have yourself a brand-new friend at the table. Inspired by the Iranian cabbage and rice dish kalam polo, *serve Cabbage Farro as is or cook up a batch of panfried Everyday Meatballs (page 260) as a topping. If you want to skip the meatballs, serve with any of the following for a complete meal: Everyday Turmeric Chicken (page 220), Saffron Chicken (page 223), or Roasted Dill Salmon (page 245).*

SERVES 6 AS A SIDE DISH

1 small or ½ large green cabbage (about 1¼ pounds), cored and thinly sliced (about ¼-inch-thick slices)

5 tablespoons olive oil, divided

2 teaspoons ground cumin

Kosher salt

Finely ground black pepper

1 medium yellow onion, diced

2 cloves garlic, chopped

1 cup farro, rinsed and drained

½ teaspoon ground turmeric

½ teaspoon ground cinnamon

2 tablespoons butter

¼ cup golden raisins

Chopped fresh basil

Lemon juice

Preheat the oven to 425°F with the rack set in the upper-third position. Line a large baking sheet with parchment paper.

In a large bowl, toss the cabbage with 2 tablespoons of the olive oil, the cumin, 1 teaspoon salt, and ¼ teaspoon pepper. Pile it onto the prepared baking sheet (if your cabbage is on the larger side, divide it between two pans), and place in the oven. Roast for 30 minutes, turning a couple of times, until soft and crisp in bits and pieces.

Meanwhile, in a medium pot or saucepan, heat the remaining 3 tablespoons olive oil over medium-high heat. Add the onion and cook, stirring frequently, until golden brown. Sprinkle the onion with a little salt, and reduce the heat to medium-low. Add the garlic, farro, turmeric, and cinnamon. Stir and cook until the spices are fragrant, about 3 minutes. Add 2 cups water, the butter, and 2 teaspoons salt. Raise the heat to high and bring to a boil. Stir, partially cover, reduce the heat to medium-low, and cook until all the water has been absorbed and the farro is cooked through, 30 to 40 minutes. Keep in mind that farro will have a bite to it. If the farro is still too hard add another splash of water and keep cooking. Remove from the heat. Fold in the raisins and cabbage, and sprinkle with the basil. Taste and give a good squeeze of lemon to brighten it up and serve.

MAKE AHEAD: The cabbage can be roasted up to 3 days in advance and stored in the fridge, but it will lose its crispiness.

Kateh Estamboli

Rice with Tomatoes and Potatoes

The comforting mix of rice and potatoes in this dish reminds me of another favorite childhood dish from our time in Rome, Italian pasta e patate—*pasta with potatoes. Here, each grain of rice is gently kissed by a hint of turmeric and saffron and a burst of tomatoes and is cooked through with creamy potatoes that melt in your mouth with every bite. Traditionally, Kateh Estamboli is also made with ground meat but my mom would often prepare it simply without the meat and instead we would top off our bowl with a* nimroo— *fried egg, sunny-side up. I loved breaking into the runny yolk and watching it lazily trace a sunny path in the red rice and hit a road block at the sight of a potato cube. Serve Kateh Estamboli simply on its own with plain yogurt, or with a fried egg and a handful of Sabzi Khordan (page 32), or top with panfried Everyday Meatballs (page 260).*

SERVES 6

¼ cup olive oil

1 leek, white and light green parts only, halved and thinly sliced

1 yellow onion, diced

Kosher salt

½ teaspoon ground turmeric

1 large Yukon Gold potato (about ½ pound), peeled and cut in ½-inch cubes

3 cups chicken broth or water (or a combination)

Ground black pepper

3 large tomatoes (about 1½ pounds), diced

2 large cloves garlic, diced

1½ cups basmati rice, rinsed and drained

¼ teaspoon ground saffron

2 tablespoons unsalted butter, cubed, or olive oil

In a large pot, heat the oil, and add the leek and onion. Cook, stirring frequently, until golden brown and fragrant, about 12 minutes. Sprinkle with a little salt, and add the turmeric. Stir and add the potatoes. Cook the potatoes, stirring occasionally, for 10 minutes.

Meanwhile, in a saucepan, bring the chicken broth to a boil (or boil 3 cups water in a kettle).

Season the potatoes well with salt and pepper, and add the tomatoes and garlic. Sprinkle the tomatoes with a good pinch of salt and cook until they just begin to release their juices, about 3 minutes. Stir in the rice and cook for 2 minutes. Add the boiling broth or water, 2 teaspoons salt, the saffron, and butter. Stir to combine. As soon as the

Kateh Estamboli *(continued)*

liquid comes to a boil, cover and reduce the heat to low. Cook just until all the liquid has been absorbed, about 15 minutes. It's okay to lift the lid to check, if you don't have a glass lid.

Wrap the lid in a kitchen towel or a couple of layers of paper towel to catch the condensation. Make sure the kitchen towel or paper towels are secured up top so they don't catch fire! Place the lid firmly back on the pot. Cook until the rice is cooked and all the flavors have melded, about 30 minutes.

PLAN AHEAD: Kateh Estamboli can be stored in the fridge (up to 3 days) and in the freezer (up to 3 months); drizzle with water when reheating to plump up the rice again.

Quinoa with Fava and Figs

A few years ago, my sister-in-law, Sarah, embraced a more healthful approach to food and cooking. When she first began this journey I very casually mentioned she should try the darling of healthy foods, quinoa, as a grain alternative. Little did I know that quinoa would become one of her staples. I always try to have some on hand for when she comes to visit while also slipping pieces of crunchy tahdig on her plate. When in season, I like to top off the dish with succulent, ripe figs for a sweet bite of summer.

SERVES 6 AS A SIDE DISH

1¾ cups chicken stock, vegetable stock, or water

1 tablespoon olive oil (plus more for drizzling)

¼ teaspoon ground saffron

Kosher salt

1 cup quinoa, rinsed and drained

1¼ cups fresh or frozen shelled fava beans

3 tablespoons slivered almonds

Large handful of mixed fresh herbs of choice (parsley, cilantro, dill, basil, mint)

1 lemon

¼ cup crumbled feta or goat cheese

6 ripe figs (if in season), quartered or halved

Ground black pepper

In a medium pot, bring the stock to a boil over high heat. Add the olive oil, saffron, and 1 teaspoon salt. Stir in the quinoa and the fava beans, wrap the lid with a clean kitchen towel or paper towels, cover, and reduce the heat to low. Make sure the kitchen towel is secured on top so the edges don't catch fire! Cook until the water has been absorbed and the quinoa is cooked through but not mushy, about 12 minutes. Gently fluff with a fork.

Transfer the quinoa to a serving dish, and mix in the almonds and herbs. Taste and drizzle with olive oil and as much lemon juice as you like to brighten up the grassy flavor of the quinoa. Season with salt and pepper, as needed. Use less salt as you'll be topping with feta or goat cheese. Top with the cheese and taste again, drizzle, squeeze, and sprinkle to make it delicious. Scatter the figs on top, if using, and serve.

MAKE AHEAD: The whole dish can be prepared a few hours in advance, but don't add the cheese or figs until you're ready to serve. The quinoa will absorb a lot of the oil and lemon juice. Taste and add more as needed.

KHORESH
Stews

SOUL

After the 1979 Iranian Revolution we left Iran for Rome, as we had done every summer. My parents had met as young students in Rome, and it had become our home away from home. Except this time, we never returned to Iran. What had started as low and grumbling tremors and rumors quickly escalated into bombs raining from the skies: the Iran-Iraq war. My parents had long since given up their Italian residency, and at the time there was no possibility of renewing it. And so began our quest for a new home. Revolution happens. War happens. Immigration happens, or so we hoped.

In less than two years, we moved three times. We were about to embark on a fourth move, what we hoped (however bittersweetly) would be our last, to what was known among the Iranian expat community as the "lucky tiny apartment." The Iranian family living in the same apartment before us had happily received their immigration papers to Canada. The family before them had been accepted to Australia. We hoped that this tiny apartment would bring us the same fortune, as we put our trust in every inch of its purported lucky walls. Of course, relying on luck to pave the way for the future is magical thinking under the best of circumstances. But when certainty, the best-laid plans, dreams, and hopes for the future are very quickly pulled out from under you, you can't help embracing luck in all its improbabilities.

The tiny apartment was quite ordinary as far as such European apartments go. The bathroom had a drain right in the middle of the floor with a shower head fixed to the wall. The door to the apartment was perpetually left open for my brother, Ramin, to stretch, pre- and post-karate. One leg balanced in the apartment, the other stretched out on the hallway banister, always precariously straddling two worlds. As expected, the tiny apartment had an equally tiny kitchen and kitchen table. It was a table meant for one, maybe two. Too big to actually fit in the kitchen, it lived just outside of it—somewhere between the entrance (and my brother's outstretched leg) and the living room (which doubled as my bedroom). The kitchen table, much like us, lingered in the in-between spaces. Not quite where it should be, where it was expected to be. But close enough.

We carried on with life, uncertainty an albatross constantly perched on our shoulders. We poured our questions and doubts into games of solitaire—*fal*. Asking the all-knowing cards to reveal our future. Would it be Canada or Australia, and what if neither country accepted us? America, of course, had very quickly and emphatically closed its doors. No amount of magical thinking could undo the damage done by a revolution, a hostage crisis, and what would become a thirty-five-year freezing of relations. So we waited, all the while, ironically, indoctrinating ourselves in all things American by way of television shows like *Dallas* and *Happy Days* dubbed in Italian. A proud Texan city and the folksy town of Milwaukee providing the soundtrack to our nightly family meals of *chelo khoresh*—rice and stew—as we gathered around our tiny kitchen table in Rome.

Khoresh, Persian stew, is the soul of Iranian cooking. Of this we can always be certain: where there is rice, there is khoresh. And the debate over how juicy a khoresh should ultimately be is always a certainty occupying much space in a Persian kitchen.

Where uncertainty consumed our daily thoughts, it was the kitchen and its two-burner stove that grounded us. There was the certainty of waking daily to the distinct smell of hot Italian coffee rising from the moka, maybe with a small pot of milk warming next to it. Come dinnertime, we could always rely on the permanent fixture of two pots, standing at attention, prepared for their marching orders. One pot was filled with plenty of salted water, ready to come to a boil for either pasta or rice. Depending on which was being served, you could always find its lover—a companion pot lounging right next to it, slowly, dreamily, simmering the day away. A sauce for the pasta, or for a taste of home, a fragrant and flavorful stew to be generously draped over the rice. Each grain of rice happily soaking up its pleasingly tart juices.

It must have been some time between the morning coffee and the simmering khoresh for dinner that it was decided Maman, my mother, would go back to Iran for a couple of weeks to tie up some loose ends. This was not a decision made lightly by my parents. We were all aware of the perils of a trip back. Would she be able to come back to us? What if they held her back, or worse? What would the cards tell us then?

The kitchen, back then, was not the domain of my architect father, Baba. But Maman's absence had hit us all hard. So Baba filled the void the only way he could think of: a faceoff with the two-burner stove, the two pots, and a heaping bag of *sabzi*—fresh herbs. The permanent lumps lodged in our throats were temporarily soothed by a steaming pot of *khoresh ghormeh sabzi*—fresh herb stew. The royalty of all Persian stews.

Baba chopped the onion with meticulous precision as my brother and I sorted through the greens. The onion sizzled golden brown, the dizzying scent sharply and quickly winding itself around the tiny Roman apartment, gently making landfall into our hearts. With a wooden spoon in one hand he nudged the onions along so they wouldn't burn, while his other hand rested on the heat knob—listening, watching, smelling, and allowing the onions to guide the way. If they got too loud and cantankerous, turning unruly shades of brown, the heat was turned down. If they went on strike and lost their sizzle (this was Italy, after all), the heat was turned up.

Next Baba added stewing beef to the onions, along with a generous pinch of turmeric, while sautéing the fresh herbs separately, releasing and intensifying their flavors before adding them to the stew. A stroll through our local Roman market back then would have definitely turned up bunches upon bunches of parsley, but cilantro and fenugreek would have been more difficult, if not impossible, to come by. So we improvised and made do, substituting where possible, always with an eye out for the postman and packages from Iran. Packages bursting with dried herbs and spices, well-traveled scents and secrets from home. Envelopes with a few perfunctory words from family (lest officials be monitoring them) and a photograph or two pulled from all the picture albums that were left behind. Substitutes for all the loved ones that were left behind. And every once in a while, in between the written words, the photographs, the spices and scents, we would pull out a package of shriveled-up, alien-like dried limes—*limoo Omani*. A distinct burst of Persian flavor, brightening up our days and the khoresh ghormeh sabzi.

Baba drizzled on the golden saffron water, and gently squeezed the limoo Omani against the side of the pot, squeezing out its tart juices, drawing out all the news and tales that couldn't be shared in the letters. All that was left to do now was wait. Time and patience are the most important and most humble ingredients of khoresh-making. Wait for the khoresh to "fall into place." Wait for an official envelope with an embassy seal. Give time for the khoresh to "find itself." Time for Maman to make her way back to us. The patience to sit back and allow the flavors to absorb its juices to its *joon*—its soul. Or to add more water to it to make it juicier—if needed.

Baba, Ramin, and I gathered around the tiny kitchen table in the tiny Roman apartment as Baba lifted the lid off the not-so-tiny khoresh pot. The scents of fenugreek, dried limes, meat, golden onions, beans, and herbs embraced us with warmth and refused to let go. As Baba ladled the khoresh onto the rice, my brother and I exchanged quick glances and then looked back to Baba again. The laughter—initiated by Baba—emerged from deep within our joon. The khoresh was quite juicy, more soup-like. Sure, we could have returned the pot to the stove, reducing its juices. But we didn't, it didn't matter. At that moment Baba's khoresh ghormeh sabzi was exactly as it needed to be. Full of love and laughter.

Maman returned to us within a couple of weeks, a few days before the postman delivered an envelope bearing an official Canadian seal. Once again, bags were packed and the lights turned off one last time on the lucky tiny Roman apartment. As we wound our way down the stairs and out the door we excitedly and hurriedly told Maman about Baba's ghormeh sabzi. It often seems like children pick the most inopportune times to launch into seemingly unimportant stories. But at that moment, on the drive from the tiny apartment to the airport, our final lap around the piazzas, our beloved *mercatos*, *gelaterias*, and *trattorias*, on our way to the unknown, Baba's juicy ghormeh sabzi story helped to fill in the silences, to ground us and provide a sense of normalcy.

These are the kinds of stews that bring us running to the family table. Whether the table is firmly planted in its destined place or lingering somewhere in between. The kind of stew that bridges the path to a new continent, a new country, a new life, a new kitchen with its own stories to tell. Just how juicy you make this khoresh is up to you, so long as you give it time to find its way, to fall into place, and to come to life.

Khoresh—vibrant pots of slowly simmered Persian stews—are refined and infused with spices and layers of flavor, but for me they are the embodiment of comfort. All khoresh, save for a couple, begins their journey with onions—*piaz daagh*—cooked until golden brown and fragrant. To this base you can then add meats, a variety of pulses, a medley of vegetables, herbs, nuts, and fruits. Typically, a khoresh can be herb-based (green) or tomato-based (red), and it is always brightened with some type of acid, ranging from lemon juice to pomegranate molasses, verjuice to tamarind.

Traditionally, most Persian stews are prepared with slowly simmered cuts of lamb or beef. These days, in our Los Angeles kitchen, we eat red meat sparingly, reserving it for special occasions, relying more on the abundance of pulses and vegetables filling out the stews.

You'll need to set aside a little time for a pot of khoresh to lazily simmer away, allowing all the flavors to meld and come to life. For a proper Persian meal serve khoresh alongside a platter of rice (see pages 104–113), but of course, you can also serve it with any grain you like.

Khoresh Karafs

Celery Stew

If you've ever wondered what to do with an entire bunch of celery, then Khoresh Karafs is the dish for you. Celery is so often overlooked, relegated to just a couple of ribs to flavor soups and stock, or as a serving vessel for peanut butter. But in this dish, it's the shining star. Khoresh Karafs is our ultimate comfort food, happily making its way from a Sunday dinner to thermoses for school lunches the next day. Traditionally, this vibrant green stew is prepared with meat. In this version I've traded the meat for chicken, which is how we now mostly prepare it. Make sure you use the entire bunch of celery, green leaves included. Serve over rice to soak up all the lovely juices, with a side of Maast-o Khiar (page 43).

SERVES 6

---

7 tablespoons olive oil, divided

1 medium yellow onion, diced

Kosher salt

2 boneless, skinless chicken breasts (about 1 pound), or 1 pound boneless, skinless chicken thighs, cut into 1-inch stewing pieces

1 teaspoon ground turmeric

Ground black pepper

1 head celery, sliced into ½-inch wide pieces

1 bunch parsley, tough stems trimmed, finely chopped

½ bunch fresh mint, stems trimmed, finely chopped (optional)

3 tablespoons dried mint (plus more as needed)

4 tablespoons fresh lemon juice (plus more as needed)

¼ teaspoon ground saffron, steeped in 2 tablespoons hot water (see page 17)

In a large pot or Dutch oven, heat 3 tablespoons of the olive oil over medium-high heat. Add the onion and cook, stirring frequently, until golden brown, about 8 minutes. Sprinkle with salt, reduce the heat to medium and add the chicken, turmeric, 1 teaspoon salt, and ¼ teaspoon pepper. Cook until the chicken takes on a little color, 3 to 5 minutes. Cover, and reduce the heat to low. Simmer until the chicken releases some of its juices, about 15 minutes.

Meanwhile, prepare the celery. In a large pan, heat the remaining 4 tablespoons olive oil over medium-high heat. Add the celery and ½ teaspoon salt, and cook for 10 minutes, stirring often, until the celery is slightly fried and fragrant. Reduce the heat to medium and add the parsley. Cook for about 5 minutes, stirring often. Add the fresh mint (if using) and cook for 3 minutes, stirring often. Rub the dried mint between your palms to release its fragrance and flavor, and add it to the celery and parsley. Give it

a quick stir and immediately turn off the heat and remove the pan off the element. Mint burns very quickly and can turn bitter. Get your nose in there and inhale. The mint should be fragrant; if not, add a little more (1 teaspoon at a time).

Transfer the celery mixture to the chicken. Turn up the heat to medium-high, add the lemon juice, the saffron water, 1 cup hot water, and ½ teaspoon salt, and bring to a very gentle boil. Partially cover, reduce the heat to low, and simmer until the celery is tender but still holding its shape and not mushy, and all the flavors have beautifully melded, 30 to 45 minutes. Taste as it simmers. Bring it to life: more hot water to make it juicier, lemon juice, salt? Too juicy? Then remove the lid and simmer to desired consistency. Serve over rice.

MAKE AHEAD: Prepare up to 3 days in advance and store in the fridge. Adjust the water and seasoning when reheating.

PREP AHEAD: The chicken, onion, celery, and parsley can be chopped, sliced, and stored in separate airtight containers in the fridge up to 1 day in advance. The celery-parsley-mint mixture can be cooked and stored in the fridge (up to 3 days) or the freezer (up to 3 months) in advance. Thaw, add to the chicken, and carry on with the recipe.

PLAN AHEAD: Perfect reheated for a school or work lunch. Or freeze any leftovers for up to 3 months and enjoy on a busy weeknight.

Khoresh Bademjan

Eggplant Stew

This is the kind of meal that makes you linger at the table just a little longer, picking at another piece of eggplant. Conspicuously gnawing on juicy saffron-and-cinnamon-scented drumsticks, while licking off jammy tomato sauce winding its way around your wrist, even though you vowed you couldn't possibly eat another bite. Use long, firm Japanese or Chinese eggplant in this vibrant Khoresh Bademjan. Their thin skin and fewer seeds make them sweeter and less bitter. Traditionally, the eggplant is first fried and then added to the stew. I prefer to roast the eggplant, skin and tender tops on. If you can find sour green grapes (see page 35), use them for a burst of flavor and color. If not, no worries; it is just as delectable with lemon juice or verjuice. A wide, deep pan with a lid is ideal for this dish.

SERVES 6

3 Chinese or 5 Japanese eggplant (1½ to 2 pounds), stems trimmed but tops on, halved lengthwise

¼ cup plus 3 tablespoons olive oil, divided

Kosher salt

8 skinless chicken drumsticks

1 medium yellow onion, diced

½ teaspoon ground turmeric

¼ teaspoon ground allspice

¼ teaspoon ground cinnamon

Ground black pepper

¼ teaspoon ground saffron, steeped in 2 tablespoons hot water (see page 17)

3 tablespoons tomato paste, diluted in ½ cup hot water

½ cup sour green grapes, ¼ cup verjuice, or 3 tablespoons fresh lemon juice (plus more as needed)

¾ cup cherry tomatoes

Preheat the oven to 450°F with the rack set in the upper-third position. Line a large baking sheet with parchment paper. Use two baking sheets if necessary.

If the Chinese eggplant is very long cut it in half crosswise. Place the eggplant halves on the baking sheet and brush with ¼ cup of the olive oil. Use more oil if necessary; eggplant absorbs a lot of oil. Liberally sprinkle the eggplant with salt and roast for 15 minutes, until softened but not completely cooked through. Move the eggplant to the top rack and broil for about 3 minutes, until lightly browned. Set aside.

While the eggplant roasts, make a couple of slits in the flesh of each drumstick. This allows the drumsticks to cook faster and for all the flavors to seep in. Set aside. In a large deep pan with a lid, heat the remaining 3 tablespoons olive oil over medium-high

Khoresh Bademjan *(continued)*

heat. Add the onion, and cook, stirring often, until golden brown, about 8 minutes. Sprinkle with a little salt, reduce the heat to medium, and add the drumsticks, turmeric, allspice, cinnamon, 1 teaspoon salt, and ¼ teaspoon pepper. Stir to combine and cook until the chicken takes on a little color, about 5 minutes. Reduce the heat to medium-low, partially cover, and simmer until the chicken releases some of its juices, 10 to 15 minutes.

Add the saffron water, the tomato paste mixture, ½ cup hot water, and ½ teaspoon salt. If you're not using sour green grapes, add the verjuice or fresh lemon juice at this point. Cover and simmer for 10 minutes.

Add the sour green grapes (if using) and cherry tomatoes, and gently nestle the eggplant into the stew so it can soak up all the delicious juices. Reduce the heat to low, partially cover, and cook until the chicken is cooked through and the eggplant, sour green grapes, and cherry tomatoes have softened but are not falling apart, 15 to 20 minutes. Taste as it simmers. Add more fresh lemon juice (or more verjuice, if using) if necessary. Add more water or salt as needed. Serve with rice or grain of choice.

MAKE AHEAD: Prepare up to 1 day in advance. Take care when reheating so that the eggplant doesn't fall apart. Adjust the water when reheating.

PREP AHEAD: The eggplant can be roasted and stored in an airtight container in the fridge (up to 3 days) or in the freezer (up to 3 months). Thaw and carry on with the recipe.

PLAN AHEAD: Freeze for up to 3 months. Adjust the water when reheating.

Khoresh Na'na Jafari

Vegetarian Mint and Parsley Stew

I always make sure I have a couple of vegetarian options available at our sofreh—table. *The beauty and flexibility of almost all Persian khoresh is that they can easily turn from a meat-based stew to a flavorful vegetarian one. In this Mint and Parsley Stew, I trade the meat and cooking time for easy-to-use frozen artichoke hearts. When in season I also like to add tangy* gojeh sabz—sour green plums (see page 352). *They provide the requisite acidity to the dish and are a fun and unexpected addition as they bob around the pot. Sour green plum season graces us but for a brief whisper of a moment in early spring. The rest of the year I prepare this stew with dried Persian sour golden prunes called* aloo Bokhara. *Available at Middle Eastern markets and online, these tart prunes are also fantastic to snack on. Just be sure to remind everyone that both the gojeh sabz and the aloo Bokhara have pits. And if those aren't an option, just stick with reliable lemon juice. Serve with rice or another grain of choice.*

SERVES 4 TO 6

¼ cup olive oil (plus more as needed)

1 medium yellow onion, diced

Kosher salt

3 bunches parsley, tough stems trimmed, finely chopped

2 bunches mint, stems trimmed, finely chopped

½ teaspoon ground turmeric

Ground black pepper

8 sour green plums or 10 sour golden prunes (optional)

1 (14-ounce) package frozen artichoke hearts, thawed

1¾ cups cooked cannellini beans, or 1 (15-ounce) can, drained and rinsed

¼ teaspoon ground saffron, steeped in 2 tablespoons hot water (see page 17)

¼ cup fresh lemon juice (plus more as needed)

In a medium pot or Dutch oven, heat the olive oil over medium-high heat. Add the onion and cook, stirring often, until golden brown, about 8 minutes. Sprinkle with a pinch of salt, reduce the heat to medium, and add the parsley, mint, turmeric, 1 teaspoon salt, and ¼ teaspoon pepper. Add more oil if the pan seems too dry. Cook, stirring often, until fragrant and reduced in volume, about 5 minutes.

Add 3 cups hot water, the sour green plums (if using) or sour prunes, artichokes, cannellini beans, saffron water, and 1½ teaspoons salt. If you are not using the sour green plums, add the lemon juice. If you are using sour green plums, hold off on the lemon juice and add it as needed later. Bring to a gentle boil, reduce the heat to low, partially cover, and simmer until the plums have softened and released their flavor and the stew has settled in, about 40 minutes. Taste as the stew simmers. Bring it to life: salt, more water, less water (remove the lid). More lemon juice to brighten it up, especially if you didn't use any sour green plums.

MAKE AHEAD: Prepare up to 3 days in advance. Adjust the water and seasoning when reheating.

PREP AHEAD: The onion and fresh herbs (see herb prep, page 12) can be chopped up to 1 day in advance and stored in airtight containers in the fridge. The onion and herb mixture can also be cooked in advance and stored in the fridge (up to 3 days) or in the freezer (up to 3 months). Thaw and carry on with the recipe when desired.

PLAN AHEAD: Freeze any leftovers for up to 3 months.

Khoresh Ghormeh Sabzi
Fresh Herb Stew

Beloved internationally, Khoresh Gormeh Sabzi could very well be the national dish of Iran. And understandably so, with its distinct Persian flavors and ingredients: a field of fresh herbs, succulent meat, dried limes, beans, the ever-present duo of saffron and turmeric, and woodsy, bitter fenugreek. Fenugreek—shanbalileh—is one of the defining flavors and aromas of Khoresh Ghormeh Sabzi. You can find fresh fenugreek at Iranian, Middle Eastern, and Indian markets, and dried fenugreek is available at most grocery stores. This is a Sunday supper kind of meal where the stew can lazily simmer away for a few hours and fill the house with the scents of the true embodiment of an Iranian khoresh.

In the Azari tradition and in homage to my mother's family (from Azarbaijan) I use black-eyed peas instead of the more commonly used red kidney beans. And please do not retreat at the sight of the abundance of fresh green herbs used in this stew; see Prep Ahead on page 156 for advice on sorting through your herbs.

SERVES 6

½ cup olive oil, divided (plus more as needed)

1 large yellow onion, diced

Kosher salt

About 2 pounds lamb shoulder chops on the bone, fat trimmed, cut into 2-inch pieces, or about 1½ pounds stewing meat (beef, veal, or lamb), fat trimmed, cut into 2-inch pieces

1 teaspoon ground turmeric

Ground black pepper

4 bunches parsley, tough stems trimmed, finely chopped

2 bunches cilantro, tough stems trimmed, finely chopped

2 bunches green onions, green parts only, finely chopped

½ bunch fresh fenugreek, leaves only, finely chopped, or 2 tablespoons dried fenugreek

1 cup dried black-eyed peas, rinsed

6 limoo Omani, (see page 349) pierced

¼ teaspoon ground saffron, steeped in 3 tablespoons hot water (see page 17)

3 tablespoons fresh lemon juice (plus more as needed)

In a large pot or Dutch oven, heat ¼ cup of the olive oil over medium-high heat. Add the onion, and cook, stirring frequently, until golden brown, about 8 minutes. Sprinkle with a little salt, and reduce the heat to medium. Add the meat, turmeric, 1½ teaspoons salt, and ¼ teaspoon pepper. Cook for 5 minutes, stirring often, until the meat takes on some color. Add 3 cups hot water and bring to a gentle boil. Cover, reduce the heat to low, and simmer until the meat is tender, about 30 minutes for stewing meat, longer if the meat is on the bone.

Meanwhile, in a large pan, heat the remaining ¼ cup of olive oil over medium heat. Add the parsley, cilantro, green onions, and fenugreek. Cook, stirring often, until fragrant and reduced in volume, about

20 minutes. Add more oil if necessary and take care not to burn the herbs. Sprinkle with a little salt and set aside.

While the meat simmers and the herbs cook, prepare the black-eyed peas. Place the black-eyed peas in a small pot and cover with 2¼ cups water and ½ teaspoon salt. Partially cover and bring to a gentle boil, reduce the heat to medium-low, and simmer for 10 to 15 minutes, until the beans have softened but not completely cooked through. They will finish cooking through in the stew. Set aside.

Turn up the heat under the meat to medium. Add the herb mixture, the beans and their cooking water, the saffron water, the limoo Omani and 1½ teaspoons salt. Bring to a gentle boil, reduce the heat to low, partially cover, and simmer for 1 hour. Add the lemon juice and continue simmering until the meat is tender, the beans are cooked through but holding their shape, and all the flavors have fallen in love, 30 minutes to 1 hour. The longer the stew simmers, the more flavorful it will be. Just keep an eye on the beans, so they keep their shape and don't turn mushy. As the stew simmers gently press down on the dried limes with the back of a spoon so they release their juices. Repeat this a couple of times. Taste as you go. If the stew needs more of a pucker, add more lemon juice accordingly. Add more water if necessary to make it juicier, or remove the lid to reduce the liquid. This khoresh shouldn't be too watered-down, but there should be plenty of juices for everyone to spoon over their rice.

MAKE AHEAD: Make the khoresh 1 day in advance, to allow the flavors to meld. Add more water when reheating and adjust the salt and lemon juice accordingly.

PREP AHEAD: The fresh herbs can be prepped (see page 12) 1 day ahead and stored in the fridge. The onion and the meat can also be cut and stored in separate airtight containers one day ahead in the fridge. The herb mixture can be parcooked and stored in the fridge (up to 3 days) or in the freezer (up to 3 months). Thaw and add to the stew as indicated.

PLAN AHEAD: Makes for great leftovers. Adjust the water and seasoning when reheating. Freeze for up to 3 months.

Khoresh Fesenjan

Pomegranate Walnut Stew

Those early years in Vancouver, after a day spent record shopping with my brother, after a lunch stop at Wendy's for a burger, fries, and milk shakes, Saturday nights were synonymous with dinner parties at our family friends' house—the Ks'. Where you could be guaranteed plenty of dancing and plenty of Mrs. K's mouthwatering Gilaki-style Khoresh Fesenjan— pomegranate walnut stew. Our parents seeking comfort in the company of other families— expats—having gone through similar travels, similar adversities. And the kids pulling out our latest music finds and swapping stories on how we managed to navigate our many worlds. Losing ourselves in a selfie slow-dance to the heartbreak that is "Careless Whisper," as a radically different sound pounded through the basement, knocking us off our feet and leaving the "Careless Whisper" sax solo whimpering in the dust. Our older brothers' music. Seamlessly shifting from milk shakes and punk rock to hip-shimmying Persian music, plat- ters of rice, and Khoresh Fesenjan.

This stew is one that I don't mess around with. I prepare it one way and one way only— Gilaki (northern Iran) style, sour, never sweet. How finely the walnuts are ground is up to personal and regional preference; in this preparation they are ground to a paste. I also like to use a combination of a sour pomegranate molasses with a not-so-sour one. Of course, feel free to use what is most convenient. But the secret ingredients, the magic to this fesenjan will always be time, patience, and respect. The respect of slowly allowing the walnuts to release their oils, bringing them out of their raw state, melding with the pomegranate molasses, transforming to a rich shade of chocolate brown and, most important, coming to life. You can prepare the sauce a day or two in advance and add the chicken the day you want to serve. This recipe makes a big pot of fesenjan, enough for a large dinner party. My feeling is that if a pot of stew sits and simmers for more than 3 hours, then it better reward for a good long while. Serve Khoresh Fesenjan over an equally magical plate of chelo-style rice (page 104), with a side of Sabzi Khordan (page 32) to cut through and better digest the richness of the walnuts.

SERVES 8

1 pound shelled walnuts

1 cup pomegranate molasses (plus more as needed)

½ teaspoon ground turmeric

Kosher salt

½ teaspoon ground cinnamon

¾ teaspoon golpar (Persian hogweed; see page 357) or ground dried rose petals (optional; see page 18)

3½–4 pounds skinless, boneless chicken pieces (any combination)

Ground black pepper

(continued)

Place the walnuts in a food processor and grind to a paste. Transfer the paste to a medium bowl and cover with 3 cups cold water. Stir well to combine and set aside.

Place the pomegranate molasses, turmeric, and 2 teaspoons salt in a large pot or Dutch oven over medium heat, and stir to combine. Keep a very close eye on it. As soon as the pomegranate molasses starts to bubble (this will happen quickly, you don't want it to burn and turn bitter) and comes to a simmer, add the walnut-water mixture. Stir, bring to a gentle boil, and keep at a rapid simmer for 5 minutes, until all the ingredients have combined. Reduce the heat to low and gently simmer the sauce, uncovered, for 2 to 3 hours. Add about ½ cup cold water every 40 minutes or so. You will know it's time to add more water as the sauce starts to thicken and the walnut oils start to rise to the surface. Skim off any oils and stir once in a while making sure nothing is sticking to the bottom of the pot. The color of the sauce will start turning from a pale beige to a rich, chocolate brown throughout this process.

While the sauce simmers prepare the chicken. Cut the chicken thighs in half, and the breasts into 4 pieces (cut on the diagonal). Season the chicken really well with salt and pepper. Set aside (refrigerate if not using within 30 minutes).

Once the sauce is ready add the cinnamon and golpar or rose petals (if using), and pepper to taste. Taste and make adjustments. Maybe a little more pomegranate molasses? Hold off on adding more salt because the chicken will be seasoned with salt. Add the chicken to the sauce, bring up the heat to medium, and bring to a gentle boil. Reduce the heat to medium-low and simmer, uncovered, stirring occasionally, for 45 minutes to 1 hour, until the chicken is cooked through and all the flavors have shared their lifelong secrets. As the stew simmers, taste for additional salt, pepper, and pomegranate molasses. The chicken will release a fair amount of juice, thinning out the sauce, but it will thicken if it sits off the heat for a little bit before serving. Alternatively, you can remove the chicken and reduce the sauce to the desired consistency.

MAKE AHEAD: The whole stew can be made 1 day ahead and gently reheated. Alternatively, you can prepare the sauce up to 3 days in advance and add the chicken when desired.

PLAN AHEAD: Khoresh Fesenjan freezes beautifully. Store any leftovers, or make a batch of the sauce, portion off, and freeze for up to 3 months—and treat yourself to a magical midweek feast.

Ghalieh Mahi

Spicy Tamarind Fish and Herb Stew

Chashnee is a word often used in Persian cooking to describe a particular ingredient that adds flavor to a dish. You'll hear people say, "Now add the chashnee." That ingredient that gives a dish its character and spirit—that makes it delicious. It can be a spice or in particular something that brightens the dish, bringing it to life, like lemon juice or vinegar. Each region in Iran leans heavily on one or two chashnee. In the Caspian region the chashnee might be pomegranate molasses; in Tabriz it can be verjuice. In the Persian Gulf region of Iran—the south—it's tamarind and spice, heat from various types of chiles. Ghalieh Mahi is a great introduction to the rich tradition of southern Iranian cooking. This stew closely resembles many other Persian stews in its use of bundles of fresh herbs, cilantro in particular. But what sets Ghalieh Mahi apart is the heat from the chile peppers and the tang from the tamarind—its chashnee. And this being the gulf region, seafood also plays a central role.

SERVES 4 TO 6

3 tablespoons olive oil

1 medium yellow onion, diced

Kosher salt

6 cloves garlic, crushed to a paste

1 teaspoon ground turmeric

1 red serrano or jalapeño chile, thinly sliced (plus more as garnish)

3 bunches cilantro, tough stems trimmed, finely chopped

2 tablespoons dried fenugreek, or ½ bunch fresh leaves, finely chopped

2 tablespoons unbleached all-purpose flour

2 tablespoons tamarind paste, dissolved in 2 cups water (plus more as needed)

2 tablespoons tomato paste

2 teaspoons brown sugar or honey (plus more as needed)

Cayenne (if needed)

2 pounds cod, halibut, or other firm-fleshed fish

Ground black pepper

In a large pan, heat the oil over medium-high heat. Add the onion and cook until golden brown, about 8 minutes. Sprinkle with a little salt, reduce the heat to medium, and add the garlic, turmeric, and chile pepper. Cook until fragrant, about 2 minutes. Add the cilantro and fenugreek and cook until fragrant, 10 to 15 minutes.

Add the flour and 2 teaspoons salt, and stir to incorporate for 1 minute. Stir in the tamarind mixture and tomato paste. Reduce the heat to medium-low and simmer for 30 minutes. Taste as it simmers and make it delicious. If it's too sour add the sugar or honey to take the edge off the tang. Taste again for salt (keep in mind that the fish will be salted), heat (add cayenne if you like), and more tang from the tamarind.

Meanwhile, cut the fish into 2-inch pieces and season well with salt and black pepper. Raise the heat to medium, add the fish, and simmer, uncovered, until the fish cooks through, 20 to 25 minutes. Stir gently to make sure nothing sticks to the bottom of the pan. If the stew gets too watered-down, remove the fish and raise the heat to reduce the sauce a little; if it's too dry add a little more water. Garnish with chiles if you like and serve with rice.

MAKE AHEAD: The stew can be prepared 3 days in advance without the fish. Reheat, adding more water and seasoning as needed, and add the fish to cook.

PREP AHEAD: See page 12 for fresh herb prep.

PLAN AHEAD: The stew can be prepared without the fish and frozen for up to 3 months. Reheat, adding more water and seasoning (as needed), and add the fish.

Khoresh Seeb-o Havij

Vegetarian Apple Carrot Stew

When I first left my family home in Vancouver for Los Angeles right out of university—chasing dreams, sunny skies, wide boulevards, and palm trees—I found myself starving within a week. This was not a romanticized "starving artist" kind of hunger—I just hadn't had a proper homemade Persian meal. I was starved for comfort and familiarity—I was starved for chelo khoresh. In those early days, I could always count on finding a few apples and carrots in my fridge (much like my children's lunch boxes these days). But what I may have lacked in fridge provisions, in furnishings or home décor, I more than made up for in my spice cupboard. And so this Vegetarian Apple Carrot Stew was born. Everyday ingredients elevated by well-traveled and well-loved spice jars. The perfect cure for a homesick heart. For lean times and more prosperous ones.

Tart green apples are great cooking apples for this stew. They hold their shape well and add the necessary Persian tang. Use canned chickpeas for a quick and soothing weeknight meal. Serve over rice or grain of choice. Or simply tuck in with a chunk of crusty bread, a dollop of plain yogurt, and any forgotten fresh herbs lingering in the back of the crisper.

SERVES 6

4 tablespoons olive oil

1 medium yellow onion, diced

4 large carrots, sliced in ¼-inch pieces (larger pieces sliced in half-moons)

1 large leek, white and light green parts only, thinly sliced

Kosher salt

3 cloves garlic, chopped

2 tablespoons tomato paste

1 teaspoon ground cumin

½ teaspoon ground turmeric

½ teaspoon ground cinnamon

½ teaspoon ground coriander

¼ teaspoon ground allspice

¼ teaspoon ground cardamom

Cayenne (as much as you like)

Ground black pepper

¼ cup verjuice, 2 tablespoons fresh lemon juice, or ¼ cup sour green grapes (page 351)

¼ teaspoon ground saffron, steeped in 3 tablespoons hot water (see page 17)

In a medium pot, heat the olive oil over medium-high heat. Add the onion, carrots, leek, and a good pinch of salt, and cook (reduce the heat to medium if necessary) until the onion is golden and the carrots and leek have slightly softened, about 10 minutes.

Reduce the heat to medium and add the garlic. Cook, stirring often, until the garlic is fragrant, about 3 minutes. Add the tomato paste, cumin, turmeric, cinnamon, coriander, allspice, cardamom, cayenne to taste, 2 teaspoons salt, and ¼ teaspoon pepper. Stir constantly until fragrant, taking care that the tomato paste doesn't burn, about 2 minutes. Add the verjuice (or lemon juice or sour grapes), saffron water, and 1½ cups hot water. Turn up the heat to medium-high

1 cup cooked chickpeas, or 1 (15-ounce) can, drained and rinsed

2 green apples, peeled, cored, and chopped into 1-inch pieces

1 tablespoon unsalted butter (optional)

2 tablespoons black raisins (optional)

Handful of fresh cilantro or fresh herb of choice

and bring to a gentle boil. Add the chickpeas and apples. Partially cover and simmer over medium-low heat, until the apples are tender, but still holding their shape and all the flavors have come to life, about 20 minutes. Taste as it simmers and help it fall into place.

Meanwhile, if using the raisins, in a small skillet, melt the butter over medium heat. Add the raisins and cook, stirring constantly, until they plump up, about 3 minutes.

Scatter the raisins and fresh cilantro over the stew and serve.

MAKE AHEAD: Prepare up to 3 days in advance. Adjust the water and seasoning when reheating.

PREP AHEAD: The onion, carrots, and leek can be chopped 1 day in advance and stored in airtight containers in the fridge.

PLAN AHEAD: Freeze leftovers (up to 3 months) and reheat gently so the apples don't fall apart.

Khoresh Gheymeh
Meat and Yellow Split Pea Stew

The most humble of dishes is often the most satisfying, and Khoresh Gheymeh is no exception. This unassuming stew of meat, yellow split peas, dried limes, and fragrant advieh *epitomizes Iranian home cooking and comfort food. Think of it as the Persian stew version of a burger and fries. Especially with the crunchy, fried potatoes heaped on top. The yellow split peas are cooked separately here so their cooking time and texture can be controlled. Some split peas cook quickly and turn into mush, some take longer to cook through. By par-cooking them separately, and then finishing them off in the stew they maintain their shape while cooking through.*

I love to serve Khoresh Gheymeh with nutty brown rice prepared in the rice cooker (page 115) or kateh-*style (page 113). And there is perhaps nothing more satisfying than the starchy, aromatic juices of the stew seeping into the creamy yogurt on the side of your plate. Khoresh Gheymeh relies on the sharp and deep tang of the limoo Omani—dried limes. Seek them out because it wouldn't be gheymeh without them.*

SERVES 6

¾ cup yellow split peas, picked through and rinsed

Kosher salt

3 tablespoons plus ¼ cup olive oil, divided

1 large yellow onion, diced

1 pound stewing meat (beef, veal, or lamb), cut into ½-inch cubes

½ teaspoon ground turmeric

½ teaspoon grated fresh ginger (optional)

Ground black pepper

¼ cup tomato paste, diluted in ½ cup warm water

½ teaspoon Advieh (page 15)

¼ teaspoon ground saffron, steeped in 2 tablespoons hot water (see page 17)

4 medium limoo Omani (dried limes; see page xx), pierced

Juice of half an orange (optional)

1 large russet or Yukon Gold potato, peeled and chopped into ½-inch cubes or sliced into matchsticks

Lemon juice

Place the yellow split peas in a small pot. Cover with 2 cups water and add 1 teaspoon salt. Partially cover and bring to a gentle boil, skimming off any foam. Keep a close eye on it so it doesn't boil over. Reduce the heat to medium-low and simmer until the yellow split peas are al dente, slightly softened but not completely cooked through (they will finish cooking off in the stew), about 10 minutes depending on the quality of your peas. Remove from the heat and set aside.

Meanwhile, in a large pot or Dutch oven, heat 3 tablespoons of the olive oil over medium-high heat. Add the onion and cook, stirring frequently, until golden brown, about 8 minutes. Sprinkle with salt, reduce the heat to medium, and add the meat, turmeric, ginger (if using), 1½ teaspoons salt, and ¼ teaspoon pepper. Cook for 5 minutes, stirring often, until the meat takes on some color. Add 1¾ cups hot water and bring to a very gentle boil. Cover, reduce the heat to low, and simmer for 30 minutes, until the meat is tender.

Turn up the heat to medium and add the tomato paste mixture, Advieh, saffron water, dried limes, the juice of half an orange, if using, and the yellow split peas and their cooking water. Partially cover, bring to a gentle boil, reduce the heat to low, and simmer for 30 to 40 minutes, until the meat is tender, the yellow split peas are cooked through but holding their shape, and all the flavors have come to life. As the stew simmers, gently squeeze the dried limes a couple of times with the back of a spoon so they release their juices. Taste as you go. Add more salt if necessary. Squeeze in a little lemon if necessary. If the stew is too watered-down, remove the lid to allow some of the juices to reduce.

While the stew simmers, fry the potato. Time this so you can serve the potatoes crispy and hot when serving the stew. In a large skillet, heat the remaining ¼ cup olive oil over medium-high heat. The oil should be hot but not smoking. Fry the potatoes, stirring often, until crispy and golden, and browned in bits and pieces, 10 to 15 minutes. Season with a good pinch of salt.

Top the khoresh with the crispy potatoes and serve over rice or grain of choice.

MAKE AHEAD: This stew tastes even better the next day. Prepare the stew (not the potatoes) up to 1 day in advance. Adjust the water and seasoning as needed when reheating.

PREP AHEAD: The onion and meat can be chopped 1 day in advance and stored in airtight containers in the fridge.

PLAN AHEAD: This is the ultimate next-day school or work lunch. Pack in a thermos and enjoy. You can also freeze the stew for up to 3 months. Prepare the potatoes fresh to garnish when reheating the stew.

Khoresh Morgh-e Torsh

Sour Chicken Stew

Khoresh Morgh-e Torsh is a tangy chicken stew, and it hails from the northern Iranian province of Gilan. This Sour Chicken Stew shows off its regional pedigree by using greater quantities of cilantro and mint, plenty of garlic, and verjuice (see page 352)—ingredients often used in the Caspian region. Seville oranges—narenj—are also often used in this area. If you happen to have one on hand come springtime, its juices are fantastic here as well. Inspired by the traditional preparation, I've taken some liberties by preparing this dish as more of a braise. Poultry is not often cooked with its skin on in Persian stews, but if you get a good sear on the chicken it can add another level of caramelized flavors to this bright and herby stew. Serve Khoresh Morgh-e Torsh with rice to soak up all the tangy, earthy flavors.

SERVES 6

8 bone-in, skin-on chicken thighs (about 3 pounds)

Kosher salt

⅓ cup yellow split peas, picked through and rinsed

6 tablespoons olive oil, divided (plus more as needed)

3 tablespoons white wine

1 tablespoon butter

1 large yellow onion, diced

4 large cloves garlic, chopped

½ teaspoon ground turmeric

2 bunches cilantro, tough stems trimmed, finely chopped

1 bunch parsley, tough stems trimmed, finely chopped

1 cup finely chopped leek greens

1 bunch mint, leaves only, finely chopped

¼ bunch fresh dill, chopped, or 2 teaspoons dried dill

¾ cup verjuice, or ⅓ cup fresh lemon juice (plus more as needed)

¼ teaspoon ground saffron, steeped in 3 tablespoons hot water (see page 17)

Ground black pepper

Season the chicken thighs with 1 heaping tablespoon salt, and set aside at room temperature while you prepare the yellow split peas. The chicken can also be salted and stored in the fridge for up to 48 hours.

Place the yellow split peas in a small pot. Cover with 1 cup water and ½ teaspoon salt. Partially cover and bring to a gentle boil, skimming off any foam. Keep a close eye on it so it doesn't boil over. Reduce the heat to medium-low and simmer until the yellow split peas are al dente, softened but not completely cooked through, 10 to 15 minutes depending on the quality of your peas. Remove from the heat and set aside.

Meanwhile, in a large wide pan with a lid or in a Dutch oven, heat 3 tablespoons of the olive oil over medium-high heat. The oil should be hot but not smoking. Brown the chicken skin-side down first, turn, and brown the other side, 5 to 8 minutes per side.

(continued)

Do this in batches if you need to so you don't overcrowd the pot. The chicken will release from the pot when it's ready, be patient, don't force it. Set the chicken aside on a baking sheet.

Carefully tip out all the oil from the pot into a small bowl and discard. Reduce the heat to medium, immediately add the wine, and scrape up any deliciousness that might have stuck to the pot. Add the remaining 3 tablespoons olive oil and the butter. As soon as the butter melts, add the onion and cook, stirring often, until the onion has softened and is golden, about 8 minutes. Add the garlic and turmeric and cook until fragrant, about 2 minutes. Add the cilantro, parsley, and leeks, and cook for 5 minutes. Add more oil if it seems too dry. Add the mint, dill, and a pinch of salt, and cook, stirring often, until all the herbs release their fragrance and reduce in volume, about 5 minutes.

Add the verjuice or lemon juice, 1½ cups hot water, the saffron water, the yellow split peas and their cooking water, 1 teaspoon salt, and ¼ teaspoon pepper. Give a stir, and nestle the chicken thighs back in the pot. Bring to a gentle boil, turn down the heat to low, cover, and simmer until the chicken is tender and all the flavors have melded, about 45 minutes. As the stew simmers, taste and make it sing. More verjuice for zing, more water to make it juicier, salt? Serve over rice.

MAKE AHEAD: Prepare up to 1 day in advance. Adjust the water and seasoning as needed when reheating. Keep in mind that the browned chicken skin will soften.

PREP AHEAD: The chicken can be salted up to 2 days in advance and stored in the fridge; bring to room temperature before browning. The herbs can be chopped (except for the mint) up to 1 day ahead and stored in an airtight container in the fridge (see fresh herb prep, page 12). The onion can be chopped up to 3 days ahead and stored in the fridge.

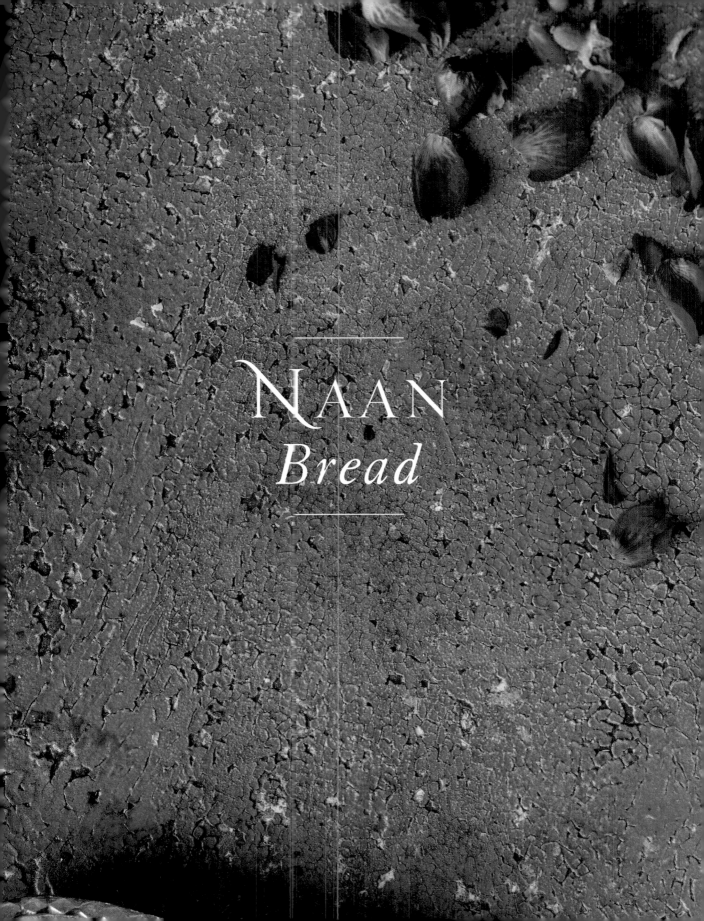

Naan
Bread

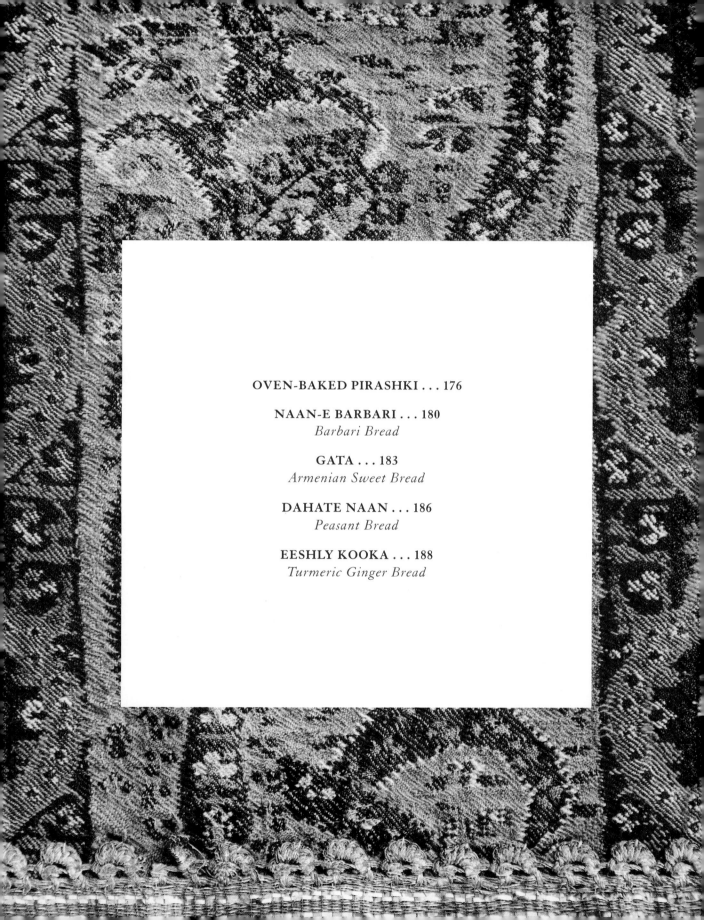

LIFE

Life in the diaspora began with little more than flour, water, yeast, a moody oven, and hearts full of resilience and determination.

We landed (officially referred to as Landed Immigrants) in Vancouver on my tenth birthday, which we celebrated twice. Once, amid tears and trepidation of what awaited us across the Atlantic, in Rome's Fiumicino Airport. Then a second time, sixteen hours later, and technically nine hours earlier, jet-lagged and dazed in Vancouver International Airport. Two birthdays in one day: not a bad start to life in the New World.

Two years earlier we had left Iran in the midst of a revolution and the beginnings of a war to now land in Vancouver, via Rome, with three over-stuffed suitcases and one sewing machine in tow. Winding our way through the airport, we made a final stop behind the frosted windows of Customs and Immigration. I have a complicated relationship with airports. A space that once held promise, the gateway to summer vacations and adventure, now makes my heart race a little faster, beat a little harder. A seemingly random red strip of tape on the ground, a dated stamp and ink pad, a place of birth forever etched on a passport, and a somber uniformed officer determine our future, our lives. These days, as I absentmindedly rush through various airports I once again pause at those red lines and frosted window panes. I wonder what new family is anxiously pacing back there, sleep-deprived and confused, hoping for that stamp to hit the ink, hoping to step into a new life.

With our paperwork officially stamped, we were welcomed to Canada by an immigration officer and just like that, we were released out into the wild. Like other immigrant families before us and surely those after us, we awkwardly pushed our luggage cart, heaped with suitcases on the verge of teetering off. Packing tape securing the lid on a lifetime condensed into three suitcases stuffed with every bit of home, memory, and spice we could fit in.

Immigration is at the very best of times undertaken by choice and at desperate times dictated by necessity and survival. For my parents it meant shelving all past hopes and expectations, professions and passions, uneventful daily routines and schedules, to quickly find a way to acclimate and provide for me and my brother in a new country. The path to provisions and providing presented itself by chance a couple of months after our initial arrival. One evening as we were acquainting ourselves with our new neighborhood of North Vancouver, we stumbled upon what we assumed was an Italian deli. Heartsick for fresh mozzarella, prosciutto, and mortadella, and in need of a respite from the never-ending Vancouver rain showers, we ducked inside. There we were greeted by the scent of cured meats and sharp cheese, and the store owner in his crisp white deli robe. Always a comforting sight. My parents greeted him with a *buongiorno*, to which he responded with a *salaam*. As it turned out, he was Persian. Introductions were made, and in the midst of exchanging pleasantries he mentioned his desire to sell more Persian goods in the store—in particular Iranian bread. My mother, without missing a beat, and quite confidently, offered her services. By the time we walked out with mortadella and pepperoncini under arm, it was agreed that she would provide the store with homemade *naan-e barbari*—barbari bread.

Barbari is one of the most popular and beloved breads in Iran, and is often eaten at breakfast with a thick slice of feta cheese and a strong cup of black tea. Barbari, *sangak*, *lavash*, and *taftoon* make up the most common breads enjoyed by Iranians. These breads are made at a *naan vayee*—a bread bakery—and handed to you hot out of the *tanoor*—a traditional clay oven. Naan vayees can be found on every other block in Iran with long lines winding out the door. *Naan* (the Persian word for "bread") at the table is not only a constant companion but a revered guest. Wheat is considered sacred, a symbol of life and the beginnings of civilization. Not a single crumb is ever to be wasted and should always be repurposed.

Maman had never baked a single naan in her life, but our lives had to be sustained. So she took inspiration from the roots of civilization and put in a call to one of the famed bakeries of her hometown of Tabriz. Long distance phone calls back in 1982 consisted of the dialing of rotary phones, a lot of crackling in the line, and plenty of yelling *allo*, *allo*, over and over again. It's an anomaly how Maman managed to transcribe the method of bread baking yelled back at her, using vast quantities of flour and water to turn out barbari in our tiny apartment kitchen with an equally tiny and incredibly grumpy oven.

There's a push and a pull to bread baking. There are many variables that can affect the process: rhythm, temperature, temperament, inspiration, timing, luck, and patience. But on those magical days when you find your rhythm, when it all flows, it's an accomplishment worthy of a celebration. Maybe even two celebrations in one day. As it turned out, Maman had a knack for bread baking and our little naan vayee business took off. When demand grew, Baba would take over to knead and stretch the dough. A 7 a.m. knock on our door became a regular occurrence, with people lining up down the apartment building hallway to pick up their daily barbari.

For a time in 1982, Maman, reputed and celebrated as the first female lyricist of Iran, proudly reinvented herself as the first baker of barbari bread in Vancouver, temporarily trading in her notebook and plume for a dusting of flour and a drizzle of water. Our lives had taken so many twists and turns that we no longer questioned the absurdity of any given situation as we woke to the smell of fresh naan, the rhythmic kneading of my architect father's arms, and the hushed murmurs of Maman, working through another rhyme. As they both punched, knocked back, dusted, drizzled, and survived.

I'm not the most natural baker and dealing with yeasted dough often sounds intimidating, but I like to remind myself that it's like any other diplomatic relationship, founded on patience, empathy, and communication. It relies on your intuition to know when to push and when to step back and give space, and, when necessary, the courage to dive right in and be firm. Respect and listen to the dough, and it will whisper back (sometimes it might yell, too) and tell you when it's ready. But at the same time, don't be scared of it—it's just dough. There will be great bread-baking days, and some that could have gone better. But even on the more challenging days you will be rewarded with fresh naan hot out of the oven. And that's always a good thing.

Besides barbari, I've included a few of our favorite yeasted, stuffed breads in this chapter. Some are savory and some sweet, and they can be enjoyed for breakfast, as a snack, or as a quick lunch.

Oven-Baked Pirashki

Once my mother's barbari baking business took off she expanded her repertoire to a variety of yeasted doughs and baked goods. The accidental baker had caught the bread-baking bug and lucky for us it all translated to after-school treats like pirashki. *Much like its Russian counterpart* pirozhki, *Persian pirashki are savory and sweet stuffed yeasted breads. Typically fried, here I prefer to bake them. By placing them right up against each other, they keep a soft bite, much like a dinner roll. Meat pirashki are most common, and we also love spinach and cheese.*

MAKES 12 PIRASHKI

FOR THE DOUGH

¼ cup lukewarm water

2¼ teaspoons active dry yeast

1 teaspoon sugar

½ cup plain yogurt, at room temperature

2 eggs, at room temperature, lightly beaten

2 tablespoons unsalted butter, melted and cooled

1 teaspoon kosher salt

3 cups (360 g) bread flour or unbleached all-purpose flour (plus more for dusting and as needed)

MEAT STUFFING (FOR 12 PIRASHKI)

2 tablespoons olive oil

1 medium yellow onion, diced

Kosher salt

2 cloves garlic, chopped

1 pound ground beef or ground dark meat turkey

½ teaspoon paprika

½ teaspoon ground allspice

¼ teaspoon ground black pepper

¼ teaspoon ground turmeric

¼ teaspoon garlic powder

Small pinch of cayenne (optional)

2 tablespoons tomato paste

½ bunch parsley, finely chopped

Place the water, yeast, and sugar in the bowl of a stand mixer, stirring to dissolve. Set aside until frothy, about 10 minutes.

Add the following to the yeast mixture in this order: the room-temperature yogurt, the eggs, melted butter, salt, and flour. Mix everything with a wooden spoon until combined, a shaggy dough forms, and it starts to pull away from the sides of the bowl. If your dough is still sticking to the sides of the bowl, add a little more flour; be conservative about this, though, and err on the side of less flour. If your dough is too dry add a sprinkle of lukewarm water. Place the mixing bowl in the stand mixer fitted with a dough hook and mix on medium speed until a soft dough forms and it starts to clean the sides of the bowl, about 3 minutes. Alternatively you can knead by hand. Cover the bowl with a plastic wrap and set aside to rise, about 1 hour.

Meanwhile, prepare either the meat stuffing or the spinach and cheese stuffing.

(continued)

**SPINACH AND
CHEESE STUFFING
(FOR 12 PIRASHKI)**

1 (16-ounce) package
frozen spinach, thawed
and drained, or equal
amount fresh spinach

2 cups crumbled white
farmer's cheese or queso
fresco

3 tablespoons olive oil

1 tablespoon fresh lemon
juice (plus more as
needed)

¼ teaspoon ground
cinnamon

¼ teaspoon ground
nutmeg

½ teaspoon ground
black pepper

½ teaspoon kosher salt
(plus more as needed)

EGG WASH

1 egg yolk

1 tablespoon milk or
yogurt

FOR THE MEAT STUFFING:

In a medium pan, heat the oil over medium heat. Add the onion and cook until soft and golden, about 8 minutes. Sprinkle with salt. Add the garlic and cook until soft, about 2 minutes. Add the meat, all the seasonings, and 1 teaspoon salt. Mix to combine, and add the tomato paste. Brown the meat, breaking it down into tiny bits, 5 to 8 minutes. Taste and adjust the seasonings. Stir in the parsley, taste again, fix again, and cook for 2 minutes. Set aside to cool completely.

FOR THE SPINACH AND CHEESE STUFFING:

Place the thawed spinach on a couple of layers of paper towel or a kitchen towel. Squeeze out all the liquid from the spinach. (If using fresh spinach, quickly steam the spinach until wilted. Set aside to cool, and then place on a couple of layers of paper towel and squeeze out all the liquid.) Place the spinach in a bowl and add the rest of the ingredients, mixing to combine. Taste and add more lemon juice and salt as needed, depending on how salty the cheese is.

ASSEMBLE THE PIRASHKI:

Place the dough back onto your lightly floured counter and knead it a few more times. Pinch off 12 equal-sized pieces (you can weigh the dough and divide for exact even pieces, or simply eyeball it), form into balls, set on the counter, loosely cover with plastic wrap or a towel, and let rise for 30 minutes.

Preheat the oven to 350°F with the oven rack in the center.

Line a large baking sheet with parchment paper and set it and the filling next to you. Lightly flour your hands, and flatten each ball with the palm of your hand into a disk about 4 inches in diameter (keep the rest of balls covered as you work). Fill half of each disk with about 2 tablespoons of the filling and, using a fork, carefully pinch and seal the other half onto it, forming an oval shape. Make sure the pirashki is well sealed so the filling doesn't burst out while baking. Place the pirashki on the baking sheet, seams down. The pirashki should be very close, almost touching each other. You should have two rows of pirashki lined up on the pan.

In a small bowl, mix the egg yolk and milk. Brush liberally over the tops and sides of the pirashki (you might not need all of the egg wash). Place the pirashki in the oven and bake for 25 to 30 minutes, rotating the pan halfway through, until the pirashki are golden brown. Remove from the oven and set aside until cool enough to handle and or until you can't stand it anymore and have to dig in. Pirashki are best enjoyed warm out of the oven.

MAKE AHEAD: Pirashki will keep in an airtight container for up to 1 day on the counter and up to 2 days in the fridge. Gently reheat in the oven. You can also freeze pirashki wrapped well in foil for up to 1 month.

Naan-e Barbari

Barbari Bread

Barbari bread is one of the most traditional and popular breads in Iran. It's distinguished by its long oblong shape and grooved indentations. For Iranians Naan-e Barbari (naan simply means "bread") is synonymous with breakfast, although, of course, it can be devoured any time of day. A typical Iranian breakfast is made of hot barbari fresh out of the tanoor (should you be so lucky), paneer (feta cheese, or white farmer's cheese), a variety of floral scented preserves such as sour cherry (see page 66), sweet butter, sarsheer (Persian clotted cream), honey, walnuts, cucumber, tomatoes, fresh fruit, and a hot cup of black tea to wash it all down with. This is the breakfast I grew up on, and it is the one I crave when in need of comfort.

 This dough is very similar to pizza dough, as my brother always likes to remind me. You'll be tempted to add more flour to the tacky, soft dough, but I urge you to hold back. If you have a stand mixer with a dough hook, it's a great idea to use it here; otherwise, roll up your sleeves and knead by hand for a good workout. A baking stone or steel is also useful but not imperative. I just turn my baking sheet upside down and bake on top of it. The glaze is called roomal. *It gives the bread its golden color and it's also a centuries-old method of creating steam in the oven. Follow these instructions, but don't get too bogged down by it all. Just move forward and bake some barbari.*

MAKES 2 LOAVES

FOR THE DOUGH

1¾ cups lukewarm water, divided

2¼ teaspoons active dry yeast

½ teaspoon sugar

4 cups (480 g) bread flour (plus more as needed for dusting)

2½ teaspoons kosher salt

FOR THE GLAZE

1 tablespoon flour

¼ cup cold water

¼ teaspoon baking soda

FOR THE TOPPINGS

1 teaspoon nigella seeds

1 teaspoon sesame seeds

Place ¾ cup of the lukewarm water, the yeast, and the sugar in the bowl of a stand mixer, stirring to dissolve. Set aside until frothy, about 10 minutes.

 Add 2 cups of the flour and the salt to the yeast mixture and mix with a wooden spoon until just combined. Add ½ cup of the water and another 1 cup of the flour, and stir. Add the rest of the water (½ cup) and flour (1 cup), and stir until combined. Place the mixing bowl in the stand mixer fitted with a dough hook and mix on medium speed until the dough just starts to slap the sides of the bowl and is no longer sticking to the sides

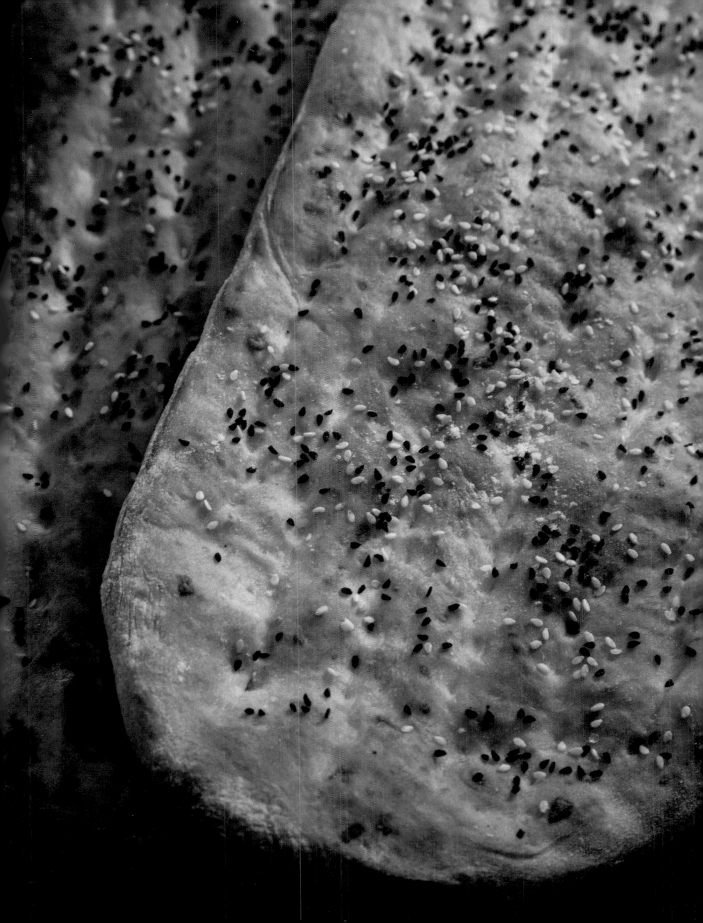

of the bowl, about 3 minutes. The dough will still be tacky and stick to the bottom of the bowl and that's okay. Just don't overknead or add more flour. Alternatively, if you don't have a stand mixer, you can knead the dough by hand. It will take 10 to 15 minutes of kneading, and it should feel like a good workout. Don't be scared of the dough, remember you're much bigger than it—and it's just flour and water!

Very lightly flour the bottom of a new bowl and transfer the dough to the new bowl, cover with plastic wrap, and rest at room temperature for about 1 hour, until doubled in size and soft; it will still feel tacky.

Use about ¼ cup flour to dust your work surface and turn the dough out onto it. You might need to use a bench scraper. Don't knead or punch it or anything of the sort— handle it as little as possible. Divide the dough in half and form each half into a ball. Lightly dust the top of the dough with flour so the plastic doesn't stick, cover with plastic wrap, and rest for 30 minutes.

Meanwhile, set the oven rack in the lowest position. If you have a baking stone, use it. Otherwise turn a rimmed baking sheet upside down and use that. Make do with what you have. Preheat the oven to 500°F and prepare the glaze.

Combine the flour, water, and baking soda in a small saucepan and cook over medium heat, whisking, until it thickens, about 2 minutes. Set aside to cool. It will thicken more as it sits.

Prepare your work space: Set the glaze, seeds, and a small bowl of water beside you. If you have a pizza peel, have it close by, otherwise use a rimless baking sheet.

Flour your hands and make sure your work surface is still floured. Otherwise dust with a little more flour. Gently shape one dough into an oval shape about 12 x 6 inches, flattening, lifting, and stretching as you go. Lift the dough with both hands and place it on one sheet of the parchment paper. Dip the fingertips of both hands in a little water and make about five indentations, ¼ inch apart, in the dough lengthwise. Press down hard but don't poke through the dough. Using your hands, lightly spread the glaze all over and sprinkle with the nigella and sesame seeds. Use the pizza peel, or the back side of a rimless baking sheet, to lift the dough and parchment paper and swiftly slip it on the pizza stone or baking sheet. Bake for 15 to 18 minutes, until golden brown. Transfer the bread to a cooling rack, wrap in a towel to keep warm, and repeat with the other dough.

Barbari is best hot out of the oven.

MAKE AHEAD: Barbari freezes well. Wrap in an airtight plastic bag and freeze for up to 1 month.

Gata

Armenian Sweet Bread

My friend and pastry chef, Fariba, helped me re-create one of my favorite childhood break-
fast breads—noon-e sheereen—Armenian Gata bread. Preparing Gata takes some time,
but it's mostly hands-off as the dough needs to rest and rise a few times. And it's quite a
forgiving dough so turning it out is not difficult. Set aside a quiet weekend morning and
enlist the kids to stir, knead, and rake designs. Gata freezes beautifully, so bake one for a
breakfast treat and save the other for another chilly afternoon to be enjoyed with a Turkish
coffee (page 308) or a hot cup of tea.

FOR THE DOUGH

1½ teaspoons active
dry yeast

1½ tablespoons plus
2¾ cups (330 g) bread
flour or unbleached all-
purpose flour, divided
(plus more as needed)

¼ cup lukewarm water

2 large eggs, at room
temperature

½ cup sugar

8 tablespoons (1 stick)
unsalted butter, at room
temperature

FOR THE FILLING

8 tablespoons (1 stick)
unsalted butter, at room
temperature

¾ cup sugar

1 vanilla bean, seeds
scraped, or 1 teaspoon
vanilla extract

¾ to 1 cup (90 to
120 g) bread flour or
unbleached all-purpose
flour (as needed)

EGG WASH

1 egg yolk

1 tablespoon milk or
yogurt

Place the yeast, 1½ tablespoons of flour, and
the water in a small bowl, stirring to dissolve.
Set aside until frothy, about 10 minutes.

Place the eggs and sugar in the bowl of a
stand mixer fitted with a paddle attachment.
Beat on medium speed until pale yellow, 5 to
8 minutes. In a small bowl, soften the butter
with a fork; it should have the consistency
of whipped cream cheese. Add it to the eggs
and sugar. Beat until well combined, 1 to
2 minutes. Add 1 cup of the flour and half of
the yeast mixture. Mix just until combined,
then add the rest of the flour and the rest
of the yeast mixture. Pulse it in using on/
off turns so the flour doesn't fly out of the
bowl. Switch to the dough hook and mix on
medium speed until a soft dough forms and
it starts to clean the sides of the bowl, 4 to
5 minutes. A little sticking is okay.

Transfer the dough to a clean bowl, cover
with plastic wrap and set aside to rise, about
1 hour.

Tip out the dough onto a well-floured
surface. Knead it a few times as follows:
Using the heels of your hands, press and
push it out from the bottom (the end closest

to you), and then pull it back it in toward you by folding the top of the dough toward you and onto itself. Turn the dough a little and repeat the process four or five times. Place the dough back in the bowl, and cover again for 1 hour.

Tip the dough out, knead a couple of times, and divide into 2 balls. Loosely wrap in plastic and leave to rest for 1 hour.

Meanwhile, prepare the filling. Place the butter and sugar in a medium bowl, and mix well. You can use a fork or just get in there with your hands. Add the vanilla and mix until the texture of wet sand. Add the flour a little bit at a time. Knead the filling in the bowl by hand until it just comes together. Set aside.

Preheat the oven to 350°F with the rack in the center. Line a large baking sheet with parchment paper.

Working with one ball of dough at a time, knead the dough a few times. Press down on the dough and roll it out with a rolling pin to about an 8-inch round, ½-inch thick. Make sure the underside of the dough is smooth, with no cracks, as the underside will eventually be the top side.

Take half of the filling and press it gently into a 6-inch round. Place the filling on top of the dough. (If the filling is too soft to roll out, press it directly on top of the dough, stopping 2 inches from the edge.) Fold in the perimeter of the dough toward the center and pinch closed until the filling is completely sealed inside. (Be vigilant about pinching so there are no openings.) Gently press with the palm of your hand and flatten the dough to about 6 to 8 inches in diameter. (You can also use the rolling pin.) Flip the dough; the top should be smooth with no cracks. Transfer the bread to the prepared baking sheet and repeat with the remaining dough and filling.

In a small bowl, combine the egg yolk with the milk or yogurt for the egg wash. Brush the top and sides of each gata with the egg wash. With a fork, make a cross design, a snowflake design, or a series of cross hatch designs covering the entire surface.

Bake for 30 to 35 minutes, until golden brown and a toothpick inserted into the center comes out clean.

MAKE AHEAD: Gata freezes very well. Enjoy one bread right away and freeze the other for a few weeks later.

Dahate Naan

Peasant Bread

One of the most thoughtful gifts I've ever received was from my cousin Laleh. She put together a small handmade recipe booklet with recipes she had collected from my paternal grandparents. A short family history accompanies each recipe, all written out and designed by hand. Stuffed "peasant" or "rustic" breads are common in all parts of Iran with slight variations to the recipe, usually in the filling, which distinguishes its provenance. My paternal grandfather—Agha joon—was Taalyishi, an Iranian ethnic group who lived in the Caspian region of Iran. This Dahate Naan—rustic bread—hails from this region. Serve with a thick slice of feta cheese and a hot cup of tea. Laleh writes, "Taalyishi women wear long and colorful dresses. I remember those days in Anzali, during summertimes, when they carried vegetables on their head, all walking together in the middle of street, speaking and singing loudly."

MAKES 6 STUFFED BREADS

FOR THE DOUGH

1 cup whole milk

2¼ teaspoons active dry yeast

8 tablespoons (1 stick) unsalted butter, melted

½ cup granulated sugar

½ teaspoon kosher salt

3¼ cups (390 g) bread flour or unbleached all-purpose flour (plus more as needed)

FOR THE FILLING

½ cup (60 g) bread flour or unbleached all-purpose flour, sifted

½ teaspoon ground turmeric

5 tablespoons clarified butter or unsalted butter, melted

¼ cup brown sugar

¼ cup walnuts or raw pistachios, finely chopped

½ teaspoon ground cardamom

EGG WASH

1 egg yolk

1 tablespoon milk or yogurt

Tiny sprinkle of ground saffron for color (optional)

In a small saucepan, gently heat the milk until it is lukewarm or at body temperature (98 to 100°F). Pour the warm milk into the bowl of a stand mixer and add the yeast, stirring to dissolve. Set aside until frothy, about 10 minutes.

Add the melted butter, granulated sugar, salt, and flour (1 cup at a time) to the yeast mixture. Mix everything with a wooden spoon until combined. Switch to the dough hook and mix on medium speed until a soft dough forms and it starts to clean the sides of the bowl, about 3 minutes. Alternatively, you can knead by hand. If your dough is still sticking to the sides of the bowl, add a little more flour; be conservative about this, though, and err on the side of less flour. If your dough is too dry, add a sprinkle of milk or water. Cover the bowl with plastic wrap and set aside to rest for about 1 hour.

Meanwhile, prepare the filling. Place the flour in a medium pan. Toast the flour over medium heat, continuously stirring and nudging the flour this way and that, until it releases its aroma and turns golden, about 8 minutes. The flour should come out of its raw state but take care not to burn it—don't go anywhere! Add the turmeric, give a stir to combine, and add the melted butter. Stir until the butter and flour are well combined. Add the brown sugar and stir to combine. Remove from the heat, and stir in the walnuts or pistachios and cardamom. Set aside until ready to use.

Preheat the oven to 350°F with the oven rack set in the center. Line a baking sheet with parchment paper.

Lightly flour the counter and scrape the dough out onto the counter. Pinch off 12 equal pieces (you can weigh the dough and divide for exact even pieces), form into balls, set on the counter, loosely cover with plastic wrap, and rest for 30 minutes.

Set the baking sheet and the filling next you. Lightly flour your hands, and flatten each ball into a disk about 4 inches in diameter. Fill 6 of the disks with the filling, using about 2 tablespoons per disk, stopping ¼ inch from the edge, place another disk on top, and fold in the edges to seal well. Place on the baking sheet. Continue with the rest of the disks.

In a small bowl, combine the egg yolk, milk, and a tiny pinch of saffron (if using for the egg wash). Brush the tops and sides with the egg wash. Place in the oven and bake until golden brown, about 25 minutes. Set aside to cool slightly and serve.

MAKE AHEAD: Dahate Naan will keep in an airtight container on the counter for up to 1 day and in the fridge for up to 2 days. Wrap tightly in a plastic bag or foil and freeze for up to 1 month. Reheat gently in the oven.

Eeshly Kooka

Turmeric Ginger Bread

These savory spiced stuffed breads are beloved in Tabriz. My mother has fond memories of snacking on Eeshly Kooka as a morning or afternoon treat as a child. These round breads are not sweet but slightly salty with a kick from the ginger and turmeric. Perfect with a cup of tea.

MAKES 6 BREADS

FOR THE DOUGH

¼ cup whole milk

1 teaspoon active dry yeast

2½ cups (300 g) bread flour or unbleached all-purpose flour (plus more as needed)

2 teaspoons sugar

1 teaspoon kosher salt

¾ cup plain full-fat yogurt, at room temperature

4 tablespoons unsalted butter, melted and cooled

¼ cup olive oil

FOR THE FILLING

½ cup (60 g) bread flour or unbleached all-purpose flour, sifted

¾ teaspoon ground turmeric

1 teaspoon ground ginger

½ teaspoon kosher salt

5 tablespoons clarified butter or unsalted butter, melted

EGG WASH

1 large egg yolk

1 tablespoon milk or yogurt

Sesame seeds for topping

In a small saucepan, gently heat the milk until it is lukewarm or at body temperature (98° to 100°F). Pour the warm milk in the bowl of a stand mixer and add the yeast, stirring to dissolve. Set aside until frothy, about 10 minutes. In a separate bowl, combine the flour, sugar, and salt.

Add the yogurt, butter, and oil to the yeast mixture, and then add the flour mix. Mix everything with a wooden spoon until combined and a dough forms. Switch to the dough hook and mix on medium speed until a soft dough forms and it starts to clean the sides of the bowl, about 3 minutes. Alternatively, you can knead by hand. Cover the bowl with plastic wrap and set aside to rise for 30 minutes to 1 hour.

Meanwhile, prepare the filling. Place the flour in a medium pan. Toast the flour over medium heat, continuously stirring and nudging the flour this way and that, until it releases its aroma, about 8 minutes. The flour should come out of its raw state but take care not to burn it—don't go anywhere! Add the turmeric, ginger, and salt. Give a stir to combine and add the melted butter. Stir until the butter and flour are well combined. Remove from the heat, and set aside until ready to use.

Preheat the oven to 350°F and place the oven rack in the center position. Line a baking sheet with parchment paper. In a small bowl, mix the egg yolk with milk for the egg wash. Set aside.

Set the baking sheet and the filling next you. Place the dough on a lightly floured counter and knead it a few times. Divide the dough into 6 equal portions, form into balls, and loosely cover with plastic wrap or a towel. Lightly flour your hands. Place a ball in your hand or on the counter and make an indentation in the middle. Fill the indentation with about 1 tablespoon of the filling. Fold in the perimeter of the dough toward the center and pinch closed until the filling is completely sealed inside. (Be vigilant about pinching so there are no openings.) Gently press with the palm of your hand and flatten the dough to about 4 inches in diameter. Flip the dough and transfer the bread to the prepared baking sheet and repeat with the remaining dough and filling. Leave room between each bread.

Design the tops of each kooka by making indentations with a small round cookie cutter or half-moons; you can also use a small glass or a spoon. Get as creative as you like and press quite hard. Brush the tops and sides with the egg wash, and sprinkle with sesame seeds. Place in the oven and bake until golden brown, and a toothpick inserted into the center comes out clean, 25 to 30 minutes. Set aside to cool slightly and serve.

MAKE AHEAD: Eeshly Kooka will keep in an airtight container on the counter for up to 1 day and in the fridge for up to 2 days. Or wrap tightly in plastic bag or foil and freeze for up to 1 month. Reheat gently in the oven.

Kookoo

Iranian Frittatas
&
Egg Dishes

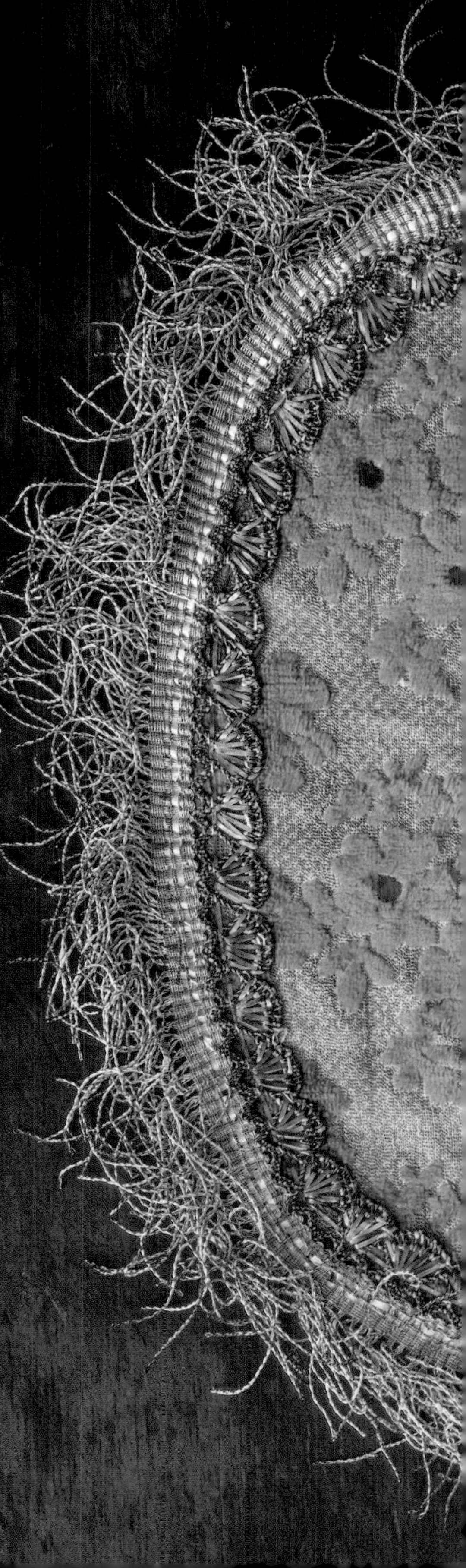

LIGHT

There's a lake just a short drive outside Vancouver. Past the cliffs, around the bend, and beyond the falls. They call her Alice. There's a distinct light that defines Alice Lake. Sharp and unyielding at high noon, soft and forgiving at dusk.

Shortly after immigrating to Vancouver in 1982, from Iran via Rome, my parents, brother, and I set out to explore our new surroundings. Vancouver was unlike any other city we had lived in. It was incredibly lush, green, and rainy; the joke among the new Iranian immigrants (all of four families back then) was "In Vancouver it rains six months of the year, and the other six months? It *really* rains." Of course, all the rain showers made for breathtaking landscapes. Anywhere you planted your feet you could turn and see the majestic mountains protectively surrounding the forest, a magical fortress guarding the city. And the city, sleepy and calm, leaning into the beaches, secretly offering it all to the Pacific. But even all this beauty surrounding us wasn't enough to soothe the anxieties and stresses of finding our footing as new immigrants. So weekends were spent packing cars and heading out of town to Alice Lake with fellow expat families. A chance to escape while discussing and strategizing how to start a new life in this brave, new, rainy world.

Iranians love nothing more than an excuse to gather outdoors, preferably next to a body of water, be it a fountain, river, lake, or sea, with plenty of food, drink, and slices of *kookoo*—Iranian-style frittatas—nestled in warm pieces of bread.

Although it had only been a few short months since we had arrived in

Vancouver, I had made it clear to my parents and anyone else within earshot that I was not budging. As much as I missed and longed for Rome, as much as I missed the warmth of family left behind in Iran, every inch of my being needed to settle and stay put. Vancouver was my last frontier. Unlike the Mediterranean or the Caspian Sea, the Pacific was cold, expansive, and desolate, and I had no inclination to find out what lay beyond it. Even talk of changing apartments was too much to bear. They say children adapt and adjust to change much easier than adults do. Like a soft ray of light settling on a pool of water, children bend and go with the flow. I was done bending and flowing. I was ready to stake my flag and enjoy endless banana splits at Dairy Queen and all-you-can-eat buffets at Sizzler.

Adapting and assimilating is always a challenge and a work in progress when your family and three others show up to a picturesque lakeside picnic hauling pots of rice, tubs of yogurt, fruit platters worthy of a Cézanne still life, and precariously sharp kabab skewers the length of a Roman general's sword. Our kookoo sandwiches bursting with the addition of cucumbers, tomatoes, feta, walnuts, pickles, and herbs were the closest thing to the neatly plastic-wrapped white bread sandwiches apparently enjoyed by our fellow Canadian picnickers. Mission Assimilation was further hindered by the sight of our group stopping in our tracks upon arrival and surveying the land en masse. Not in admiration and awe of Alice and all her charms, but with the laser-sharp precision of explorers scanning for the perfect spot to claim as our own, loudly discussing and discerning the merits and shortcomings of each.

There's something that happens to the newly displaced. Whatever power or choice that was stripped away in the process of reluctantly leaving one's homeland is fervently reclaimed in other situations, and honing in on the best spot to sit and enjoy a meal, be it at a restaurant or a lakeside, takes on the utmost importance. Not too close to the restroom, but close enough—just in case. Never with your back to an open door or window, as the cool breeze will weaken your kidneys and your hot tea. Always a safe distance from the water, be it fountain, river, lake, or sea, because you never know when a sudden gust of wind might pick up, enraging the sea and summoning the waves to crash into your *sofreh*—picnic cloth—and carry away the pots, pans, the perfectly stuffed bites of kookoo, and very possibly even you. If nothing else, we were always prepared for any and all circumstances and with plenty of provisions to see us through.

Eventually, once the perfect spot was agreed upon, we settled in as if making one last immigration. A large colorful sofreh was spread out and everyone made themselves at home around it. Where our Canadian neighbors lounged next to each other facing the magnificent view, we sat in the round, facing one another and, more important, facing the sofreh and all its delectable offerings. A hot tea thermos weighing down the sofreh in one corner and a game of backgammon in another. Handfuls of ground meat were expertly slapped on the skewers, while someone else fanned the hot coals with pieces of cardboard. Kookoo sandwiches were nibbled in between dips in the cool lake, and inevitably someone would always get up and carry the fruit platter over to our neighbors. An offering of sorts. Whatever hesitation I might have felt earlier dissipated as soon as we settled into our picnic routine, around the sofreh with Alice and all her beauty surrounding us.

All these years later, I now make an annual pilgrimage to Alice Lake with my own family and lifelong friends, six families in total. Picnics have turned into camping trips. We leave the precarious kabab skewers at home, but I have been known to show up with a pot of rice. As we set up camp, all the children run from campsite to campsite, sneaking a bite of chili here, a sip of hot chocolate there, Swedish pancakes smeared in Nutella three camps down, with marshmallows and graham crackers available at every stop. Alice graciously welcomes us all, with all our foods and quirks. And just before we lose the light we rush her waters for a sunset swim, bending to her grace and charms. Always with plenty of kookoo sandwiches in tow—just in case.

Unlike a frittata or an omelet, kookoo is less about the eggs and more about the filling. Just enough eggs are added to bind the vegetables, herbs, and sometimes meats together, until the batter is the consistency of thick yogurt or soft-serve ice cream. Typically, one ingredient is the star of a kookoo, like zucchini, potatoes, or a crisper full of herbs or green beans. Kookoo not only makes for perfect picnic fare, but is regularly enjoyed as a light lunch, dinner, appetizer, or, my favorite, end-of-week clean-out-the-fridge meal. It's fantastic served at room temperature with a quick *kateh*-style rice (page 113), or alongside a salad with a dollop of yogurt, and a hit of something tart like Torshi Liteh (page 68) or sumac. A dash of hot sauce, although not traditional, is never a bad idea.

The same concept applies to the other egg dishes in this chapter. Whip up a pan of minty scrambled eggs for breakfast or for a quick, light dinner served with a side of rice or simply scooped up with some *lavash* bread.

Kookoo Sabzi

Fresh Herb Kookoo

The bunches upon bunches of green herbs that take over our kitchen table on a regular basis are mixed here with a few eggs and spices for a fragrant, fresh, and vibrant Kookoo Sabzi. Use this recipe as a guide for all the greens and spices that can be thrown in. This kookoo is prepared traditionally on the stovetop, which is the best way to brown the outside, but you can also place the pan in a 350°F oven for 30 to 40 minutes until set, and broil for a couple of minutes to brown the top. If you prep the greens ahead of time, like the night before, then you can whip up a batch quickly and without much fuss. You can serve Kookoo Sabzi any which way you like. Serve warm or at room temperature for a light lunch or dinner alongside some plain rice and yogurt, or wrap in a piece of lavash or sangak bread with some sliced tomatoes, feta cheese, and a few nuts. Cut it in smaller bite-sized pieces for an appetizer spread, or serve with all the sides for brunch.

SERVES 6 TO 8

1 bunch parsley, tough stems trimmed

1 bunch cilantro, tough stems trimmed

1 bunch dill, tough stems trimmed

1 bunch Swiss chard or spinach, stems removed

1 bunch green onions

1 clove garlic, chopped

½ cup walnuts, roughly chopped (optional)

⅓ cup barberries, picked through, soaked for 10 minutes and drained

1 teaspoon dried fenugreek, or a few fresh leaves, finely chopped (optional)

1 teaspoon dried tarragon, or 1 sprig of fresh tarragon, leaves chopped (optional)

1¼ teaspoons kosher salt

½ teaspoon ground turmeric

¼ teaspoon ground cinnamon

¼ teaspoon ground saffron (optional)

¼ teaspoon ground dried rose petals (see page 18)

¼ teaspoon ground black pepper

8 large eggs

⅓ cup plus 2 tablespoons olive oil, divided

Working in batches, finely pulse the greens in a food processor, until finely chopped but not mushy. Alternatively, use a sharp knife and large cutting board. Set the greens in a large bowl. Finely chop the green onions. You can do this in the food processor, but take care (green onions quickly turn mushy). Add the green onions and the rest of the ingredients *except* for the eggs and the oil to the green herbs and give a stir to combine. Add the eggs and mix well to combine. The batter should have the consistency of thick yogurt or soft-serve ice cream.

In a large (10- or 12-inch) nonstick frying pan with a lid, heat ⅓ cup of the olive oil over medium heat. Add the batter, and spread evenly. Cook the kookoo until the oil starts to bubble along the sides, about 3 minutes. Cover and cook until the kookoo starts to set, and the bottom is browned,

12 to 15 minutes. Cut the kookoo evenly into 4 large pieces, and using a wide spatula flip each piece over one at a time. You can also set a dish beside you, take one piece of kookoo out to make room, flip the other pieces, and place the piece back in. Drizzle 2 tablespoons of oil in between all the cuts, reduce the heat to medium-low, and cook, uncovered, until cooked through, about 10 minutes. Cut the kookoo into desired pieces and serve warm or at room temperature.

MAKE AHEAD: Prepare up to 3 days in advance. Serve at room temperature or gently heat through in the oven.

PREP AHEAD: The greens (except for the green onion) can be prepped and chopped 1 day in advance. See fresh green herb prep (page 12).

PLAN AHEAD: Freeze portions wrapped tightly in foil (for up to 3 months). Heat through in the oven.

Kookoo Kadoo

Zucchini Kookoo

The mix of fragrant spices, the tart barberries, and the orange zest give this kookoo its Persian touch. I love serving this elegant Kookoo Kadoo as an appetizer or for brunch. It also makes for a decadent picnic sandwich. Be sure to wring out as much moisture from the zucchini as possible so you don't end up with a loose and falling-apart kookoo.

SERVES 6 TO 8

2 medium zucchini plus 2 medium yellow squash (or any combination; about 2 pounds total), ends trimmed

2¼ teaspoons kosher salt, divided

7 tablespoons olive oil, divided

1 medium yellow onion, diced

1 teaspoon dried mint

3 tablespoons unbleached all-purpose flour

⅓ cup barberries, picked through, soaked for 10 minutes, and drained (page 358)

2 cloves garlic, chopped

¼ teaspoon ground cinnamon

¼ teaspoon ground turmeric

¼ teaspoon ground dried rose petals (see page 18)

⅛ teaspoon ground saffron

⅛ teaspoon ground nutmeg

⅛ teaspoon ground black pepper

Zest of 1 small orange

5 large eggs

Preheat the oven to 375°F with the rack positioned in the center.

Grate the zucchini and yellow squash using the shredding disk of a food processor. You can use the large holes of a box grater as well, but I prefer the food processor because it releases less liquid. Place the zucchini in a colander over a bowl, and sprinkle with 2 teaspoons of the salt. Toss, and set aside to release liquid.

In a small pan, heat 2 tablespoons of the oil over medium-high heat. Add the onion and cook, stirring often, until golden brown, about 12 minutes. Sprinkle with salt and turn off the heat. Rub the dried mint between your palms to release its fragrance and flavor, and add it to the onion. Give it a quick stir and remove the pan from the element. Transfer the onion-mint mixture to a small bowl and set aside to cool.

Place all the grated zucchini and squash in a cheesecloth or a clean dishtowel. Wring out all the excess liquid over the sink. Squeeze with all your might, and when you think you can't squeeze any more, ask a friend or a child to take over. The less moisture, the happier the kookoo. *(continued)*

Kookoo Kadoo *(continued)*

In a large bowl, combine the wrung-out zucchini and squash, the onion-mint mixture, and all the rest of the ingredients *except* for the eggs and remaining olive oil. Stir to combine everything. Take a moment to marvel at all the colors and scents. Add the eggs, and stir to combine. The batter should have the consistency of thick yogurt or soft-serve ice cream.

Add 4 tablespoons of the olive oil to an 8 x 8-inch baking pan (preferably glass), swirl around and up the sides, and place in the oven to heat through for 1 minute. Pour the batter into the pan and spread evenly. Bake in the oven for 20 minutes, until the kookoo has mostly set. Remove the pan from the oven and carefully cut the kookoo into 8 equal portions, or 16 bite-sized pieces. Drizzle the remaining 1 tablespoon oil in between the cuts. Place back in the oven and bake for an additional 15 minutes, until the kookoo has fully set and is golden on top, and the edges are slightly crisp. Run a spatula along the sides and in between the cuts to make sure it doesn't stick to the pan. Allow the kookoo to cool slightly in the pan before serving.

MAKE AHEAD: Prepare up to 3 days in advance. Serve at room temperature or gently heat through in the oven.

PREP AHEAD: The onion-mint mixture can be cooked and stored in the fridge for up to 3 days or in the freezer for up to 3 months.

PLAN AHEAD: Freeze portions wrapped tightly in foil for up to 3 months. Heat through in the oven.

Kookoo Loobia Sabz

Green Bean Kookoo

Kookoo Loobia Sabz makes for a great clean-out-the-crisper dish. The last of the carrots, a nub of onion, half a munched-on bell pepper, and a bag full of green beans you never got around to using are all brought to life and reinvigorated with a sprinkling of bright and tart sumac. Wrap a slice in a warm piece of sangak, *pita, or a thick slice of sourdough, with sliced tomatoes, a couple of walnuts, a crumbling of feta and a bit more sumac for extra vim and vigor and devour with a side of Torshi Liteh (page 68). Or serve with a dash of hot sauce and call it a day.*

SERVES 6 TO 8

1 pound green beans, trimmed

½ cup olive oil, divided (plus more as needed)

½ medium yellow onion, finely chopped

Kosher salt

2 teaspoons plus 1 tablespoon sumac, divided (plus extra for sprinkling)

6 large eggs

1 small carrot, grated on the large holes of a box grater or shredded in the food processor

1 large clove garlic, finely chopped

½ red bell pepper, chopped

¼ teaspoon ground black pepper

Preheat the oven to 375°F with the rack positioned in the center.

Give the green beans a rough chop and place them in a food processor. Pulse about 15 times or until the green beans are very finely chopped but still holding their shape, not mushy. You can also do this with a sharp knife and a little more time and patience. Set aside.

In an 8- to 10-inch cast-iron or nonstick pan, heat 3 tablespoons olive oil over medium-high heat. Add the onion and cook, stirring often, until golden brown, about 12 minutes. Sprinkle with a little salt. Add the green beans, 2 teaspoons of the sumac, and 1 teaspoon salt. Cook, stirring occasionally, until the green beans are slightly cooked through and fragrant, about 5 minutes. Add more oil if the pan gets too dry. Transfer the green bean–onion mixture to a large bowl and set aside to cool. Don't wash out the pan.

In a small bowl, lightly whisk the eggs. Once the green beans are cool enough, so as not to scramble the eggs, add the eggs, remaining 1 tablespoon sumac, garlic, red pepper, and 1 teaspoon salt. Stir to combine. The batter should have the consistency of thick yogurt or soft-serve ice cream.

Add ¼ cup olive oil to the pan. Heat the oil on medium heat, and pour in the batter and spread evenly. Transfer the pan to the oven and bake for 30 minutes, until the kookoo has mostly set. Remove the pan from the oven and carefully cut the kookoo in eight equal wedges. Drizzle 2 tablespoons oil in between the cuts. Place back in the oven and bake for an additional 10 minutes, until the kookoo has set and the edges are slightly crispy. Turn on the broiler and broil for 2 to 3 minutes for a golden surface. Sprinkle with sumac to serve.

MAKE AHEAD: Prepare up to 3 days in advance. Serve at room temperature or gently heat through in the oven.

PREP AHEAD: The onion and green beans can be sautéed and stored in an airtight container in the fridge for up to 3 days or in the freezer for up to 3 months.

PLAN AHEAD: Freeze portions wrapped tightly in foil for up to 3 months. Heat through in the oven.

Varagheh

Eggplant and Tomato Kookoo

Varagheh means "layers," which is a perfect description of this layered eggplant and tomato frittata bursting with summer sun. Varagheh is essentially a northern Iranian–style eggplant kookoo. In this version I combine roasted and slightly crisped eggplant with late summer's sweet, juicy tomatoes and salty sour capers. A welcome companion to the bite of the tarragon and garlic. This dish is a hit for a weekend brunch. Serve with a side salad, a little bread, and a big dollop of yogurt.

SERVES 6 TO 8

2 large Chinese eggplants or 4 Japanese eggplants (about 1¼ pounds), sliced into ½-inch pieces

¼ cup plus 1 tablespoon olive oil, divided

Kosher salt

6 large eggs

4 cloves garlic, crushed to a paste

Leaves from 1 stem tarragon, minced (about 1 teaspoon; plus more leaves as garnish)

1 tablespoon capers, rinsed and roughly chopped

Ground black pepper

2 tablespoons unsalted butter

4 medium tomatoes (about 1 pound 6 ounces), sliced into ¼-inch rounds

Fresh green herbs, such as mint, basil, cilantro

Yogurt for serving

Preheat the oven to 425°F with one rack set in the upper-third position and a second rack in the lower-third position. Line two large baking sheets with parchment paper.

In a large bowl, toss the eggplant with ¼ cup of the olive oil and ¾ teaspoon salt. Divide the eggplant slices between the baking sheets. Try not to crowd the pans. Roast for 20 minutes, turning once halfway through and rotating the sheets. Remove from the oven and set aside. Turn down the oven to 400°F and position one rack in the center of the oven.

While the eggplant roasts, add the eggs, garlic, tarragon, capers, 2 teaspoons salt, and ⅛ teaspoon pepper to the same bowl you used for the eggplant. Beat well to combine and set aside.

Heat a 10- or 12-inch cast-iron or non-stick pan over medium-high heat and add the butter and remaining 1 tablespoon olive oil. As soon as the butter sizzles place one layer of tomatoes in the pan. It's okay if they

overlap slightly. Sprinkle the tomatoes lightly with salt and layer with eggplant slices. Repeat with another layer of tomatoes (sprinkled with salt) and one more layer of eggplant. Pour the egg batter over the whole thing and place in the oven to bake for 20 minutes, until the kookoo has set and the edges are slightly browned.

Set aside to cool slightly. Garnish with fresh herbs (whatever you have on hand), and slice into wedges or squares. Serve with a dollop of yogurt.

MAKE AHEAD: Preare up to 3 days in advance. Serve at room temperature or gently heat through in the oven.

PREP AHEAD: The eggplant slices can be roasted and stored in an airtight container in the fridge (up to 3 days) or in the freezer (up to 3 months).

PLAN AHEAD: Freeze portions wrapped tightly in foil for up to 3 months. Heat through in the oven.

Kookoo Sibzamini

Potato Kookoo

You can enjoy Kookoo Sibzamini as they are with a simple dollop of yogurt, or bring out the whole cavalry of sides and dips as accompaniment. I love having a batch in the fridge to snack on, especially around that precarious 4 p.m. hour. You can also make smaller patties and serve them hot off the pan as a mazeh—*a little bite for an appetizer spread—with a tall, frosted glass of beer. Serve with a side of spicy yogurt, or Maast-o Khiar (page 43), or alongside Arugula Orange Fennel Salad (page 54). Use any type, and as much hot sauce or paste you like. We're partial to Calabrian hot pepper sauce or the North African chili paste harissa.*

MAKES 16 PATTIES

FOR THE KOOKOO

2 pounds Yukon Gold potatoes (about 4 large potatoes), peeled and halved

Kosher salt

5 large eggs

¾ teaspoon ground turmeric

½ teaspoon baking powder

½ teaspoon ground black pepper

⅛ teaspoon ground saffron (optional)

Olive oil for frying

FOR THE SPICY YOGURT (OPTIONAL)

1 cup Greek yogurt

Kosher salt

Hot sauce or paste of choice, as much as you like

Handful of fresh parsley, roughly chopped

Place the potatoes in a large pot. Cover with water (about 6 cups) and add 1 teaspoon salt. Partially cover and bring to a boil. Cook on medium-high until the potatoes are fork-tender, about 20 minutes. Drain and return the potatoes to the hot pot for a couple of minutes to steam dry. Transfer the potatoes to a large bowl. When the potatoes are cool enough to handle, grate them on the large holes of a box grater. Set aside to cool.

Meanwhile, prepare the spicy yogurt, if desired. Place the yogurt in a small bowl. Season with salt and stir in hot sauce of choice. Sprinkle on the chopped parsley and set aside.

In a small bowl, lightly whisk the eggs. Set aside. Add the turmeric, baking powder, pepper, saffron, and 2½ teaspoons salt to the potatoes. Mix and add the eggs and fold to combine well. The mixture should have the consistency of thick yogurt or soft-serve ice cream.

(continued)

Kookoo Sibzamini *(continued)*

In a large pan, heat ¼ cup olive oil over medium-high heat. The oil should be nice and hot but not smoking. Stick the end of a wooden spoon handle in the oil. If small bubbles form around it, the oil is hot enough and ready. Reduce the heat to medium and drop in ¼ cup of the batter with a spatula. If you'd like more uniform patties you can use a round 3-inch mold. Fry until golden, 3 to 5 minutes per side. Work in batches, and add more oil as needed. Place the patties on a paper towel to drain and serve with a side of spicy yogurt, if you like.

MAKE AHEAD: Store in the fridge for up to 3 days. Serve at room temperature or gently heat through in the oven.

PLAN AHEAD: Freeze with parchment paper in between each patty and wrapped tightly in foil or place in an airtight container. Heat through in the oven.

Persian Omelet

This combination of juicy, jammy tomatoes and eggs is what Iranians refer to as an omelet, despite its departure from the traditional French version. Persian Omelet is a staple at an Iranian breakfast table. Sometimes the tomatoes are cooked completely down to a sauce, sometimes the eggs are scrambled in, and sometimes salty slices of saucisse—sausage—*are added. We love this variation bursting with tomatoes cooked in hot butter just until they start falling apart and releasing their juices. Use any and all combinations of tomatoes, large and small. I love a combination of heirloom and smaller cherry tomatoes. And don't skimp on the fresh herbs, which add a needed crisp and fresh bite. Here I use green onions and mint; use what you like and what you have on hand. Serve right away with bread to sop up all the buttery tomato juices and yolky deliciousness.*

SERVES 4

---

2 tablespoons unsalted butter

3 or 4 large tomatoes, sliced into ¼-inch slices

1 cup cherry tomatoes (about 10), halved

Kosher salt

8 large eggs

Ground black pepper

Green onions

Fresh mint

Melt the butter in a large pan (a 12-inch pan works well here) over medium-high heat. As soon as the butter starts sizzling, add all the tomatoes to the pan in a single layer covering the entire pan; a little overlap is okay. Season the tomatoes well with salt and cook for 5 minutes, until the tomatoes start falling apart slightly, releasing all their juices. Don't stir, just let the tomatoes do their thing and melt into the hot butter.

With a spatula make a space for the eggs and crack the eggs into the spaces. Gently give the egg whites a little jiggle to help them spread and set. Try not to break the yolk, but if you do, no worries. Season with salt and pepper, and cook for about 10 minutes. The last couple of minutes, cover with a lid until the whites have set but the yolk is slightly runny, or until desired consistency. Lift the lid every 30 seconds to check. Remove from the heat, and garnish with green onions and mint. Serve immediately.

Scrambled Eggs with Dried Mint and Yogurt

In our house eggs were never relegated to a breakfast-only dish. A simple and typical meal of rice—kateh—and a sunny-side-up egg fried in olive oil or butter with a few sliced and salted tomatoes on the side is, and always will be, our quick and comforting go-to lunch or dinner. Soft scrambled eggs, with dried mint and yogurt, is another of those unfussy dishes that has the comfort of my mother's embrace wrapped all around it. To this day, if I'm feeling a little blue, tired, or generally out of sorts, I'll whip up these eggs in a matter of minutes and hear my mother's wise and steady voice telling me that there's always a way. "Onward" is her constant motto. The dried mint and the tangy yogurt are the surprises here that transform everyday scrambled eggs. Don't substitute fresh mint here as it won't work. Sometimes it's best to stick to the old and the trusted. Especially when it comes to scrambled eggs. Serve right away with Naan-e Barbari—Barbari Bread (page 180) or your favorite bread, and a nice cup of black tea.

SERVES 4

8 large eggs

1 teaspoon dried mint

1¼ teaspoons kosher salt

Ground black pepper

2 tablespoons butter

1 to 2 tablespoons plain yogurt (optional)

Crack the eggs into a medium bowl. Add the mint, salt, and a sprinkling of pepper. Beat with a fork to combine. Melt the butter in an 8- or 10-inch nonstick pan over medium-low heat. Stir with a wooden spoon and scramble until the eggs are loosely set (if not using yogurt, scramble until desired consistency). Add the yogurt (if using) and stir quickly to incorporate, about 2 minutes. You might need to turn up the heat slightly so the yogurt doesn't release too much water. These eggs should be soft and slightly runny because of the yogurt.

Yeralma Yumurta

Smooshed Potato and Egg

I always knew I was in for a day of adventure and rebellion when my maternal grand-mother used to babysit back in Iran. My mother would take out a container of khoresh—*stew—from the freezer and ask her to serve it with some rice for our lunch. But as soon as my parents left for work the khoresh would go right back in the freezer, and we'd go about setting and breaking our own rules. A quick boiled potato and egg smooshed on a piece of lavash or* sangak *bread, drizzled with plenty of olive oil, and sprinkled with dried mint for lunch was our little act of rebellion. This simple treat is regular street fare in Tabriz, my grandmother's hometown. Years later and oceans away, this is still my preferred "fast food" lunch or dinner, always prepared with a twinkle of rebellion in my eye.*

SERVES 1

1 medium Yukon Gold potato (about 4 ounces), peeled and cut in half

Kosher salt

1 large egg

Olive oil for drizzling

Ground black pepper

1 piece of lavash or sangak bread

Dried mint for sprinkling

Feta cheese, crumbled (optional)

Fresh herbs, chopped (optional)

Place the potato in a small pot. Cover with water (about 2 cups), and add ½ teaspoon salt. Partially cover and bring to a boil over high heat. Reduce the heat to medium and cook until the potato is fork-tender, 15 to 20 minutes.

In the final 5 minutes cook the egg. Place the egg in a small pot, cover with water, and bring to a boil over high heat. Turn off the heat and cover the pot for 4 to 5 minutes, for a soft-boiled egg with a runny yolk. If you prefer your yolk not as runny, cover for 6 to 8 minutes, or cook up to 10 minutes for a hard-boiled egg. Set aside to cool slightly and peel.

Place the potato in a small bowl and mash it with a fork. Drizzle with a glug of olive oil. Sprinkle with a pinch of salt and black pepper. The olive oil and salt are key here, so don't skimp. Place the mashed potato on top of the bread, place the egg on top, and mash or cut in half so the yolk oozes out. Sprinkle with salt and pepper. Top with dried mint, feta, and herbs, if you like. Give another light drizzle of olive oil, roll up the bread, or fold it over, and eat.

Meat, fish
&
vegetables

MEMORY

"Welcome, have you had anything to eat?" my paternal aunt—Ammeh Fakhri—inquires softly, as I walk through the doors of my cousins' home in Vancouver. She curiously searches my eyes and greets me with a warm smile, and then repeats the familiar Persian greeting.

"Befarmayeed, ghaza khordeen?"

The road from Tehran to Gilan, the northern Iranian province referred to as Shomal (North), twists and turns, at times dangerously winding its way along narrow misty roads with wide-open cliffs and brilliant green valleys on one side and jagged, imposing sheets of rock jutting out on the other. It's a stunning landscape, but one that requires the full attention of all drivers. On our drives up to Ammeh Fakhri's *bagh*—orchard—my mom recalls I would chitchat nonstop from the backseat, most likely driving Ramin, my brother, crazy. Maybe it was because I had a lot to share, as most six-year-olds do, or maybe it was to calm my nerves about the breathtaking but perilous scenery.

I don't recall my incessant chatter, but I do remember the sudden stillness that would wash over us without warning, as every proud, solid mass of rock softened, humbly brought down to its knees by the welcoming scent of orange blossoms. The scent of Shomal! The sweet perfume wound its way across the rice paddies and welcomed us back to Gilan and my father's hometown of Bandar-e Anzali. Back to the Caspian Sea—Darya-yeh Khazar.

"Welcome," the orange blossoms whispered, "have you had anything to eat?"

Ammeh Fakhri's bagh burst at the seams with wild poppies, sour green plum trees, drooping pomegranate trees, fruit in various stages of cooking or drying under the sun in preparation for a tangy sweet-and-sour snack called *lavashak*—fruit leather. Ripe mulberry trees—*shahtoot*—provided just enough shade for an afternoon nap, as the Caspian Sea—five minutes away—proudly crashed and thundered. As dusk set, the familiar scent of charcoal heating up for a casual meal of *kabab torsh*—pomegranate kabab—roused us sleepy-eyed travelers from our slumber under mulberry skies.

I was six years old the last time we made our way north to Shomal. I haven't been back since, but every time I crack open a bottle of orange blossom water, splinters of memories spill out. The mist, the sea, the lush green forests, the tangy pomegranates, and the orange blossoms whispering a familiar refrain.

Back at my cousin's house in Vancouver, they tell me how much Shomal has changed. New developments, roads, and summer vacation villas have taken over much of the green lush valleys and forests. The salty, stick-to-your-lips-and-hair scent of the Caspian is barely recognizable from the bagh anymore. "It's not like how you remember it anymore," my cousin tells me.

I kneel down and take Ammeh Fakhri's hands in mine. I look deep into her puzzled eyes and tell her my name. I remind her that I am her brother's daughter, Nazzy, Nazgol. Her eyes dart back and forth and she just smiles. She now calls my father, her brother, *agha*, sir. She calls her daughters, my cousins, *khanoom*, lady. I know she no longer recalls who I am, so I reintroduce myself and assure her that I have eaten, but will stay for a cup of tea and a taste of my cousin Fahimeh's homemade *zoghal akhteh* jam, cornelian cherry. The jam isn't imported from Shomal but foraged from a single tree on the side of a highway in Vancouver. Apparently, all the Iranians know of the presence of this tree. This kind of vital information spreads quickly in an immigrant community. Which tree, which street corner, which fruit, vegetable, or herb.

As my cousin scrolls through her phone showing me recent pictures of the bagh and Gilan, Ammeh Fakhri fixes her gaze beyond us and out the window. From where we're sitting you can catch a sliver of the Pacific on the horizon.

"Every once in a while, she comes back," my cousin Fattaneh says.

She returns to her daughters ever so briefly. It's an unplanned visit, sudden and without warning, but just long enough for a quick kiss and a warm embrace. I'd like to think in those moments she's guided back by the distant scent of orange blossoms, ushering her across rice paddies. Or maybe it's the crashing sound of the waves in the Pacific rumbling in the same low baritones of the Caspian, or perhaps a neighbor's barbecue heating up next door conjures a charcoal grill burning bright for kabab torsh.

Then, just as quickly, she's gone again. Back on the twisting and winding road to Shomal, back to Gilan and the Caspian, back to her bagh. Her memories scattered and trapped under the weight of the jagged and imposing sheets of rock. But not before she asks, one more time, the one question that is set deep in every Iranian's blood and soul, the hospitable greeting that can never be forgotten.

"Befarmayeed, ghaza khordeen?"

This chapter is a collection of the meat and fish main dishes and vegetable sides that can be served on their own or alongside many of the rice dishes. Many of these dishes such as Everyday Turmeric Chicken (page 220) or Roasted Dill Salmon (page 245) are our go-to staples for a weeknight dinner. Some, like Braised Lamb Shanks (page 225) and a variety of kababs require a little extra time but make for a presentation-worthy dish for entertaining.

Kababs are what most people primarily associate with Middle Eastern food. Juicy cuts of meat, chicken, or fish grilled to perfection over hot charcoal. In our house, and for many Persian families I grew up with, grilling kababs was not an everyday occurrence. It was a special-occasion meal laced with plenty of ritual, hoopla, and various pieces of cardboard paper to fan the coals for the grill. These days it's much more common to get together for a festive barbecue, and it's in that spirit that I share a couple of the kababs we like to throw on the grill to celebrate with friends and family.

Morgh ba Zardchoobeh

Everyday Turmeric Chicken

If turmeric is the workhorse of our spice cabinet, this dead simple and flavorful turmeric chicken dish is the workhorse of our weeknights. It's the dish Drew consistently makes for the girls whenever I travel, and it's the dish my mother would prepare when she didn't want to think about what to cook. Everyday Turmeric Chicken is as perfect for a weeknight meal as it is for an impromptu dinner party. You can take the meat off the drumsticks when serving or serve on the bone, as we do, so the kids (and the adults) can gnaw on and suck out all the lovely mustardy yellow and lemony juices. You can ask your butcher to remove the chicken skin or do it yourself easily: hold the bottom of the drumstick with a paper towel with one hand as you slip the skin off with a paper towel with the other hand.

Use this recipe as your canvas and add to it as you like. A few sprigs of rosemary can add a fresh, earthy note, or stir in a little tomato paste (maybe with a little more water) for a richer red sauce. Put on a simple kateh*-style steamed rice (page 113) or Sheveed Polo—Dill Rice (page 124), plop down the yogurt container, or toss together a quick ends-and-bits salad, and call it a night.*

SERVES 4 TO 6

10 skinless chicken drumsticks (about 3 pounds)

1 teaspoon ground turmeric

2½ teaspoons kosher salt (plus more as needed)

¼ teaspoon ground black pepper (plus more as needed)

3 tablespoons olive oil

1 medium yellow onion, diced

2 cloves garlic, chopped

Splash of white wine (optional, if you happen to have some open)

2 tablespoons fresh lemon juice (about ½ lemon plus more as needed)

Parsley, as a garnish (optional)

Make a couple of slits in the flesh of each drumstick. This allows the drumsticks to cook faster and for all the flavors to seep in. In a bowl, season the drumsticks with the turmeric, salt, and pepper. Set aside.

In a large pan with a lid (12-inch works well), heat the oil over medium heat. Add the onion, sprinkle with a little salt, and cook, stirring occasionally, until soft and golden, about 8 minutes. Add the garlic and cook for 2 minutes. Splash with the wine (if using).

Add the drumsticks to the pan. It's okay if they overlap a little, just scoot them around once in a while. Cook until the chicken takes on a little color, about 3 minutes on each side. Add the lemon juice and a scant ¼ cup hot

water. Turn the chicken pieces in the sauce to coat all sides, and scrape up all the crispy bits. Reduce the heat to medium-low, partially cover, and simmer, turning once in a while, until the chicken is cooked through and tender, about 35 minutes. Taste as it cooks and make delicious. More salt, pepper, lemon juice? Garnish with parsley, if using, and serve.

MAKE AHEAD: A few hours in advance, but leave the chicken in its juice in the pot. You might need to drizzle in a little more water when reheating.

PLAN AHEAD: Can be stored in the fridge for up to 3 days or in the freezer for up to 3 months.

Morgh ba Z'afaran

Saffron Chicken

Saffron chicken is a decadent yet effortless dish that regularly accompanies any number of rice dishes at our table. A simple drizzle of brilliant saffron water lets it transcend everyday chicken to become a Tuesday-night family feast. If you're feeling particularly poetic and drunk on life, steep the ground saffron in a combination of water and a touch of rose water, for a light floral accent. You can also prepare this with bone-in, skinless chicken thighs. Use a little more oil and increase the cooking time. Serve with your favorite rice—Chelo ba Tahdig (page 194), Kateh (page 113), or Sheveed Polo—Dill Rice (page 124). Or fold the chicken pieces in sangak or pita bread, tuck in fresh herbs, with a sprinkling of sumac and a drizzle of lightly salted plain, garlic, or dill yogurt.

SERVES 4 TO 6

3 tablespoons olive oil

1 medium yellow onion, sliced into ¼-inch-thick half-moons

4 cloves garlic, chopped

8 skinless, boneless chicken thighs (about 2 pounds), cleaned and cut in half

2½ teaspoons kosher salt (plus more as needed)

¼ teaspoon ground black pepper (plus more as needed)

¼ cup fresh lemon juice (plus more as needed)

¼ teaspoon ground saffron, steeped in 1 tablespoon hot water (see page 17)

In a large pan with a lid, heat the oil over medium heat. Add the onion and cook, stirring occasionally, until soft and golden, about 8 minutes. Add the garlic and cook for 2 minutes.

In a small bowl, season the chicken well with the salt and pepper. Add it to the pan, a little overlap is okay, and cook until the chicken takes on a little color, about 3 minutes on each side. Drizzle on the lemon juice and the saffron water, making sure you get every last drop of the saffron water. Add a few more drops of water to the glass or bowl, swirl it around, and use. Turn the chicken pieces well in the brilliant sauce to coat all sides, reduce the heat to medium-low, partially cover, and cook, turning once in a while, until the chicken is cooked through and tender, about 30 minutes.

If the chicken makes too much juice, remove the lid and reduce the sauce. Taste and make delicious.

MAKE AHEAD: A few hours in advance, but leave the chicken in its juice in the pot. You might need to drizzle in a little more water when reheating.

PLAN AHEAD: Can be stored in the fridge up to 3 days or in the freezer up to 3 months.

Maheecheh

Braised Lamb Shanks

Save these celebratory succulent Braised Lamb Shanks for a weekend dish when time is not a concern. Most of the preparation here is hands-off as the shanks slowly simmer away, filling your kitchen with scents of just about every spice in the Persian pantry. Serve Maheecheh with Baghali Polo—Fava Bean Rice (page 129) or Sheveed Polo—Dill Rice (page 124) or plain rice prepared any which way you like.

SERVES 4 TO 6

3½ pounds lamb shanks (about 4 large shanks), fat trimmed

1 teaspoon ground turmeric

Kosher salt

Ground black pepper

3 tablespoons olive oil

3 tablespoons white wine

1 large yellow onion, chopped

6 cloves garlic, chopped

3 tablespoons tomato paste

1½ teaspoons Advieh (page 15)

Zest and juice of 1 large orange

Zest and juice of 1 large lime, plus more as needed

¼ teaspoon ground saffron, steeped in 2 tablespoons hot water and 1¼ teaspoons orange blossom water

Fresh green herbs (such as mint or parsley)

Place the lamb in a large bowl. Season well with the turmeric and salt and pepper. Cover and refrigerate for 24 hours or at least 2 hours. Bring back to room temperature 30 minutes before cooking.

In a large pot or Dutch oven, heat the oil over medium-high heat. When the oil is hot but not smoking, brown the shanks on both sides, about 5 minutes per side. You might have to do this in batches so you don't overcrowd the pot. The shanks will release from the pot when it's ready, be patient, don't force it. Set the shanks aside on a baking sheet.

If there is more than 3 tablespoons of oil in the pot, tip some out until you're left with about 3 tablespoons. Add the wine, scraping up any stuck-on bits and pieces, and reduce the heat to medium. Add the onion and sprinkle with salt and cook until softened, about 8 minutes. Add the garlic and cook for about 2 minutes. Stir in the tomato paste and Advieh, and cook until fragrant, about 3 minutes. Take care not to burn the tomato paste. Add the orange zest, orange juice, lime zest, lime juice, saffron–orange blossom water, 2½ teaspoons salt, and ¼ teaspoon pepper, give a quick stir to incorporate, and place the shanks back in. Pour in 1 cup water, bring up to a gentle boil, cover the pot, reduce the heat to low, and simmer until the shanks are tender, 2 to 3 hours. (Alternatively, you can also transfer the pot to a 350°F oven and cook for 2 to 3 hours.)

Once in a while check and make sure there is enough juice, if not add a little more water. Remove the shanks and place them on a serving platter. With a spoon skim any fat off the sauce. Taste the sauce and add more salt, pepper, a squeeze of lime, or a drop of orange blossom water, if necessary. Pour the sauce over the shanks, garnish with any green herbs you like, and serve.

MAKE AHEAD: Prepare up to 1 day in advance. Reheat, adjusting the liquid and seasoning as needed.

Sumac Cauliflower

When my kids respond positively to an ingredient, I start incorporating it in everything. This was the case with sumac, which for a while appeared on our table every single night. We even had to travel with a jar for a while. Soups, popcorn, even pasta. We have this Sumac Cauliflower to thank for starting the girls' love affair with the bright, sharp, crimson spice. Sumac also symbolizes the color of sunrise—a new day. You will typically find a jar of sumac present on the table of all Persian restaurants. A healthy sprinkling of sumac on chelo kabab—the iconic rice and kabab dish—is mandatory. Here I play off of the charred flavors of kabab with crispy panfried cauliflower florets. The trick is to not overcrowd the pan so the florets can properly crisp up and char in bits and pieces, rather than steam each other. Add a healthy sprinkling of sumac, and serve as a side dish or as a snack to tide everyone over until dinner is ready.

SERVES 4

¼ cup olive oil

1 small head cauliflower, cored and chopped into small florets

2½ teaspoons sumac

½ teaspoon kosher salt

Ground black pepper

In a large cast-iron or nonstick pan, heat the oil over medium-high heat, until hot but not smoking. To test the oil, put one cauliflower floret in the middle of the pan; as soon as it starts to sizzle, add the rest of the cauliflower. Spread out the florets in a single layer. Fry the cauliflower, stirring occasionally, until it starts to brown, about 15 minutes. Add the sumac and salt, reduce the heat to medium, and cook for 5 to 10 minutes, until crispy and cooked through. Taste as the cauliflower crisps, and add more sumac, salt, and pepper to make it delicious.

Alternatively, you can toss everything together and roast on a baking sheet in a 425°F oven for about 35 minutes, but it won't be quite as crisp and charred as on the stovetop.

PREP AHEAD: The cauliflower can be chopped up to 1 day in advance and stored in a resealable bag in the fridge.

Mahi Shekampor

Stuffed Branzino

Whole fish stuffed with fresh green herbs, dried fruits, and nuts is traditionally prepared all over Iran with various regional interpretations. This is a summer take on a classic stuffed fish from the Caspian region. Fresh peaches or nectarines and raisins add a sweet bite to the tangy mix of the pomegranate molasses and the lime or Seville orange juice. If peaches are not in season use dried peaches and use any combination of green herbs you like. Seville oranges are available for a brief period of time in early spring. Scoop some up if you can and use their fragrant juice to flavor and perfume fish dishes like this one, but of course lime or lemon juice can be used instead.

SERVES 6

2 tablespoons olive oil (plus more as needed)

2 cloves garlic, thinly sliced

1 green onion, finely chopped

Handful of fresh mint, stems trimmed, finely chopped

Handful of fresh parsley, tough stems trimmed, finely chopped

Handful of fresh basil, finely chopped

¼ cup raw shelled pistachios, finely chopped

1 small ripe but firm peach or nectarine, pitted and diced

2 tablespoons golden or dark raisins

2 tablespoons fresh Seville orange or lime juice

1 tablespoon pomegranate molasses

Kosher salt

Ground black pepper

2 tablespoons butter

¼ teaspoon ground saffron

4 whole large branzino, scaled, cleaned, and butterflied

Lime or Seville orange wedges to serve

Preheat the oven to 450°F with the rack in the center position. Line a large baking sheet with parchment paper and lightly oil.

In a medium pan, heat the olive oil over medium-low heat. Add the garlic and cook until lightly golden, about 3 minutes. Take care not to burn the garlic. Turn up the heat to medium and add the green onion, mint, parsley, basil, pistachios, peach, raisins, Seville orange juice, and pomegranate molasses. Lightly season with salt and pepper. Stir and cook just until fragrant, 3 to 5 minutes. Set aside to cool so it's not too hot when added to the fish.

Meanwhile, melt the butter in a small saucepan. Stir in the saffron and set aside.

(continued)

Mahi Shekampor *(continued)*

Place the fish on the baking sheet and drizzle all over, inside and out, with olive oil. Season well with salt and pepper. Stuff each fish with the peach-and-herb mixture. Tie the fish closed with kitchen twine, no fancy knots or technique required here, just make sure it's secure enough so the stuffing doesn't spill out. Drizzle the top of each fish with the butter-saffron mixture. Roast until the fish is cooked through and just beginning to flake, about 15 minutes. Serve with lime or orange wedges.

PREP AHEAD: See page 12 for fresh herb prep. The peach-and-herb stuffing can be made up to 1 hour in advance; partially cover to make sure it doesn't dry out.

Bamiyeh

Roasted Okra

Okra is traditionally prepared as a stew in a tomato-based sauce. Like many, as a child I was never a big fan of bamiyeh—okra. I had written it off until it started popping up in our weekly farm box and I decided to treat it like most anything else in our kitchen: when in doubt, roast it. Roasted okra is a revelation for a doubter like me. Slightly browned, salty, and smoky, these bamiyeh call out for a tall pint of beer. Look for the elegantly twisted shaped ones when in season. They resemble dancers bending and stretching their way across the baking sheet. Serve on its own or with the accompanying sweet-and-sour tamarind dipping sauce and/or yogurt and dill sauce. Just make sure you serve and eat the okra hot out of the oven, before it regresses to its old, soft, squishy ways.

SERVES 4 TO 6

FOR THE OKRA

1 pound okra

2 tablespoons olive oil

Kosher salt

Ground black pepper

FOR THE TAMARIND DIPPING SAUCE

¼ cup tamarind concentrate

2 tablespoons maple syrup

Cayenne pepper

FOR THE YOGURT DILL SAUCE

¼ cup plain yogurt

Small handful of fresh dill, finely chopped, or 1 teaspoon dried dill

Kosher salt

1 tablespoon Greek yogurt (optional)

Preheat the oven to 425°F with the rack set in the upper-third position. Line a baking sheet with parchment paper.

Place the okra in a large bowl and toss with the oil, salt, and pepper. Transfer to the baking sheet and spread out in a single layer. Roast in the oven until crisp and slightly browned, about 15 minutes.

Meanwhile, prepare the dipping sauces. In a small saucepan, combine the tamarind, maple syrup, and a sprinkling of cayenne pepper over medium heat. Stir and just heat through, about 3 minutes. Add more cayenne pepper to taste, and transfer to a small bowl. In another small bowl, combine the plain yogurt, dill, and salt. If your yogurt is too runny add the Greek yogurt to thicken.

Serve the roasted okra hot out of the oven with the dipping sauces.

Kabab Raminy

Pan Kabab

These simple pan kababs were (and still are) a favorite of my brother, Ramin, when he was a little boy growing up in Rome. Ever since, rather than being called by their proper name—kabab tabei—they are called Kabab Raminy. The method of preparing these patties is as much a part of my family tradition as is the name. The rhythmic tap-tapping of the knife across the meat, tenderizing and flattening the meat to a very thin patty, provides the percussive soundtrack to our lives. As do the memories of blue-lined sheets of loose-leaf paper borrowed from our school binders to pound the meat on. I've traded in the school paper for parchment paper here. Pounding the meat on the paper makes it easier to transfer the very thin patties to the pan without them falling apart. There's nothing to preparing these juicy, slightly charred kabab. Once you get the hang of the knife tapping, make a big batch and freeze them raw with a piece of parchment paper separating each patty. Throw in a hot pan and serve in a matter of minutes. Serve Kabab Raminy chelo kabab–style with rice (page 104), a side of grilled tomato, Sabzi Khordan (page 32), and plenty of sumac for sprinkling. Or for a quick lunch wrap a kabab in a warm piece of lavash or sangak *bread slathered with mayo and stuffed with plenty of fresh greens.*

MAKES 4 THIN PATTIES

---

1 pound ground beef, at least 15% fat

1 small yellow onion, grated on the large holes of a box grater

1¼ teaspoons kosher salt

¼ teaspoon ground black pepper

Olive oil for frying

Sumac for sprinkling

Cut four pieces of parchment paper into 5 x 7-inch rectangles and set aside.

Place the meat, grated onion, salt, and pepper in a bowl. Get your hands in there and combine really well. Pound, pummel, and thump the meat into the bowl several times. Divide the meat into 4 equal portions. Set up your work space. You'll need a knife, a cutting board, the parchment pieces, and the meat mixture. Place a parchment square on the cutting board. Place 1 meat portion in the middle of the square and flatten it with your hand or the back of a spoon. Tenderize and flatten the meat with the sharp end of the knife by constantly hitting it from one end to another, in a repeated motion. Fold in the sides slightly and flatten out again with the knife; repeat this process a few times until the patty is shaped into a thin kabab. Set aside, and repeat with the rest of the meat.

In a large cast-iron or nonstick pan over medium-high heat, heat 1 tablespoon olive oil, make sure the oil is nice and hot, but not smoking. Lift the kabab with the parchment paper and quickly slap it into the pan. The parchment paper helps in the transfer of the thin kabab to the pan. Fry the kabab for about 1 minute 30 seconds on each side, until juicy and cooked through with slightly crisp sides. Repeat with the rest of the patties, adding oil as needed. If your pan is large enough you can fry 2 patties at a time because they shrink as soon as they hit the hot oil; just add a little more oil. Serve hot off the pan with a good sprinkling of sumac.

PREP AHEAD: The patties can be frozen for up to 1 month.

Joojeh Kabab

Chicken Drumettes Kabab

Juicy and tender on the inside and charred and smoky on the outside, dripping with saffron and spiked with lime juice, Joojeh Kabab is the stuff of summertime barbecue dreams. The drumettes (which look like tiny drumsticks, also referred to as wings) are served over a layer of lavash bread. The bread happily soaks up all the smoky, sweet joojeh juices and sends all hands reaching in to tear away at both the succulent kabab and the bread. Long, flat metal skewers (can be purchased online or at Iranian markets) come in handy here so the drumettes don't twist and turn while grilling; otherwise, you can use double skewers. These kabab really need an overnight marinade, so plan ahead. Serve with Chelo ba Tahdig (page 104) or Kateh (page 113), and a heaping basket of Sabzi Khordan (page 32).

SERVES 6

4 pounds chicken drumettes

1 large yellow onion, sliced into half-moons

1¼ cups plain yogurt

½ cup fresh lime juice

5 cloves garlic, crushed to a paste

¼ cup olive oil

½ teaspoon ground saffron, steeped in 2 tablespoons hot water (see page 17)

4 teaspoons kosher salt

1 teaspoon ground black pepper

FOR THE BASTE

4 tablespoons clarified butter, unsalted butter, or olive oil

Juice of 1 small lime

Kosher salt

Ground black pepper

6 small tomatoes

Lavash bread for serving

Sumac for serving

Place the drumettes and the onion slices in a large container or in a large resealable plastic bag. In a medium bowl, combine the rest of the ingredients and pour over the chicken. Turn the chicken a few times to coat well in the marinade. Cover the container or seal the bag and marinate in the fridge for 24 to 48 hours. Turn the chicken pieces around a few times while marinating.

Remove the chicken from the marinade and skewer. This can get messy so have a few paper towels on hand. Skewer the tomatoes separately.

In a small pot, melt the butter or heat the oil for the baste. Stir in the lime juice and season with salt and pepper. Heat a hot grill and grill the chicken and the tomatoes, turning and basting the drumettes, until the chicken is cooked through and charred in parts on the outside, about 15 minutes. Place the chicken and grilled tomatoes on the lavash bread. Sprinkle sumac on the chicken and tomatoes and serve.

Kabab Torsh

Sour Pomegranate and Walnut Kabab

Pomegranates and walnuts go hand in hand in northern Iranian cuisine, whether mixed with olives in Zeytoon Parvardeh (page 40), in stews like Khoresh Fesenjan (page 157), or as a marinade in these tangy kabab. The meat is initially pounded with the blunt edge of a knife to tenderize it, similar to the technique in Kabab Raminy (page 234). You can skip this step, but it really adds to the delicate texture of the kabab. Serve Kabab Torsh with rice and plenty of fresh greens and alliums—Sabzi Khordan (page 32)—to ease the digestion of the red meat. These kabab need the overnight marinade, so plan accordingly.

SERVES 6

FOR THE KABAB

2 pounds beef top sirloin, fat trimmed, cut in half crosswise

1 onion, cut into eighths

1 cup walnuts

3 large cloves garlic, roughly chopped

1¼ cups pomegranate molasses

¼ cup fresh lime juice or Seville orange juice

¼ cup fresh mint leaves (about 20 leaves), or 1 teaspoon dried

3 tablespoons olive oil

2 teaspoons kosher salt

½ teaspoon ground black pepper

Pomegranate seeds, as a garnish (optional)

FOR THE BASTE

4 tablespoons clarified butter or unsalted butter or olive oil

¼ cup fresh lime juice or Seville orange juice

Kosher salt

Ground black pepper

Tap each piece of meat vertically with the blunt edge of your knife. Don't cut through the meat, just tap lightly back and forth to flatten and tenderize the meat. Cut the pieces against the grain into 1¼-inch kabab pieces. Set aside.

Place the onion, walnuts, garlic, pomegranate molasses, lime juice, mint leaves, oil, salt, and pepper in the bowl of a food processor. Blitz to a paste. Place the meat in a large resealable plastic bag or a container and slather with the marinade. Place in the fridge and marinate for 24 hours.

Remove the meat from the fridge 30 minutes before grilling. Skewer the kabab on large flat metal skewers or double skewers. Brush off any excess marinade so as not to burn it on the grill. In a small pot, melt the butter or heat the oil for the baste. Stir in the lime juice, and season with salt and pepper. Set aside.

Heat a grill until hot and oil the grates. Grill the meat, turning and basting, until desired doneness of meat, 8 to 10 minutes. Serve hot off the grill. Garnish with pomegrante seeds, if using.

Mixed Veggie Kabab

I always try to have some mixed veggie kabab ready to go when we grill for a pop of color and to balance the chicken and meat. A well-suited accompaniment to Joojeh Kabab (page 237) or Kabab Torsh (page 238), these veggies are brought to life with earthy cumin, oregano, and a squeeze of lemon or lime juice. If grilling isn't an option, a quick roast on a sheet pan in a hot oven does the trick, too.

SERVES 4 TO 6

1 large red onion, chopped into 2-inch chunks

1 green bell pepper, chopped into 2-inch pieces

1 red bell pepper, chopped into 2-inch pieces

1 yellow bell pepper, chopped into 2-inch pieces

1 zucchini, sliced into ½-inch pieces

1 yellow summer squash, sliced into ½-inch pieces

1 cup cherry tomatoes

2 cloves garlic, crushed to a paste

2½ teaspoons kosher salt

½ teaspoon ground black pepper

3 tablespoons olive oil

⅓ cup fresh lemon or lime juice or verjuice

2 teaspoons ground cumin

1 teaspoon ground dried oregano

½ teaspoon garlic powder

Place all the vegetables in a large bowl. In a small bowl, combine the garlic with the rest of the ingredients. Pour over the vegetables and combine well. Set aside to marinate for 15 to 30 minutes.

Heat a grill until hot and oil the grates. Skewer the vegetables (don't discard the marinade), and grill until slightly charred and tender, about 15 minutes. Baste with the marinade as you go. Serve hot off the grill, and drizzle with any remaining marinade, if you like.

MAKE AHEAD: Although best hot off the grill, the veggie kabab can be stored in the fridge for up to 3 days.

PREP AHEAD: The vegetables can be chopped and stored in the fridge up to 1 day.

Balal

Grilled Corn on the Cob

Corn on the cob is the most iconic street food worldwide. On the streets of Iran, just as dusk approaches, it's grilled until smoky and charred and then immersed in a hot, briny salt bath. The scent of charred and blackened Iranian street corn dipped in a bucket of salt water is one that always unapologetically grabs me by the waist and hurls me back to scattered recollections of Tehran. A pat of melting butter is not necessary or traditional, but my kids do like to slather it on. My memories weaving into theirs, or theirs into mine, depending on who is telling the story. Serve as a snack or as a side.

SERVES 4

4 ears corn, shucked

Kosher salt

Unsalted butter
(optional)

Heat a gas or charcoal grill until hot.

Place the corn on the hot grill. Grill the corn, rotating often, until the corn is tender and charred, about 10 minutes. (Alternatively, you can also grill the corn directly on a gas stovetop burner.) While the corn grills, fill a pot, just large enough to fit the corn, halfway full of water. Bring to a boil and add a heaping handful of salt, enough to make the water briny. Allow the salt to dissolve, cover, and turn off the heat.

Using tongs, quickly dunk the corn in the salty water and remove. Serve hot as it steams, smoky and salty. Serve with a pat of butter, if you like.

Roasted Dill Salmon

My stepmother, Kumi, is a phenomenal home cook, and her oven-roasted salmon is what we always look forward to when visiting Vancouver. She's always experimenting with flavors, incorporating her native Japanese ingredients with Iranian ones, like pomegranate molasses. Her Japanese love of seafood nicely complements that of my northern Iranian father's. She typically prepares this roasted salmon with a splash of sake, but here I've traded in the sake for lime juice or Seville orange juice. This dish comes together in under 20 minutes, just about the time it takes to put on a quick pot of rice to serve with it. Make sure to drizzle plenty of the pan juices over the salmon and the rice. Serve with Sheveed Polo—Dill Rice (page 125), Baghali Polo—Fava Bean Rice (page 128), or a side of Drew's Paprika Oven Fries (page 251).

SERVES 4 TO 6

1½ pounds center cut salmon fillet (king, sockeye, or coho), pin bones removed

1¼ teaspoons kosher salt

¼ teaspoon ground black pepper

¼ cup fresh lime juice or Seville orange juice

1 large clove garlic, crushed

2 tablespoons olive oil

2 tablespoons soy sauce

2 tablespoons maple syrup

1 tablespoon dried dill or 3 tablespoons chopped fresh dill

¼ teaspoon ground turmeric

⅛ teaspoon ground saffron (optional)

Lime or Seville orange wedges, for serving

Preheat the oven to 425°F with the rack in the center position. Choose a baking sheet that is just big enough to fit the salmon (so the juices don't disperse and burn) and line it with parchment paper. Place the salmon flesh-side up on a baking sheet and season well with the salt and pepper.

Combine the rest of the ingredients in a small bowl, and spoon over the salmon. If you have an extra 15 minutes, let the salmon sit in the marinade, flesh side down. Roast the salmon skin side down until cooked through to your liking, anywhere between 9 and 12 minutes, depending on the thickness of the fillet. Serve with extra lime or Seville orange wedges, and drizzle the pan juices over rice.

PREP AHEAD: The marinade can be prepared 30 minutes in advance.

Baghali Pokhteh

Fava Beans with Mint and Pistachio Sauce

The arrival of spring brings heaping mounds of favas to Iranian street food stalls. Whole pods are boiled in water and vinegar, sprinkled with a generous dose of golpar and eaten whole or shelled. Favas are grilled or roasted here first, and topped with a bright and crunchy mint-and-pistachio sauce. The first-of-the-season young favas can be eaten whole, pod and all. Or if you like, you can pop the beans out with your fingers or, even better, and messier, scrape them out with your teeth. If you prefer to keep things a little more civilized and tidy, and if young favas have passed you by, grill or roast the favas and then pop the beans out and mix with the sauce. You can also do this year-round by steaming or quick boiling frozen fava beans or edamame beans and adding them to sauce. The mint-and-pistachio sauce, which I prepare cheshmy—"by eye"—is also fantastic on any grilled meat, chicken, fish, or veggies.

SERVES 4 TO 6

1 pound favas in the pod, rinsed and dried

Olive oil

Kosher salt

½ bunch mint, stems trimmed

¼ cup roasted and salted shelled pistachios

1 large clove garlic

Ground black pepper

White wine vinegar

Golpar (Perisan hogweed; see page 357; optional)

Heat a grill until hot, or preheat the oven to 450°F with the rack set in the upper-third position. If roasting, line a baking sheet with parchment paper.

Place the favas in a medium bowl and drizzle with olive oil (about 2 tablespoons). Sprinkle well with salt, and toss to coat. Place the favas on the grill or on the baking sheet. Grill or roast, turning a few times, until the pod softens and the bean inside is tender, 15 to 20 minutes.

Meanwhile, place the mint, pistachios, garlic, and a small pinch each of salt and pepper in a mortar and pestle, and pound a few times to break up. Add a splash of vinegar (about 1 teaspoon), a drizzle of olive oil (about 2 tablespoons), and a pinch of golpar (if using). Pound to form a rough paste, with pieces of broken-up pistachio still visible, here and there. Taste, sprinkle, splash, and drizzle more of everything as needed. Alternatively, you can pulse everything in a small food processor. Transfer the sauce to a bowl, add the hot favas, and turn with tongs to coat. Sprinkle the top with more golpar, if using. Or pop the beans out first, add to the sauce, and mix to coat. Dig in with plenty of napkins on hand.

Roasted Squash and Grapes

Many Iranian sauces balance sour with a touch of sweet, much like the combination of tangy vinegars with a hint of sugar or honey in Italian agrodolce *sauces. Here, maple syrup takes the edge off the pomegranate molasses. Warm spices such as cinnamon, allspice, and cardamom, draped over meaty squash and shriveled-up sweet grapes make us look forward to cooler weather and cozy evenings. I love the texture and flavor of red kuri squash, but any winter squash, such as butternut, kabocha, or acorn, will work here. Serve as a vegetable side or alongside rice as a main meal.*

SERVES 6

12 ounces red seedless grapes, off the stem (about 1½ cups)

5 tablespoons olive oil, divided

Kosher salt

Ground black pepper

1 large red kuri squash (about 2½ pounds), seeded and chopped into 1-inch pieces

1 tablespoon unsalted butter

⅓ cup pomegranate molasses

2 tablespoons maple syrup

½ teaspoon ground cinnamon

¼ teaspoon ground allspice

1 medium red onion, cut into ¼-inch-thick slices

Handful of fresh mint

Preheat the oven to 425°F with the racks set in the upper-third and lower-third positions. Line two large baking sheets with parchment paper.

Place the grapes in a large bowl, and toss with 1 tablespoon of the olive oil and a pinch each of salt and pepper. Scatter the grapes on the baking sheet and roast on the upper rack for 15 minutes.

Meanwhile, place the squash in the same bowl as you used for the grapes. Toss with 3 tablespoons of the olive oil and a good pinch each of salt and pepper, and set aside. In a small saucepan, combine the butter, pomegranate molasses, maple syrup, cinnamon, and allspice over medium-low heat. Heat through until all the flavors meld, about 3 minutes. Toss the squash with a quarter of the sauce. Set aside.

Remove the pan from the oven and carefully add the squash to the grapes. You'll need to scoot the grapes this way and that to make room. Use two pans if necessary so the grapes and squash don't steam each other.

(continued)

Roasted Squash and Grapes *(continued)*

Place the pan back in the oven and roast for 20 to 25 minutes, until the grapes are shriveled and sticky, and the squash is tender.

Meanwhile, in a small pan, heat the reamining 1 tablespoon oil over medium-high heat. Add the red onion. Cook, stirring often, until fragrant and browned in parts, about 10 minutes. Sprinkle with a little salt, reduce the heat to medium-low, and cook for 15 minutes until caramelized and crispy in parts. Add a splash of water if the pan gets too dry.

Remove the pan from the oven. Transfer the squash and grapes to a serving dish and drizzle with as much sauce as you like. You might not use all the sauce. Scatter the caramelized red onion and the fresh mint over it all, and serve.

MAKE AHEAD: The whole dish can be prepared a few hours in advance and gently reheated in the oven right before serving. Set aside the sauce to drizzle on when serving.

PREP AHEAD: The red onion can be caramelized and stored in the fridge in an airtight container for up to 3 day or in the freezer for up to 3 months. Gently reheat before serving.

Sole in Parchment Paper with Drew's Oven Fries

Stuffing fish with fresh herbs, fruits, and nuts, as in Mahi Shekampor (page 230) is a classic Iranian preparation. In this version, I take the herb stuffing out of the fish and use it as an aromatic topping for one of my favorite ways of serving fish—all wrapped up like a parcel in parchment paper. This is my salute to fish-and-chips. Clearly it bears no resemblance to true fish-and-chips, but eating the fish out of the parchment paper with a side of Drew's paprika-stained fries always conjures up memories of my first taste of fish-and-chips served on newspaper, by the sea at English Bay in Vancouver.

Once you set up your parchment squares assembly line, this dish comes together very quickly. If serving with the oven fries, get the potatoes in the oven first and roast the sole in the final 11 to 13 minutes. Barberries are available online and at Middle Eastern and Iranian markets. They lend a distinct sour pop and a burst of color to this dish. You can substitute unsweetened dried cranberries or unsweetened dried sour cherries, which lean more sweet than sour. Serve with extra lemon or Seville orange wedges, and a side of Drew's oven fries to dip in the golden juices.

SERVES 6

DREW'S OVEN FRIES

4 Yukon Gold potatoes (about 2 pounds)

2 tablespoons olive oil

2 teaspoons kosher salt

1 teaspoon paprika

¼ teaspoon ground black pepper

Preheat the oven to 450°F with racks set in the upper- and lower-third positions. Line two baking sheets with parchment paper.

Cut the potatoes into ¼-inch-wide sticks. Place the potato sticks in a large bowl, add the rest of the ingredients, and toss well to combine. Spread out the potatoes on the baking sheets in a single layer. The more space between the potatoes, the crispier they'll get. Roast for 20 minutes. Toss the potatoes and rotate the baking sheets, and roast until crispy, about 10 minutes more. You can combine the potatoes on one sheet in the final 12 minutes to make room for the sole.

While the fries are baking, cut six 15-inch square pieces of parchment paper.

(continued)

FOR THE SOLE

2 tablespoons olive oil (plus more for drizzling on fish)

6 cloves garlic, thinly sliced

½ bunch cilantro, finely chopped (about ½ cup)

½ bunch fresh mint, finely chopped (about ½ cup)

¼ bunch parsley, finely chopped (about ¼ cup)

3 sprigs of tarragon, finely chopped (about 1 tablespoon)

¼ cup barberries, picked through and rinsed

Kosher salt

18 fillets of dover sole (about 2.6 ounces each, roughly 2½ pounds total)

Ground black pepper

4 tablespoons fresh lemon juice or Seville orange juice

Tiny pinch of ground saffron

In a small pan, heat the oil over medium-low heat. Add the garlic slices and cook, stirring frequently, until the garlic is fragrant and golden, taking care not to burn the garlic, about 3 minutes. Add the herbs and cook until just fragrant, about 3 minutes. Add the barberries and a sprinkle of salt, stir, and cook until the barberries plump up, 2 minutes. Remove from the heat and set aside. Partially cover if not using immediately.

Set up your work station. Lay out the parchment paper. You will most likely take over the kitchen island or dining table. Place 3 sole fillets in the middle of each parchment paper, a little overlap is okay. In a small bowl, combine 2½ teaspoons salt and ¼ teaspoon pepper, and season the fish. Drizzle each fish packet with 2 teaspoons of the lemon juice, a drizzle of olive oil, the ground saffron (evenly sprinkle the saffron over the fish, it doesn't take much saffron), and the herb mixture.

Bring the two sides of the parchment together and fold. Keep folding until you get a tight seal. Twist the other two sides shut like a candy wrapper. Place the packets on a baking sheet and bake for 11 to 13 minutes. (Set the rack in the lower-third position if you're also making the fries. Otherwise, use the center rack.) You can take a peek inside one to see if the fish is cooked to your liking. Be careful of the steam when you open it. Place a packet on each dish for each person to unravel, and serve with the oven fries.

STUFFED
&
ROLLED

HOME

TABRIZ, 1979

I learned to properly pound, pummel, and stuff a batch of ground meat at my grandfather Baba Ghomboli's house in Tabriz. *Baba Ghomboli* means "chubby daddy." My family has a penchant for assigning nicknames, and this was what we lovingly called my maternal grandfather.

With both parents holding jobs in Tehran, my brother and I would hook arms and travel to the northwest of the country, escaping the suffocating heat of the capital and apartment living, to spend the summer with family in Tabriz.

Walking through the gates of Baba Ghomboli and my step-grandmother Roohi jan's house, I fancied myself as Alice dropping into Wonderland. The house was a traditional Iranian home, punctuated every few feet by thick, proud columns, wrapping around a central courtyard, dripping with bougainvillea, fruit and nut trees, grape vines, potted flowers and herbs. The stained-glass windows encircling the courtyard reflected and bounced off the *hoz*—a small, decorative, shallow, and ornate turquoise pool—in the center of the courtyard. At the right time of day, if I stood on the lip of the hoz and spun fast enough, I could create my own kaleidoscope of dream-like images and colors.

My days were spent chasing butterflies round and round the cool, colorful courtyard. Weaving in and out of the rosebushes, ducking under the grape arbors, and leaping high in hopes of either finally making contact with the winged creature, or picking a cherry or two off the cherry trees. Both equally tantalizing and eventful. As my steps picked up speed and momentum, somewhere beyond the walls of Baba Ghomboli's house,

I could hear the faint but growing sounds of street demonstrations—the drumbeat of revolution well underway. The chants and slogans echoing like nursery rhymes through the alleys and bazaars. The *click-clack* of my sandals keeping time to the repeated cries and protests.

Making my rounds, I always made sure to briefly pause and greet Roohi jan at the entrance to the kitchen, as she thumped the living daylights out of a mound of ground meat. Awakening and binding the meat for our dinner of *koofteh tabrizi*—an awe-inspiring stuffed meatball of Wonderland-like proportions. If meatballs were to star in a Tim Burton film, koofteh tabrizi would take the lead. Like a seasoned ball player, Roohi jan slapped the meat from one hand to another, once in a while raising it high in the air and thumping it back into the bowl. Like a runner at the starting line, I took my cue off the thump of the dropping meat and sped off again, in search of my butterfly and edible garden treats.

Once the meat had been sufficiently pounded and kneaded, we'd all gather to help with the stuffing. If it was a special occasion, a whole bone-in poussin—which itself had been stuffed with an egg—would be encased in the ground meat. A Russian nesting doll meatball. Rolling, wrapping, and stuffing are cooking projects that make very specific demands of us. Primarily, the demand to slow down and sit down. Not exactly my strong suits as a child. As Roohi jan patted and smoothed the meat around the poussin, my brother, Ramin, our twin aunts, Zarin and Farin, and I would play a game of tug-of-war with the garden hose. Each team on either side of the hoz. Ramin, the perpetual prankster, would suddenly let go and cannonball into the hoz, leaving us all in a fit of giggles.

When we were ushered in to clean up and gather around the *sofreh*, I gave my butterfly one last chase around the courtyard. Only this time she flew up, over the wall and out of sight. The street protests had grown into a crescendo. Their chants, slogans, and raised fists punching through the clear Tabriz skies, sending every bird and winged creature ducking for cover. Unaware that this would be our last summer in Tabriz, or that my butterfly-chasing days had come to an end, I kicked off my sandals and gave one last look up and beyond the stained-glass windows. As I watched through squinted eyes, the setting sun momentarily forget herself, gently laying her lips one last time on Wonderland and the cool turquoise tiles of the hoz.

The tradition of stuffing vegetables and rolling ground meat into all sizes and shapes is ingrained in Iranian food culture. Eggplant, grape leaves, cabbage, peppers, and tomatoes are but a few examples of vessels worthy of stuffing. Fillings vary and are dictated by region and household, some meat-based, some grain-based, some a combination of both, as is the specific *advieh*—spice blend.

There is something about the ritual of forming meatballs and patties, or wrapping little parcels of grape leaf, that reminds me most of the comforts of home. Maybe it's because of the care and love that goes into preparing these dishes, or maybe because it usually takes the help of friends and family to gather and get rolling and wrapping together.

There's a mental hurdle to get over when considering making Dolmeh Barg (page 265) or Koofteh Tabrizi (page 282). There are usually a number of cooking components to consider when preparing for these dishes. The stuffing, various fillers and binders, like the combination of rice and yellow split peas for Koofteh Tabrizi, or meat and potatoes for Kotlet (page 275). But once you give in to the process it can be quite meditative and even enjoyable. These days I get my girls to form our Everyday Meatballs (page 260). It can get messy and meatball sizes will not be uniform, but it's a fun way to get kids involved in the kitchen and for everyone to lend a hand. The task of rolling and stuffing is also a much-needed break from the frenzied rhythm of the day.

Goosht Ghelgheli

Everyday Meatballs

Meatballs, or Goosht Ghelgheli as I grew up calling them, are a staple comfort food in just about every culture. Sometimes rolled as tiny as marbles, and sometimes large enough to encase an entire poussin, meatballs appear in a variety of sizes in many Persian dishes. Add them directly to aash *in dishes like Aash-e Dogha (page 76), or panfry and top off rice or grain dishes like Cabbage Farro (page 132). A harried weeknight dinner at our house is dependent on quick baked meatballs served with a salad and a simple* kateh-*style rice, and Cranberry Quince Sauce (page 273) when in season. Persian-style meatballs are typically simply prepared with salt, pepper, and turmeric. I also like to add a few more aromatic spices, such as cinnamon and allspice. You can use any type of meat you prefer: ground beef, lamb, turkey, or chicken. Leave out the egg and bread crumbs if adding the meatballs directly to aash. And keep in mind ground turkey will be wetter and stickier to roll; wetting your hands really helps the rolling process.*

SERVES 4 TO 6

1 pound ground beef, lamb, turkey, or chicken

1¼ teaspoons kosher salt

⅛ teaspoon ground turmeric

⅛ teaspoon ground cinnamon

⅛ teaspoon ground allspice

¼ teaspoon dried mint

¼ teaspoon ground black pepper

½ large yellow onion, grated

2 cloves garlic, crushed to a paste

¼ cup bread crumbs (leave out for aash)

1 egg (leave out for aash)

Place the meat in a large bowl and spread it out, creating a flat surface, to ensure the spices are evenly distributed across the meat mixture. Sprinkle all the spices evenly over the meat. Add the onion, garlic, bread crumbs, and egg. Mix everything well, getting out all the clumps.

Set up your work space. Place a baking sheet and a small bowl of water next to you. Wet your palms a little so the meat doesn't stick to your hands, and roll into a walnut-sized ball (about 1 tablespoon of meat mixture per meatball). Place the meatballs on the baking sheet. If you have time, place them in the fridge, uncovered, to rest for 30 minutes. If not, prepare them as you like.

BAKED MEATBALLS: Preheat the oven to 425°F with the rack in the center position. Place the meatballs on a baking sheet, lined with foil or parchment paper if you like. Drizzle the meatballs with a little olive oil and bake until cooked through and slightly browned on top, about 20 minutes, depending on the size of the meatball. Garnish with chopped herbs of choice, and serve.

PANFRIED: Coat a large frying pan with olive oil. Heat over medium heat, and add as many meatballs as you can without crowding the pan. Fry the meatballs until browned on one side. Turn and fry the other side and cook through, about 5 minutes per side, depending on the size of the meatballs. Transfer to a serving plate, and carry on with the next batch. Garnish with chopped herbs of choice, and serve.

Garni Yarikh

Stuffed Eggplant

Garni Yarikh is a specialty of Azarbaijan province. My aunt Zarin shared this recipe with me from Tabriz via text, as I photographed every step of the preparation and texted back for her approval. Thankfully, she appreciated my California-inspired tweaks and riffs on a classic. Garni Yarikh is the Turkish name for this meat-stuffed eggplant. The Persian name is shekam pareh, *both of which mean "split belly," in reference to the splitting of the eggplant. This is the kind of dish that seduces and beckons as silky eggplant collapses into well-browned and delicately spiced meat, all simmering over a rich tomato-based sauce. Even the youngest eggplant skeptics in our household have been swayed by the wonders of these split bellies. And when they've had their fill of trying suspicious eggplant they simply scoop up the meat sauce with pieces of* lavash *bread—a* loghmeh *to suit every palate. Serve Garni Yarikh with just-warmed-through lavash bread and a side of plain yogurt for lunch or dinner.*

SERVES 4 TO 6

6 Italian or baby eggplant (about 2 pounds)

½ cup olive oil, divided

10 cloves garlic, thinly sliced

1 yellow onion, finely diced

Kosher salt

1 pound ground beef

6 tablespoons tomato paste

½ teaspoon ground cinnamon

¼ teaspoon ground allspice

⅛ teaspoon ground cloves

Ground black pepper

½ bunch parsley, tough stems trimmed, chopped (set a little aside for garnish)

½ cup cherry tomatoes, sliced in half

Preheat the oven to 425°F with the rack set in the center position. Line a large baking sheet with foil or parchment paper and lightly oil.

Peel the eggplant in stripes, with the stem and cap on. Leaving 1 inch off the top and the bottom, cut a shallow split lengthwise in the belly of the eggplant, without piercing right through, stopping about 1 inch from the bottom. Place the eggplant in a large bowl and with a teaspoon drizzle a little of the olive oil in each slit and sprinkle generously with salt. Rub the rest of the oil all over the eggplant, and season with a good pinch of salt and a little pepper. Place the eggplant on the baking sheet and bake for about 35 minutes, until fork-tender. Set aside to cool.

(continued)

While the eggplant roasts, prepare the filling. Bring a kettle of water to a boil, and keep at a simmer. In a large pan, heat ¼ cup olive oil over medium-low heat. Add the garlic and cook very gently, constantly stirring, until slightly softened, but taking care it doesn't take on any color, about 5 minutes. The garlic slices should resemble slivered almonds. Transfer the garlic to a small bowl, leaving the oil in the pan, and set aside. Turn up the heat to medium and add the onion to the pan and the garlicky oil, and cook until softened, about 8 minutes. Sprinkle with a little salt, turn up the heat to medium-high, add the meat, and brown for about 5 minutes. Stir in the tomato paste, and cook with the meat for 2 minutes. Reduce the heat to medium and add the cinnamon, allspice, cloves, 1 teaspoon salt, and ½ teaspoon pepper. Give a stir and add ½ cup water from the kettle. Reduce the heat to medium-low, and cook until the meat is cooked through and all the flavors come to life, about 5 minutes. Taste and make delicious. Remove from the heat, and stir in the parsley and garlic slices.

With a fork, gently push the eggplant flesh to either side, making room for the filling, and sprinkle with a little more salt. Fill each eggplant with about 2 tablespoons of the filling, depending on the size of the eggplant. You'll have filling left over in the pan. Place the pan back on the stove over medium heat, add the cherry tomatoes and ½ cup water from the kettle. Give a stir, and bring to a good simmer. Taste and add more salt or spices, as needed. Gently nestle the eggplant boats in the sauce, spoon a little sauce over the eggplant, cover, and reduce the heat to low. Cook until the tomatoes collapse and release their juices, and the eggplant is completely tender and everything is luscious, 35 to 45 minutes. Once in a while spoon a little sauce over the eggplant. Add a little more water if needed, but remember this is supposed to be a somewhat thick, meaty sauce. Garnish with parsley and serve.

MAKE AHEAD: Prepare up to 3 days in advance and gently reheat. You might need to add a little more water to the sauce and adjust seasoning.

PREP AHEAD: The eggplant can be roasted a few hours in advance, and the meat sauce can be prepared 3 days in advance. Assemble and finish cooking through.

PLAN AHEAD: The meat sauce can be frozen for up to 3 months.

Dolmeh Barg

Stuffed Grape Leaves

If there was ever a time to call up friends and sit around a table chatting, sipping on a mid-day aperitif, and laughing about who stuffs their grape leaf the best (or, in my case, in the most oddly creative) way, this is it. Set aside a weekend morning for "project dolmeh."

Stuffing grape leaves is an exercise in patience and letting go. You might put the kettle on for a hot cup of tea or you might decide that if there was ever a time to pour yourself a drink, this would be it, regardless of what the clock says. You'll call up your mother, 1,200 miles away, hoping she'll somehow magically have the answer to your current situation. But then, something happens just as you turn on the music and sit yourself down in front of the mixing bowl and thirty grape leaves. There's a sudden shift as the wooden spoon digs into the bowl for the first time, bringing together all those lone ingredients, stirring up all the scents and secrets of your spice cupboard. It's not a sharp assault of the senses but more of a dizzying, hypnotic trance, knocking you off-balance. And that's when you let go and settle in to stuff and fold bundles of dolmeh.

Dolmeh Barg, Persian-style stuffed grape leaves, set themselves apart from the various other preparations of dolmeh spanning the Mediterranean and heading east, in the method of wrapping the leaf and the distinct presence of the sharp scent of the herb marzeh—*summer savory (see page 354). Fresh savory might be hard to come by, but you can use dried, which is available at most grocery stores.*

Iranian grape leaves are wrapped like a square bundle or a package. Within Iran preparations for the stuffing vary depending on region, home, and personal preference. Many preparations use a meat filling or a tomato broth. Some preparations lean sweet with the addition of raisins. This recipe is more pleasantly tangy and herb-heavy, and combines both rice and bulgur as its stuffing. These bundles came my way directly from Tabriz. I don't often have access to fresh grape leaves, but if by any chance you do, use the young and more tender leaves. Look for fresh grape leaves around May. Dolmeh can be served as an appetizer but we also eat them as a main meal served with some lavash *or* sangak *bread.*

MAKES ABOUT 30 GRAPE LEAVES

7 ounces fresh, young tender grape leaves, or half of a 23-ounce jar, in brine (about 30 leaves)

FOR THE FILLING

¼ cup yellow split peas, picked through and rinsed

1 teaspoon kosher salt (plus more as needed)

2 tablespoons olive oil

2 large shallots, minced

½ cup jasmine rice, soaked for 1 hour and drained

(continued)

Dolmeh Barg *(continued)*

¼ cup medium (#3) bulgur wheat, soaked for 1 hour and drained

5 green onions, finely chopped

½ bunch fresh dill, finely chopped

Scant 1½ teaspoons dried summer savory or ¼ cup chopped fresh

1½ teaspoons ground dried rose petals (see page 18)

1½ teaspoons ground cinnamon

½ teaspoon ground black pepper

3 cloves garlic, crushed to a paste

3 tablespoons plain yogurt

2 tablespoons unsalted butter, melted

Olive oil

¼ cup sour green grapes

FOR THE BROTH

½ cup chicken stock or water

¼ cup verjuice or fresh lemon juice (plus more as needed)

Kosher salt

FOR THE GARNISH (OPTIONAL)

1 tablespoon clarified butter or unsalted butter

1 small yellow onion, sliced into ¼-inch-thick half-moons

2 tablespoons barberries, picked through, rinsed, and drained

Tiny pinch of sugar

½ cup plain yogurt

1 clove garlic, crushed to a paste

A few drops of saffron water (page 17; completely optional and only if you have some on hand)

If using brined leaves: Place the grape leaves in a colander, place the colander in a large bowl, and cover with cold water. Soak for 5 minutes to wash off the salty brine. Drain, give another rinse, and set aside to drain.

If using fresh leaves: Bring a pot of water to a boil. Turn off the heat. Place the grape leaves in a colander and submerge in the hot water. Soak just until they change color, 5 to 10 minutes. Set aside to drain.

Meanwhile, for the filling, place the yellow split peas in a small saucepan. Cover with about 1 cup water and add ½ teaspoon salt. Partially cover and bring to a gentle boil, skimming off any foam, keeping a close eye on it so it doesn't boil over. Reduce the heat to medium-low and simmer until the yellow split peas are parcooked, tender but still firm, and holding their shape, about 10 minutes, depending on the quality of your peas. Drain and set aside.

In a large frying pan, heat the olive oil over medium-high heat. Add the shallots and cook, stirring occasionally, until golden brown, 8 to 10 minutes. Reduce the heat to medium. Add the rice, bulgur, yellow split peas, green onions, dill, savory, dried rose petals, cinnamon, salt, and pepper. Stir to combine, and cook just until fragrant, about 2 minutes. Transfer to a mixing bowl, and add the garlic, yogurt, and melted butter. Mix to combine.

(continued)

Dolmeh Barg *(continued)*

To wrap the grape leaves: Prepare your work station. Drizzle the bottom of a medium-sized pot with olive oil and cover with a few of the larger, tougher grape leaves so the dolmeh don't burn. Place the pot, the grape leaves, the filling, kitchen scissors, and a plate beside you. Place a grape leaf, vein-side-up, on the plate with the bottom stem end toward you. Trim the stem with scissors. Place anywhere between 1 teaspoon to 1 tablespoon of the filling, depending on the size of the leaf, in the center. You don't want to overstuff the dolmeh, or it might burst open.

Wrap the dolmeh into a tight little bundle (but not too tight so the rice has space to expand) or package, by folding in the right side, then the left, and then the top and bottom. Place each dolmeh seam-side down, snugly against each other at the bottom of the pot. Make sure you don't leave any spaces between the dolmeh so they don't open up while cooking.

Place a few sour green grapes on top of the first layer and continue stuffing, wrapping, and layering all the dolmeh with sour green grapes sprinkled in between each layer. Place a heatproof plate face down over the top to hold them down so they don't move around.

Make the broth. In a bowl, combine the stock, verjuice, and a pinch of salt. Pour it into the pot over the dolmeh, cover, and bring to a boil over medium-high heat. As soon as it comes to a boil, reduce the heat to low and cook until the rice and bulgur are cooked through, and most of the liquid has been absorbed by the dolmeh, 30 to 45 minutes. You can test a dolmeh; if it's not ready, add more liquid to the pot, and keep cooking until the rice is tender. Check in on the dolmeh; once in a while and taste the broth, and add a little salt and verjuice, if necessary, to make it delicious. Set the dolmeh aside to rest in the pot, uncovered, for about 10 minutes before serving them.

While the dolmeh rests, prepare the garnish. In a medium pan, melt the butter over medium-high heat. Add the onion and cook, stirring frequently, until golden, about 10 minutes. Reduce the heat to medium and continue cooking until golden brown, not too dark, 5 to 10 minutes. Reduce the heat to medium-low. Add the barberries and a tiny pinch of sugar, and stir to heat through and plump up the barberries, about 2 minutes. Remove from the heat (barberries burn very quickly). Set aside until ready to use.

In a bowl, combine the yogurt and the garlic.

To serve, arrange the dolmeh on a platter. Top with the barberries and drizzle with a little garlic yogurt. Drop a few drops of saffron water on the yogurt drizzle, if you like. Serve the rest of the yogurt on the side.

MAKE AHEAD: The dolmeh can be prepared up to 3 days in advance. Gently heat through in the oven or serve at room temperature.

PLAN AHEAD: Dolmeh freeze well. Make a big batch, portion off, place parchment paper between each layer, freeze, and have on hand for a quick appetizer or meal. Thaw and gently heat through in the oven.

Baked Feta with Cranberry Quince Sauce

Every year around the holidays I bust out my contribution to the holiday meal—Cranberry Quince Sauce. It was love at first pop when I first discovered cranberries as a child in Vancouver. These little, sour, crimson pops must have Persian roots somewhere. Sprinkled with a little salt or golpar they make for the ultimate Persian-style movie watching snack. Combined with the sweet perfume of quince and orange blossom water, the sauce is a festive addition to any holiday meal, and a Swedish imposter of a companion to Everyday Meatballs (page 260) or Kotlet (page 275). This feta parcel was inspired by my desperate need to use up the last few grape leaves sadly left behind in the jar, after an epic Dolmeh Barg (page 265) feast. A block of feta is bundled up in grape leaves, then left to soften and quiver in the oven. Top with the slightly sweet and tangy Cranberry Quince Sauce, and a new holiday favorite is born. You can use any sauce or preserves you like to enjoy any time of year, but the Cranberry Quince Sauce adds just the right note of sweet-and-sour against the bold and briny flavors of the feta. Serve with a soft flatbread, like lavash or sangak, to easily scoop up the gooey, juicy, molten cheese and sauce.

SERVES 6 AS AN APPETIZER

This will make more sauce than is needed here. Use the leftover sauce as an accompaniment to meatballs, roast chicken or Thanksgiving turkey, yogurt topping, or simply enjoy it by the spoonful as a snack.

½ cup apple juice

⅓ cup plus 1 tablespoon sugar

1 large quince, peeled, cored, and diced

⅓ cup fresh orange juice

8 ounces fresh or frozen cranberries

¼ teaspoon orange blossom water (optional)

8 large grape leaves, stems trimmed

1 (8-ounce) block feta cheese

Olive oil for drizzling

In a small pot, combine the apple juice and ⅓ cup sugar over medium-high heat. Bring to a gentle boil to dissolve the sugar. Add the quince. Reduce the heat to medium-low, cover, and simmer until the quince softens, about 15 to 20 minutes. Add the orange juice and cranberries, and simmer uncovered until the cranberries pop, about 10 minutes. Remove from the heat and add the orange blossom water, if using. Set aside to cool to room temperature and refrigerate. It will thicken as it sits.

Preheat the oven to 400°F with the rack in the center position.

(continued)

If using brined leaves: Place the grape leaves in a colander, place the colander in a large bowl, and cover with cold water. Soak for 5 minutes to wash off the salty brine. Drain, give another rinse, and set aside to drain.

If using fresh leaves: Bring a small pot of water to a boil. Turn off the heat. Place the grape leaves in a colander and submerge in the hot water. Soak just until they change color, 5 to 10 minutes. Set aside to drain.

Set aside 2 grape leaves. Line the bottom of a small (6 x 6-inch) baking or casserole dish with the rest of the leaves, overlapping them. Or you can use a small baking pan lined with parchment paper. Place the feta in the center and drizzle with a little olive oil. Fold the grape leaves over the feta and, place the reserved grape leaves on top, so it's nicely wrapped. Place in the oven and bake for about 40 minutes, until the feta has softened and is molten, begging to be scooped up with some bread. Peel it open, top with the cranberry quince sauce, and serve.

Oven-Baked Kotlet

Meat and Potato Patties

At about the 20-minute mark into baking kotlet, my daughters, Luna and Soleil, will chime in unison, "I know that yummy smell!" That yummy smell is the distinct scent familiar to anyone who loves the humble meat and potato patties known as kotlet. Traditionally, kotlet is fried in batches on the stovetop. In this version I bake the patties in a hot oven all in one go, skipping babysitting them as they cook on the stovetop. I make and form the patties earlier in the day, give them time to rest in the fridge, and stick them in the oven around dinnertime. Just in time for everyone to inquire about the yummy smells. If you don't have Advieh (page 15)—spice blend—on hand, look at some of the spices used in the blend and add whichever you have (in smaller, tip-of-a-knife amounts) in your spice cupboard. I highly recommend mixing a batch of Advieh, though.

Serve Oven-Baked Kotlet with pickled cucumber, sliced tomatoes, avocado, and any fresh, crunchy vegetables you like. Kotlet also makes a fantastic sandwich. Slather your favorite bread, like a baguette, with mayo and top with a piece of kotlet, greens of choice, avocado, sliced pickles, tomatoes, and thinly sliced red onion. Grab a few napkins and dig in.

MAKES 12 PATTIES

1 pound Yukon Gold potatoes (about 2 large potatoes), peeled and quartered

Kosher salt

1 cup bread crumbs

1 pound ground beef or ground turkey

1 teaspoon ground turmeric

½ teaspoon Advieh (page 15)

¼ teaspoon ground black pepper

1 medium onion, grated on the large holes of a box grater or in the food processor

2 large eggs

Large handful of fresh parsley, finely chopped (about ¼ cup)

⅓ cup olive oil (plus more as needed)

Place the potatoes in a small pot. Cover with water (about 2 cups), and add 1 teaspoon salt. Partially cover and bring to a boil. Cook on medium-high until the potatoes are fork-tender, about 15 minutes. Drain and return the potatoes to the hot pot (with the heat off) for a couple of minutes to steam dry. Transfer the potatoes to a large bowl and mash really well; the back of a fork works just fine for this. Set aside to cool, so the eggs don't cook when added to the potatoes.

Line two large baking sheets with parchment paper.

Set up your work space before you get your hands in the meat: place the baking sheets and a small bowl of water next to you to use as needed to wet your hands so the

Oven-Baked Kotlet *(continued)*

meat mixture doesn't stick to your hands (especially if using ground turkey). Scatter the bread crumbs on a large plate and set next you. Place the meat in a large bowl and spread it out, creating a flat surface, to ensure the spices are evenly distributed across the meat mixture. Sprinkle the turmeric, Advieh, pepper, and 2 teaspoons salt evenly across the meat. Add the mashed potatoes, onion, eggs, and parsley. Use your hands to knead the mixture until really well combined.

If there are any friends or children around, enlist them to help form the patties. If not, sit yourself down in front of the television or, better yet, turn on your favorite music, and get rolling. Grab a small handful (about ⅓ cup or 3 ounces) of the meat mixture and form a small ball, about the size of a very small orange. Flatten and shape the ball in your hand into an oval shape, about 4 inches long. The oval shape is the traditional shape, but no one will be offended if the patties are round. Coat each side of the patties in the bread crumbs and place the patties on the baking sheet, leaving space between each kotlet. You should end up with 12 kotlet. Place the kotlet in the fridge, uncovered, for 30 minutes (or up to 5 hours) to set. You can skip this part if you're in a mad, hungry rush.

Preheat the oven to 400°F with the oven racks set in the upper-third and lower-third positions. Brush both sides of the kotlet with the olive oil, and bake both sheets for 20 minutes. Flip the patties, rotate the pans, and bake for an additional 20 minutes, until sizzling, browned, and cooked through. Serve warm or at room temperature.

MAKE AHEAD: Prepare up to 3 days in advance. Serve at room temperature or heat through in the oven.

PREP AHEAD: Form the patties up to 5 hours in advance and store in the fridge on the baking sheets ready to bake in the oven.

PLAN AHEAD: The cooked patties can be stored in the freezer for up to 3 months in an airtight container or resealable bag. Place a small piece of parchment paper between each patty so they don't stick to each other. Heat through in the oven. Makes for a perfect last-minute school lunch, quick dinner, or late-night snack.

Kotlet-e Sardine

Sardine Fish Cakes

Canned sardines save dinner at our house on a weekly basis. These Kotlet-e Sardine are a jazzed-up version of our staple, with a nod to the seafood-rich cuisines of the Caspian and Persian Gulf regions of Iran. Like a meat kotlet, *they are bound by potatoes and eggs, and flavored with fragrant fresh herbs and spices. The tamarind in the mango salsa delivers the acidity and flavor, but if you don't have any on hand you can use fresh lime juice as needed. Kotlet-e Sardine make a quick light lunch or dinner. Serve with lemon wedges or the tangy mango salsa for a hit of color and burst of flavor, or simply serve with a side salad.*

MAKES 8 PATTIES

1 pound Yukon Gold potatoes (about 2 large potatoes), peeled and quartered

2 teaspoons kosher salt

2 (4.4-ounce) cans whole sardines in olive oil

½ bunch parsley, tough stems trimmed, finely chopped

½ bunch cilantro, tough stems trimmed, finely chopped

1 teaspoon dried mint

Zest of 1 lemon

¼ teaspoon ground fennel (optional, but tasty)

¼ teaspoon ground turmeric

¼ teaspoon ground black pepper

Cayenne pepper (start with ⅛ teaspoon, add more as you like)

2 tablespoons bread crumbs

2 large eggs, at room temperature

Olive oil for frying

Lemon wedges for serving

Place the potatoes in a small pot. Cover with water (about 2 cups) and add 1 teaspoon salt. Partially cover and bring to a boil. Cook on medium-high until the potatoes are fork-tender, 10 to 15 minutes. Drain and return the potatoes to the hot pot (off the heat) for a couple of minutes to steam dry. Transfer the potatoes to a large bowl and mash. The back of a fork works just fine for this. Set aside to cool, so the eggs don't cook when added to the potatoes.

Completely drain the sardines of oil, place in a large bowl, and flake into very small pieces. Add the rest of the ingredients *except* for the olive oil. Combine well, and form 8 3-inch patties. Place the patties on a small baking sheet and chill in the fridge for 30 minutes, or up to 2 hours.

FOR THE MANGO SALSA

1 ripe mango, peeled and diced (about 1½ cups)

2 tablespoons finely diced red onion

½ to 1 small jalapeño pepper, minced

Kosher salt

1 teaspoon tamarind concentrate (plus more as needed)

¼ teaspoon golpar (Persian hogweed; page 357; plus more to taste; optional)

Drizzle of honey (if needed)

Handful of fresh cilantro, chopped (about 2 tablespoons)

⅓ cup pomegranate seeds

Meanwhile, prepare the mango salsa. In a small bowl, combine the mango, red onion, jalapeño, small pinch of salt, tamarind paste, and golpar. Taste and drizzle on a little honey to balance the acids if necessary, depending on how sweet the mango is. Add the cilantro and pomegranate seeds, and sprinkle with a little more golpar if you like.

In a large pan, heat the oil over medium-high, until hot but not smoking. Add the patties and cook until browned on each side, 3 to 4 minutes per side. Serve with lemon wedges and mango salsa.

Shami Rashti

Yellow Split Pea and Meat Patties

Rasht is the capital of Gilan Province in the north of Iran. Rashti-style doughnut-shaped meat patties are simply prepared with slowly simmered stewing meat, yellow split peas, a dash of turmeric, all bound with a few eggs, and fried in oil. The ratio in weight of the meat to the yellow split peas is crucial here. As is the number of eggs used to just bind the mixture. If you use too many eggs, the patties will crack and fall apart. Rumor has it in Tehran they use a larger amount of split peas than meat. Which may raise a few eyebrows in Rasht. Thousands of years of regional differences celebrated and debated in a simple, economical, and filling meat patty with a hole in the middle. Shami is traditionally served in Gilan with a side of feta cheese, crisp lettuce, tomatoes, fresh herbs, and pickles. On this side of the globe we might also like to dip our "doughnuts" in mayo or ketchup, or a mix of both. Which may raise a few eyebrows somewhere else.

MAKES ABOUT 15 PATTIES

---

1 pound stewing meat (beef, veal, or lamb), cut into 1-inch pieces

1 large yellow onion, roughly chopped

Kosher salt

1 teaspoon ground turmeric, divided

½ teaspoon ground black pepper

1 pound yellow split peas, picked over, rinsed, and drained

2 teaspoons Advieh (page 15)

¼ teaspoon ground saffron (optional)

1 teaspoon baking soda

2 large eggs

Olive oil for frying

Place the meat and onion in a medium pot, and cover with water (about 2 cups). Bring to a boil over high heat, skimming off any foam. Add 1 teaspoon salt, ½ teaspoon of the turmeric, and black pepper, to taste. Reduce the heat to medium-low, cover, and cook until the meat is completely cooked through and tender, about 1 hour. Drain, reserving the broth, and transfer the meat and onion to a large bowl.

In the final 30 minutes of the meat cooking, prepare the yellow split peas. Place the yellow split peas in a medium pot, and cover with 4½ cups water and 1 teaspoon salt. Partially cover and bring to a gentle boil, skimming off any foam, and keeping a close eye on it so it doesn't boil over—seriously, keep an eye on it. Turn down the heat to medium-low and simmer until the yellow split peas are tender, 25 to 35 minutes.

Drain and add the split peas to the meat. Mash the meat and split peas into a stretchy paste using an immersion blender or a food processor. Set aside to cool slightly before adding the spices and eggs.

Add the Advieh, saffron, baking soda, and remaining ½ teaspoon turmeric to the meat mixture. If the mixture is too dry, add a spoonful of the reserved meat broth (store any leftover broth to use in soups or *aash*). At this point you can cover the meat mixture and rest in the fridge for up to 24 hours. When ready to cook the shami, add the eggs, one at a time, to the mixture. Knead the mixture well with your hands until you form a soft paste.

Prepare your work station. Place the meat mixture and a small bowl of water next to you at the stove. Line a large baking sheet with paper towels and set it next to you. In a large frying pan, heat ¼ cup olive oil over medium-high heat until hot but not smoking. Wet your hands, roll a ball of the meat mixture to the size of a walnut (about 3 ounces), and flatten it in your hand, about 3 inches in diameter.

Poke a hole in the middle of the patty, like a doughnut, and gently slip the patty into the hot oil. Continue with the rest of the mixture, working in batches and adding more oil as needed. Fry on each side for 3 to 5 minutes, until browned. Place the patties on the baking sheet. Serve warm or at room temperature.

MAKE AHEAD: Prepare up to 3 days in advance and store in the fridge.

PREP AHEAD: The meat and yellow split pea mixture can be prepared and combined without the addition of the eggs and frozen for up to 3 months. Thaw, add the eggs, and cook.

Koofteh Tabrizi

Stuffed Meatballs

These quintessential Iranian stuffed meatballs are awe-inspiring in flavor, presentation, and preparation. As their name would suggest, they hail from the city of Tabriz, Azarbaijan Province. Traditionally, a poussin is stuffed with a cooked egg, dried fruits, and nuts. The poussin is then encased in the meatball mixture, to form a gigantic meatball, and slowly cooked in a fragrant tomato sauce.

In our humble home kitchen, we love making the more streamlined, but equally presentation worthy and flavorful, Koofteh Tabrizi. We forgo the poussin and the egg, and stuff more manageable-sized meatballs with walnuts and a few dried fruits. This recipe has many components, which makes it ideal to prepare on a day when time and hungry children are not poking at you. But if you set up your ingredients and prepare your work station beforehand, it all comes together quite efficiently.

The most important note on making Koofteh Tabrizi is to make sure that the meat mixture doesn't crack or fall apart as it cooks in the sauce. Which is why the ingredient ratios are very specific. Please don't alter these amounts. It is also imperative that the meat gets a good workout; knead, thump, and pummel into the bowl to ensure it binds well with the rest of the ingredients. Although it is now common to do this in the food processor I prefer to work all the ingredients the old-fashioned way—by hand. The meat mixture can turn tough and pasty in the food processor. Just get your hands in there and squish, squash, and thump.

To serve, ladle a little sauce in a bowl, and top with a koofteh and any of the garnishes. Enjoy with sangak *bread and a side of Torshi Liteh (page 68) and Sabzi Khordan (page 32). Also, quite spectacular the next day as a sandwich, smashed between crusty sourdough bread served au jus, as my husband, Drew, likes to prepare it.*

SERVES 4 TO 6

FOR THE MEATBALLS

½ cup yellow split peas, picked through and rinsed

1 very small Yukon Gold potato (about 2 ounces), whole and unpeeled

Kosher salt

½ cup white jasmine rice, rinsed

⅛ teaspoon ground saffron

1 pound ground beef, at least 15% fat

2 large eggs, at room temperature

2 teaspoons dried summer savory (optional)

Place the yellow split peas and the potato together in a small pot. Cover with just enough water to cover the potato, about 2 cups, and add ½ teaspoon salt. Partially cover and bring to a boil over high heat. Reduce the heat to medium and cook until both the yellow split peas and the potato are cooked through, 15 to 20 minutes. Drain and set aside to cool.

(continued)

Koofteh Tabrizi *(continued)*

¼ teaspoon Advieh
(page 15)

¼ teaspoon ground black
pepper

2 tablespoons barberries,
rinsed and dried

4 dried apricots,
quartered

4 dried prunes, quartered

8 walnuts, halved

FOR THE SAUCE

¼ cup olive oil

1½ large yellow onions,
diced

2 tablespoons tomato
paste

1½ teaspoons kosher salt

¼ teaspoon ground black
pepper

⅛ teaspoon ground
allspice

GARNISH (OPTIONAL)

½ tablespoon butter

1 tablespoon barberries

Tiny pinch of sugar

Meanwhile, place the rice and ½ teaspoon salt in a small pot, cover with 1 cup water, and bring to a boil. Reduce the heat to low, sprinkle in the saffron, and give a stir. Cover and cook until the rice is cooked through and all the water has been absorbed, 12 to 15 minutes. Transfer to a small bowl and set aside to cool.

While the yellow split peas/potato and rice cool, start on the sauce. In a large pot, heat the oil over medium-high heat. Add the onion and cook, stirring often, until really golden brown, about 12 minutes. Set aside 2 heaping tablespoons of the browned onion for the meatball stuffing. Reduce the heat to medium, add the tomato paste, and stir for 1 minute, taking care not to burn the paste. Add 4 cups water, the salt, pepper, and allspice. Bring to a gentle boil, reduce the heat to low, and simmer for 10 minutes. Taste and add more salt if necessary. Partially cover and set aside.

While the sauce simmers, peel the cooked potato. Place it and the cooked yellow split peas in a food processor, and blitz until pureed. Set aside. Place the ground meat in a large bowl. Knead and massage the meat really well with your hands. Bring the meat to life. Add 2 teaspoons salt to the meat and mix to combine. Add the pureed potato and split peas, the cooked rice, the eggs, savory (if using), Advieh, and pepper to the meat. Pack all the meat in your hands and pummel it down back into the bowl. Really thump it back into the bowl. Knead and repeat several times until the mixture binds. This process ensures the meatballs don't open up and fall apart while cooking. Set aside.

Set up your workspace to form the meatballs: place the reserved 2 tablespoons browned onion, the barberries, dried fruit, walnuts, small bowl of water, and a large plate or baking sheet next to you. Divide the meat mixture, onion, dried fruit, and walnuts into 8 equal portions. Wet your hands a little and form a meatball the size of a small orange. Make an indentation in the ball, stuff the meatball with a little bit of the onion, barberries, apricots, prunes, and walnuts. Don't overstuff the meatball or it might burst open when cooking. Seal the meatball by gently pinching it closed, until the stuffing is fully covered, and roll back into shape. Place on a baking sheet and repeat with the remaining meat and stuffing. Place in the fridge to rest for 30 minutes.

Remove the meatballs from the fridge. Bring the sauce back up to a gentle boil over medium-high heat, and carefully slip the meatballs into the sauce. The sauce should come about three-quarters of the way up the sides of the meatballs. Spoon a little bit of the sauce over the meatballs, reduce the heat to medium-low, and simmer, uncovered, for 15 minutes. Occasionally, spoon more of the sauce over them. Partially cover and continue cooking, occasionally spooning more sauce over them, until the meatballs are cooked through, about 1 hour. If you feel confident the meatballs won't crack, gently turn them once halfway through; otherwise leave them be.

Just before serving, prepare the barberry garnish. In a small pan, melt the butter over medium-low heat. Add the barberries and a tiny sprinkling of sugar and stir to warm through, about 2 minutes.

To serve, spoon a little bit of the sauce into individual bowls and place a meatball on top of each. Garnish with the barberries, and serve.

MAKE AHEAD: Prepare up to 3 days in advance. You might need to add more water and seasoning to the sauce when reheating.

PREP AHEAD: Measure out all your ingredients and set up your workspace in advance.

PLAN AHEAD: Store for up to 3 months in the freezer. Add water and adjust the seasoning for the sauce when reheating.

DRINKS

WATER

"Nazzy joon, the future looks bright."

That's how my maternal grandmother would begin every Turkish coffee cup reading for a then five-year-old me. She would hold the tiny cup in front of her, tilting it this way and that, peering deep into its caverns and caves, its walls etched with difficult to decipher patterns, signs, and symbols.

We didn't call her grandma; she wouldn't have any of that. Instead we called her Maman Ghashangi—"beautiful mama." Maman Ghashangi was all life and spirit, refusing to submit to the restrictive and judgmental edicts of her surrounding society and culture. She was known for her spirited Lezgi dance (a traditional dance of the Caucasus region), her beautiful smooth hands, her love for her one glass of *veesky* on ice, her perfectly applied lipstick, her midmorning Turkish coffee gatherings, and her weekly rummy-playing sessions. Her reputation for seeing the future in a tiny cup of thick, soothing, aromatic coffee was well known. Many years later, she would tell me that she didn't really read the cup, but she read the people. And although we knew the readings were just for fun, she was always spot on with almost every prediction.

She was the first to predict our eventual departure from Iran, as she peered into my mother's cup and saw a bird, or maybe it was an airplane, or maybe it was a creature, part human, part bird, in flight, across open skies, to distant lands, never to return again. The plane, bird, or flying creature was headed toward open waters—symbol of light and life—but leaving behind a heavy heart, symbolized by the thick, dark paste smeared at the bottom of the cup.

I always looked forward to the days that Maman Ghashangi babysat. It meant throwing out all the rules and setting our own schedule. She would make us a little *hazeri*, something quick, fast, and fun. Usually a sandwich, slathered with plenty of mayo and topped with ham, pickles, the works. Or she would quick boil a potato, drench it in olive oil, top it with an egg, sprinkle it with salt, pepper, and dried mint, and smoosh it all together between a piece of *lavash* bread. And to wash it all down she would pour us a sweet and fragrant *sharbat*—a fruit or floral syrup mix diluted with water, and served over ice. Particularly refreshing on those hot Tehran summer days.

Come midmorning the *chezve*, the long-handled small pot used to prepare Turkish coffee, was placed on the stovetop as she slowly stirred in the coffee grounds. The foam was always scooped out for me, and although my cup of coffee was prepared with plenty of sugar, we also nibbled on a little something sweet as we slurped back the future. Then came the moment of truth. Just as we reached the gritty, muddy, thick layer at the bottom, we covered the cup with the saucer, and quickly flipped it. Allowing the thick remnants to drip down the sides of the cup, etching our future on the walls.

I never questioned why my cup had such bright and positive tales to tell. I simply accepted it as so. According to Maman Ghashangi, my cup was painted with white doves (love), lots of travel (planes and birds), beautiful open fields, intermingled hearts, and flowing streams and rivers—water. At the very end of the reading I would take my index finger, make a wish, and make a deep indentation at the bottom of the cup. I loved licking the gritty, bitter-sweet paste off my fingers. This final picture would often tell the story of me coming home from my very important job, to quickly get changed and emerge in a gold velvet cape and run out in my impossibly high heels to meet my tall and handsome American date, who had just pulled up in his shining new Cadillac. Maman Ghashangi was enamored with all things America. My date and I would then drive to a café for a night of dancing (Lezgi, of course, which my American date was curiously an expert at) and sipping on rose-scented sharbats.

Maman Ghashangi left us before I could tell her that as usual, she was spot-on with her predictions. She never got a chance to meet my husband, Drew, and his sky blue 1975 Buick LeSabre, which was gifted to him by his grandmother. She didn't get to see how he kicked up a storm dancing all our traditional dances at our wedding. I think they would have gotten along swimmingly, sipping on Turkish coffee by day and veesky on ice by night.

These days, on occasion, we make a cup of Turkish coffee in Drew's chezve that he picked up in Turkey years ago before we met. We sip our coffee. and make a tiny cup for Luna, who loves the stuff. Then we all attempt telling each other's futures. I begin Luna's with stories of doves, and then launch into important jobs, travel, hearts, and a bright and flowing body of water. Sometimes I even throw in flowing gold capes, dancing, and tall glasses of sharbat.

Because the future looks bright.

In keeping with the hot and cold concept of maintaining balance in the body (see page 24), Iranians love drinking various fruit juices and sharbat for their purported medicinal properties and to cool and hydrate the body. Think of sharbat as the ancient predecessor to lemonade. It is a concentrated syrup mix of fragrant flower and fruit essences, usually brightened with something sour, and sweetened with honey or sugar. The concentrated syrup—the sharbat—is used to flavor drinks or frozen treats. Western words such as *sherbet*, *sorbet*, *syrup*, and *sorbetto* all derive from the word *sharbat*.

And regardless of how hot or cold the weather may be, a pot of Persian chai is always at a brew. It's the first and last thing to be offered to a guest. Whenever Baba, my father, visits I always know to light the kettle for Baba's post-dinner digestif: a cup of chai with a couple of dates.

Sharbat-e Sekanjebeen
Honey and Vinegar Sharbat

Sharbat-e Sekanjebeen is a centuries-old concoction of honey (or sugar) and white wine vinegar simmered until slightly thickened, infused with fresh mint, diluted with water, and served chilled over ice and garnished with cucumber. Sharbat-e Sekanjebeen is touted for its healing benefits of cooling and restoring balance to the body. Our friends call this bright, refreshing, and hydrating summer drink Persian lemonade. Like lemonade, the sweet honey softens the tang from the vinegar. But be warned, the simmering honey syrup is a siren call to all the neighborhood bees, tapping at the windows, hoping this one time they'll be welcomed in. You can garnish sekanjebeen the traditional way with grated (or sliced) cucumber, or with any summer fruits that catch your eye, such as strawberries, cherries, or watermelon. To make a sekanjebeen cocktail, try a splash of vodka or a dry, crisp Lambrusco.

SERVES 8

---

1 cup mild-flavored honey, such as clover or orange blossom

⅔ cup plus 1 tablespoon white wine vinegar

1 small bunch mint (plus extra for garnish)

Grated or sliced cucumber

In a medium saucepan, bring the honey and 1 cup water to a boil over medium-high heat, stirring to dissolve. Stand close by, as the mixture can boil over very quickly. Reduce the heat to medium-low, and simmer briskly for 10 minutes. Add the vinegar, raise the heat to medium-high, and bring back to a boil. Reduce the heat to medium-low and simmer for 20 to 30 minutes, stirring occasionally, until the syrup thickens slightly.

Remove from the heat, add the mint, and cool to room temperature. At this point you can discard the mint or keep the mint and infuse overnight. Transfer the sharbat (about 1 cup syrup concentrate) to a glass jar, cover, and store in the fridge. Remember to discard the mint the next day. The sharbat will keep in the fridge for 1 month or longer.

TO MAKE A PITCHER: In a large pitcher, combine the sharbat with 6½ cups water, add a handful of cucumber slices (or grated cucumber) and mint leaves or any other summer fruits you like. Taste and dilute with more water if needed. Keep in mind that this sharbat should have a pleasant tang. Keep in the fridge to chill. Serve over ice.

FOR INDIVIDUAL SERVINGS: In a glass, combine ¼ cup sharbat with about ¾ cup water and serve over ice.

Sharbat-e Golab

Rose and Lime Sharbat

Besides Sharbat-e Sekanjebeen (page 292), this the most sought after sharbat in our house. If sekanjebeen cools and hydrates, and seduces the bees, Sharbat-e Golab calls for bare feet and sunsets. This drink is an elixir for the soul. You can make a concentrated syrup as with the other sharbat, but I prefer to prepare the simple syrup and add the fresh lime juice and rose water directly to the pitcher for a fresher taste.

SERVES 6

¾ cup sugar

⅓ cup fresh lime juice (about 2½ juicy limes)

2 tablespoons rose water (plus more as needed)

Fresh mint leaves (optional)

Lime slices (optional)

Rose petals, fresh or dried (optional; see page 18)

In a small saucepan, combine the sugar and ¾ cup water over medium-high heat. Stir and simmer until the sugar completely dissolves and comes up just to a quick boil, 3 to 5 minutes Remove from the heat, and set aside to cool. At this point you can store the simple syrup in a covered glass jar in the fridge until ready to use. (Makes about 1 cup syrup.)

To serve, in a large pitcher combine the simple syrup, lime juice, 6 cups water, and the rose water. Stir, taste, and add more water and rose water if necessary. Chill in the fridge for a few hours. Stir well, and garnish with mint leaves, lime slices, and rose petals (if using). Serve over ice.

Chai

Persian Tea

When I was little, my sweetened breakfast chai (colloquially pronounced cha-ee*)—tea— was poured into a small, curvy glass cup. I would then carefully pour a little bit into the matching saucer. This way the tea cooled off faster as I took small sips right from the saucer. Once in a while I would slip a rough and jagged sugar cube between my teeth and imitate the older gentlemen I had seen sipping tea at the tea houses. Pouring the boiling hot tea from cup to saucer, then loudly sipping from the saucer while slurping in the melting sugar cube between their teeth—*ghand pahloo*. The sugar cube slowly melting with every slurp in a 2/4 rhythm.* Slurp, smack, slurp, smack, slurp, smack.

A fresh pot of tea is always brewing in a Persian home. It's drunk throughout the day, and it is always, always served out of a glass cup. The color of the tea is just as important as its fragrance and flavor. When serving tea, you ask your guests how light or dark they would prefer their tea. Traditionally, the tea would be brewed in a samovar. In modern times it's brewed on the stovetop with a large kettle simmering with boiled water on the bottom and a smaller teapot with a concentrated amount of tea steeping on top. Something of a samovar replica. This way you can pour a small amount of concentrated tea in individual cups and top with hot water according to how light or dark each person prefers their tea. If your kettle's handles don't collapse you can simply steep the tea in a smaller teapot off the heat, and keep the water in the large kettle simmering on the stove.

The challenge as a kid was to remember who wanted what shade of chai, not to mention transferring a tray holding upward of ten dainty glasses of hot tea to its destination without causing any severe injury to myself or to our guests. Clink, clank, clink, clank *went the tea glasses;* slurp, smack, slurp, smack *went the tea drinkers. The sounds and rhythm of my childhood.*

SERVES 2 TO 4

2 teaspoons loose-leaf black tea, such as Earl Grey

Nabat (Persian rock candy), honey, or a sugar cube, for serving

ADDITIONAL OPTIONAL FLAVORINGS

Whole cardamom pods, bruised, or a touch of ground cardamom

Rose water

Orange blossom water

Fill a large kettle with water, and bring it to a boil. Pour a little boiled water into a smaller teapot, swirl it around to warm the teapot, and then pour it out, or pour back into the kettle. Place the tea leaves in the teapot, or in a strainer in the teapot. Fill the teapot halfway with the kettle water (about

Chai *(continued)*

4 cups), and add any additional flavorings to the teapot. Place the kettle back on the heat, and reduce the heat to medium-low, so the water gently simmers. If the handle on the kettle collapses, collapse the handle, remove the cover, and place the teapot on top of the kettle to brew for 10 minutes. If that's not possible, set the teapot aside, cover with a tea cozy, and steep for 10 minutes.

To serve, pour the concentrated tea from the teapot a quarter or halfway up a glass, depending on how light or dark you prefer, and top with hot water from the kettle. Serve hot with nabat, honey, or a sugar cube, if you like.

Sharbat-e Reevas
Rhubarb Sharbat

Iranians love the tang of rhubarb and use it often in savory stews. This rosy-hued sweet-and-sour sharbat is a lovely way to usher in spring. Make sure you save the rhubarb pulp after straining to spread on toast, stir into yogurt, or simply eat by the spoonful. Mix with either still or sparkling water.

SERVES 6

1 pound rhubarb (about 7 stalks), cut into 2-inch pieces

1 cup sugar

3 tablespoons fresh lime juice

1 teaspoon rose water (optional)

Place the rhubarb in a heavy-bottomed, nonreactive pot. Add the sugar, and set aside to macerate for 1 hour. Add 5½ cups water, stir to combine, and bring to a boil over high heat to dissolve the sugar. Reduce the heat to medium-low, and simmer for 20 minutes. Strain into a bowl. Scrape all the good stuff stuck to the bottom of the strainer into the liquid, and remember to save the pulp. Return the strained liquid to the pot, add the lime juice, and simmer on medium-low for 10 minutes, until slightly thickened. Remove from the heat, stir in the rose water (if using), and set aside to cool. Transfer the sharbat to a glass jar, cover, and keep in the fridge for up to a couple of weeks.

TO MAKE A PITCHER: In a large pitcher, combine the sharbat with 5 cups cold water. Stir, taste, and dilute with more water as needed. Store in the fridge to chill. Stir (the sharbat settles at the bottom) and serve over ice.

FOR AN INDIVIDUAL SERVING: Mix ¼ cup sharbat with ¾ cup water. Taste and add more sharbat or water, if necessary. Serve over ice.

Paloudeh Talebi

Cantaloupe Slushy

Los Angeles really starts to heat up in September. Just as everyone else seems to be readying for sweaters and boots, we crank the air conditioner and pull out the blender to blitz this refreshing and super-simple icy cantaloupe slushy. Paloudeh Talebi is sold at street stalls at the height of summer in Iran, and it is slurped back on rotation at the first signs of fall in our house in Los Angeles. This drink is all about the melon, so make sure you use a very sweet and ripe cantaloupe. If your cantaloupe isn't quite sweet enough you can gently sweeten it with a light drizzle of honey, or maple syrup, or a dusting of sugar. But prime summer melons shouldn't need any additional sweetening. You can also make this slushy with honeydew and watermelon.

SERVES 4 TO 6

1 large sweet and ripe cantaloupe

1 cup crushed ice (plus more as needed)

1 teaspoon rose water (optional)

2 fresh mint leaves (optional; plus extra for garnish)

Honey, maple syrup, or sugar (optional)

Place all the ingredients in a blender and blitz. You may need to give the cantaloupe a little push and shove at first to get the blender going. Taste and sweeten if necessary, and add more ice if needed. Blitz again, garnish with mint leaves, and serve right away.

Rosé-Dipped Strawberry Rose Ice Pops

Whoever came up with the idea of dipping ice pops into adult beverages has my personal gratitude. This is a fun way for both adults and kids to enjoy a light and bright drink/dessert, lightly perfumed with a hint of rose water, on those summer evenings begging for something cool and sweet. The kids can enjoy the ice pops as is. And the adults can pour themselves a fancy glass of crisp rosé and tint it deeper with dips of rosy strawberry ice pops. Everyone happily sipping and slurping away.

The ice pops shouldn't need any additional sweetening if you use sweet, ripe, in-season strawberries. If the strawberries need a little perking up, you can drizzle in a touch of honey, or maple syrup, or a sprinkling of sugar. Alternatively, you can set the strawberries aside to macerate in a little sugar and then use.

SERVES 8

---

2 pounds ripe, sweet, height-of-the-season strawberries, halved

A splash of rose water, to taste

Sweetener of choice, honey, maple syrup, or sugar (optional)

1 bottle rosé wine

Fresh mint leaves

Place the strawberries in a blender, drizzle with rose water, and blend until smooth. You might have to stop and nudge the strawberries around a little to get them going. Taste and sweeten a little, if you like. Evenly pour the mixture in eight ice pop molds and freeze overnight.

To serve, pour a crisp rosé wine into widemouthed cocktail glasses or wine glasses, dip in an ice pop, garnish with mint, and serve right away.

MAKE AHEAD: The ice pops can be prepared up to 3 days in advance.

Sharbat-e Tambreh Hendi

Tamarind and Orange Blossom Sharbat

If you love Mexican agua frescas, Sharbat-e Tambreh Hendi will definitely hit the spot. The tart bite of tamarind is lightly perfumed here with a hint of orange blossom water. My mother-in-law, Susan, and I came up with the Tambreh Hendi cocktail after an epic day of cooking, and it quickly became our favorite aperitif. Look for a tamarind concentrate (see page 352) without any added ingredients, which can alter the overall taste.

SERVES 6

FOR THE SHARBAT

1 cup sugar

¼ cup tamarind concentrate

1½ teaspoons orange blossom water

Orange slices

In a medium saucepan, combine the sugar and 1 cup water over medium-high heat. Stir and simmer until the sugar completely dissolves, 3 to 5 minutes. Add the tamarind concentrate, reduce the heat to medium-low, and simmer for 5 minutes. Turn off the heat and stir in the orange blossom water. Set aside to completely cool. Transfer to a glass jar, cover, and keep in the fridge until ready to use. Makes about 1½ cups syrup.

TO MAKE A PITCHER: In a large pitcher combine the sharbat with 5 cups cold water. Stir, taste, and dilute with more water if necessary. Add a few sliced oranges, and store in the fridge to chill. Stir (the sharbat settles at the bottom), and serve over ice with extra orange slices as garnish.

FOR INDIVIDUAL SERVINGS: Mix ¼ cup sharbat with ¾ cup water. Taste and add more sharbat or water, if necessary. Serve over ice and garnish with a couple of orange slices.

FOR THE COCKTAIL

1 to 1¼ ounces tequila

1 ounce tamarind sharbat

4 ounces sparkling water

Orange slice

Ice

FOR INDIVIDUAL COCKTAILS: Combine the tequila, sharbat, and sparkling water in a glass. Stir well, garnish with an orange slice, and serve over ice.

Anar Aablamboo

Squeezed Pomegranate Juice

If Khoresh Gormeh Sabzi (page 154) is considered Iran's national dish, then pomegranates are Iran's national fruit. This ancient ruby-red fruit is native to Iran, and symbolism and mythology drip from its jewel-like seeds. Pomegranates symbolize a crimson new dawn during the celebration of the winter solstice called Shabeh Yalda. They're also known to represent life, fertility, and beauty. But symbolism and mythology aside, every Persian child will tell you that their favorite way to drink pomegranate juice is right out of the fruit, by placing their mouth right on the skin and squeezing its tangy sweet juices right into their mouths. It's no different in our house. Come late fall, my husband, Drew, is in charge of squeezing and softening the fruit, until the seeds crunch and pop, and then handing it off to the girls to juice right into their mouths. It can get messy, but it's pure, life-affirming joy.

Look for a pomegranate with bulging skin, rather than a smooth skin. This means the pomegranate is ripe and juicy. If you are new to juicing pomegranate in this manner I recommend doing it over the kitchen sink, or outdoors, to begin with, until you get the hang of it. You might also want to slip on an apron.

1 pomegranate

Gently but firmly squeeze the pomegranate with both hands to release the juice inside the seeds. As the seeds crunch and pop under your fingers, the fruit will soften. Work your way through the entire fruit. You want the pomegranate to soften, but take care not to overdo it or the fruit will burst. And take care not to break the skin. But if you do—don't panic—try to recover as much of the juice as possible right away.

Once the pomegranate has softened, poke a small hole in the skin with the tip of a sharp knife. BE READY. The juice is going to come gushing through. Immediately put the fruit to your mouth and squeeze out the juice. And when you think you've squeezed it all out, squeeze a little more—there's always a little more left. You can use this same method to squeeze the juice into a glass. Not as fun, but a little less messy.

Ghaveh Tork

Turkish Coffee

Iranians are tea drinkers through and through, but there is also a deep tradition of enjoying Turkish coffee in homes and coffeehouses. The ritual of a late-morning Turkish coffee is not one to be rushed. If you're going to do it, take the time to sit and enjoy it, preferably shared with a friend or two. Turkish coffee is prepared in a chezve—a pot with a long handle— and served in small espresso-type cups. It's a rich and aromatic coffee, made with Arabica beans. It's quite potent, so one small cup is all you need.

First, clear your palate with a small glass of water. Then take your time and slowly sip the thick, rich coffee, with the creamy foam on top, accompanied with a small bite of something sweet, maybe a small piece of Baghlava Cake (page 316). Sip just until you get to the thick, muddy layer at the bottom. Then flip the cup over and allow figures and pictures to drip and form on the side of your cup, a window into your future. Peer deep into your cup, or better yet have a friend look into your cup and tell you all about it. Because "the future looks bright," as my grandmother Maman Ghashangi always told me.

Turkish coffee

Sugar (optional)

For each person measure out 1 Turkish coffee cup (the one you'll be drinking from) of room-temperature water and pour it in the chezve. Add 1 heaping teaspoon Turkish coffee per person. If anyone would like sugar, measure out a scant teaspoon of sugar and add it to the chezve. You will have to make a separate pot for those who do not want sugar. Place the chezve over low heat and slowly heat up, stirring to dissolve the sugar. As soon as it comes to a quick boil a layer of foam rises up to the top. Remove the chezve from the heat (don't turn off the heat). With a small spoon evenly divide the froth between the coffee cups. Return the chezve to the stove and heat again just until it foams and rises again. Remove from the heat and evenly divide the remaining coffee in the coffee cups. Don't stir the coffee once you serve it, as it will disturb the thick layer on the bottom and the coffee will taste gritty. Don't drink the thick layer at the bottom of the cup. That stuff is going to tell your future. Clear your palate with a small glass of water first, and then slowly sip and enjoy your Turkish coffee with a bite of something sweet.

SWEETS

LOVE

I hike up my gown and join Drew, my new husband, sitting on the curb looking off into the hills. If I stand back up and perch on my toes I might catch a glimpse of the Pacific shimmering in the distance. All the guests and family have left, and the waterproof candles floating in the small pool slowly burn off.

Just a few hours earlier, as I was getting primped for our wedding ceremony, I noticed friends and family speaking in hushed tones, and from the wide windows looking out to the grassy fields, I watched as Drew worriedly ran his hands through his hair, in deep conversation with his groomsmen and groomswoman. Something was amiss, and I was not in on it. After a little prodding, it was finally revealed that the people delivering our wedding cake had lost their way and were on their way back to the bakery, about two hours away. Our thoughtful Persian caterer, Mr. Rahbar, had found out about this calamity just as he, his crew, and the entire wedding feast were making their way up to the reception, and in an effort to save the cake they turned around to retrieve it. For Mr. Rahbar, the moment was thick with symbolism and he was not about to let our future be tainted with the bad omen of a missing wedding cake.

At the Persian table, *shirini*—sweets—symbolize love.

Like a game of telephone, messages were delivered back and forth between me and Drew. At this point, having lost both our caterer and the cake, my husband-to-be wanted to assure me that he'd figure something out. In the midst of all the commotion, it occurred to me that I could simply walk outside and speak to Drew myself, reassuring him that we would work this out together, just as we had everything else leading up to this moment. Instead, I played along and asked my bride's squire to let him know that I was not worried at all and that I had a plan. We would find the closest McDonald's and buy them out of all their burgers and sundaes—dinner and dessert.

The platters of saffron steamed rice, *khoresh fesenjan*, *baghali polo*, *khoresh na'na jafari*, the kababs, the fruit platters, and tubs of *bastani-yeh gol-o bolbol* (saffron and rose ice cream) and *faloudeh*, flashed right before my eyes. All the planning, and debate over what to serve, had all come to this: McDonald's to the rescue. Like an old spaghetti western with Clint Eastwood riding into town, cheroot hanging off his lip, ready to save the day.

Having settled on our plan B, we decided to get on with the ceremony. I linked arms with Maman on one side and Baba on the other as we made our way down to Drew, our families, friends, and the *sofreh aghd*—the traditional Persian wedding table.

Unlike the symbiotic companionship of the rice pot and the pot of stew, my parents' marriage existed either at the deafening silences of a barely there simmer or the thunderous storms of a high boil. But sometimes, on an agreeable day, there was the gentle warmth of mutual respect. And during those most trying of times, from Iran to Italy to Canada, they stood shoulder to shoulder, their love and devotion to their children never faltering. So once again, they took their places next to me and guided me down a grassy path, a new life on the shores of the Pacific, and potentially, a feast of cold burgers and fries.

The theme from *Il Postino* echoed off the hilltops as my stomach churned with joy, love, and the fear of my four-inch heels sinking deep into the grass as our threesome slowly approached Drew, the anxious groom. On cue, the guests rose, and suddenly there was a collective gasp. My veil had caught on a branch and I was stuck. In an instant Drew leaped over the decorative table dotted with sweets perfumed with rose water and cardamom, his pant legs just missing the flames from the candles, and untangled me from the twigs and branches. Laughter spread as we took the last few steps together, hand in hand, bride and groom. And just as we sat in front of the sofreh aghd, reflected in the *ayenehyeh bakht* (mirror of fortune), we caught a glimpse of our caterer's van pulling up, wedding cake and Persian feast in tow.

Sweets for a sweeter life.

At the end of the night, as I join Drew on the curb, he stretches his legs and reaches for the large container of gol-o bolbol ice cream left behind by Mr. Rahbar. Gol-o bolbol—flowers and nightingales—the messengers of love. The scents of rose water, saffron, fresh cream, and pistachios drift out into the still, dark August night. We take stock of our surroundings. Not a single spoon, fork, or cup to be found. The groom looks to his bride. He rolls up his sleeves as I secure the new ring on my finger. We smile at each other, a look of cahoots, a look that will carry us through thick and thin for years to come. We lean into each other and dig, one finger at a time, into the sweet churned ice cream.

Persian sweets range from delicate pastries to puddings, compotes, cream- and fruit-filled cakes, frozen treats, and intricate traditional dishes like Halva (page 340). Most of these sweets are often enjoyed with a midmorning or afternoon cup of tea. And some, such as Shir Berenj—Persian Rice Pudding (page 338) can be served for breakfast.

Typically, heavy desserts aren't served after a Persian meal. Instead we might put out a few dates or small bites of Baghlava Cake (page 316) to enjoy alongside an after-dinner chai. And nothing satisfies a Persian sweet tooth more than an abundant fruit platter. Iranians love snacking on fruit all day long and take great care in arranging a company-worthy fruit platter boasting all kinds of in-season fruits, with Persian cucumbers tucked in between. Growing up we actually had a place setting for fruit, complete with fruit forks and knives.

In this chapter I've handpicked some of our favorite Persian and Persian-inspired treats, including my childhood favorites like Roulette Cake (page 322), Napoleon Cake (page 335), and Faloudeh Shirazi (page 319). You'll find many of these confections perfumed with rose water and cardamom. Think of them as the ubiquitous equivalent of vanilla and cinnamon in Western desserts.

Baghlava Cake

For as long as I can remember, my mom has always had Baghlava Cake at the ready in the freezer to serve with tea just in case someone stops by. Little diamonds or squares of this cake also make an appearance at our Nowruz (Persian New Year) table. Baghlava is the Persian pronunciation for baklava. This cake is for those of us who are not quite up to rolling out sheet after sheet of phyllo for the more traditional baklava. Here I've traded out the butter or vegetable oil for olive oil, which, along with the almond flour, makes for a more tender cake. Make sure to use almond flour and not almond meal. Serve with a cup of tea or Turkish coffee.

FOR THE CAKE

1 cup (120 g) unbleached all-purpose flour

1 teaspoon baking powder

½ teaspoon baking soda

¼ teaspoon kosher salt

3 large eggs, at room temperature

½ cup sugar

½ cup olive oil

¼ cup rose water

1½ to 2 teaspoons ground cardamom, to taste

2 cups (192 g) almond flour

FOR THE GLAZE

¼ cup sugar

2 tablespoons rose water

TOPPING

1 tablespoon raw pistachios, finely chopped

Preheat the oven to 350°F with the rack set in the middle position. Lightly grease a 9 x 13-inch cake pan. Line the pan with parchment paper with enough overhang to be able to easily lift the cake out.

In a small bowl, combine the all-purpose flour, baking powder, baking soda, and salt. Set aside. In the bowl of a stand mixer fitted with the paddle attachment, or by hand, beat the eggs and sugar until well combined. Add the olive oil, rose water, and cardamom, and combine. Add the all-purpose flour mixture and the almond flour in alternating batches. Mix until just combined, but don't overmix. Spread the batter evenly into the prepared pan. It will spread thick, so make sure you get all the corners. Bake until lightly golden on top and a toothpick inserted into the middle of the cake comes out clean, about 30 minutes.

While the cake bakes, prepare the glaze. In a small pot, combine the sugar and ½ cup water over medium-high heat. Stir and bring

to a very gentle boil to dissolve the sugar (stay close, as this happens quickly). Keep at a rapid simmer for 3 minutes. Remove from the heat, and stir in the rose water. Set aside.

Remove the cake from the oven. Gently lift the cake out of the pan using the overhanging parchment, and set it on a board. Cut the cake into diamonds or about 1½-inch squares. Using a spoon, drizzle the glaze evenly over the hot cake. Pause in between drizzles to allow the cake to absorb the glaze. Sprinkle the top with the pistachios. Allow the cake to completely cool. Serve at room temperature, or store in the fridge in an airtight container and serve chilled.

MAKE AHEAD: This cake freezes very well. Store in an airtight container with pieces of parchment paper in between and freeze for up to 1 month.

Faloudeh Shirazi with Roasted Rhubarb

Faloudeh Shirazi, or paloudeh *as we call it in my house, is my personal favorite Persian dessert. It's reputed to be the oldest dessert, the original granita or sorbet, and the inspiration for all frozen treats to follow, including ice cream. And after millennia it still holds its own. Faloudeh is a sweetened and perfumed* sharbat—syrup—*frozen with thin pieces of rice vermicelli. It's served drizzled with lemon juice or sour cherry juice, something tart to cut through the sweetness. I've topped it here with roasted rhubarb for a hint of color and that touch of something sour. The rhubarb topping is optional, as it's seasonal; simply serve with lemon juice if not using the rhubarb. You can prepare faloudeh much in the same way granita is prepared. Start a few hours before you want to serve, and rake with a fork every couple of hours. If not serving right away, store the faloudeh in an airtight container in the freezer, and set out to thaw for about fifteen minutes before serving.*

SERVES 6 TO 8

FOR THE FALOUDEH

1¼ cups sugar

¼ cup rose water

1½ ounces rice vermicelli

Fresh lemon juice, to serve

FOR THE ROASTED RHUBARB

½ pound rosy rhubarb stalks, cut into ½-inch pieces

¼ cup sugar

In a small saucepan, combine the sugar and 2 cups water over medium-high heat. Stir and simmer until the sugar completely dissolves and comes up to a quick boil. Keep at a rapid simmer for 5 minutes. Remove from the heat, drizzle in the rose water, and set aside to cool to room temperature. Transfer to a freezer-safe bowl, and place in the freezer until it just begins to freeze, about 1 hour.

Meanwhile, prepare the noodles. Time this so the noodles can be added to the just-beginning-to-freeze syrup. In a small pot, bring 4 cups water to a boil. Add the noodles, reduce the heat to medium, and simmer until they soften, 5 to 10 minutes. Immediately drain and rinse with cold water, and add a couple of ice cubes on top to stop the noodles from cooking. Squeeze the noodles well to drain. With kitchen scissors, snip them into

Faloudeh Shirazi *(continued)*

1- to 1½-inch pieces. Add the noodles to the freezing syrup, stir gently to combine, separating the noodles the best you can, and place back in the freezer. Scrape the faloudeh with a fork, like a granita, every 1 to 1½ hours and place back in the freezer. Repeat until the faloudeh has fallen into place like a granita or a sorbet, about 5 hours total.

While the faloudeh freezes, you can prepare the rhubarb. Preheat the oven to 350°F with the rack in the center. Place the rhubarb and the sugar in a bowl, and macerate for 30 minutes. Transfer the rhubarb and all its juices to a baking dish in a single layer. Cover with foil, and roast for 15 to 20 minutes, just until the rhubarb is tender but not falling apart. Set aside to cool, and store with its juices in a container to use as needed.

Serve the faloudeh in individual bowls. Drizzle with fresh lemon juice, and top with roasted rhubarb (if using) and a drizzle of the rhubarb juice, if you like.

Roulette Cake

Right around the holidays, I start looking forward to the predictable and obligatory European Yule log cake. Most likely because it reminds me of the cream-filled rolled cakes I loved in Iran. Roulette Cake is very similar to a Swiss roll. It is light and pretty, and it's not annoyingly sweet. Once the cake bakes it needs to be rolled in a clean, damp towel, to help in the rolling process without the cake breaking and crumbling. I've added strawberries to the filling for a fresh pop of color and a bite of early summer. You can mix and match any berries you like, or simply serve with only the cream filling. This cake can be made one day in advance and sliced at the table for a beautiful and festive finish to a dinner party.

SERVES 8

4 large eggs, at room temperature

½ cup granulated sugar

½ teaspoon vanilla extract, or ½-inch vanilla bean, seeds scraped

½ cup (60 g) unbleached all-purpose flour, sifted

1½ cups heavy cream

3 tablespoons powdered sugar (plus more for dusting)

2 teaspoons rose water

1 pound sweet, in-season strawberries, hulled, halved or quartered depending on size

Dried rose petals (optional; see page 18)

Slivered or roughly chopped raw pistachios (optional)

Preheat the oven to 350°F with the oven rack in the center. Lightly oil a 9 x 13-inch baking sheet and line with parchment paper.

Separate the eggs. Place the egg yolks and the granulated sugar in the bowl of a stand mixer. Set the egg whites aside in a small bowl (you'll use them shortly). Using the whisk attachment, beat the yolks and the sugar on medium-high, until pale yellow and creamy, 4 to 5 minutes. Stir in the vanilla to combine, transfer to a large bowl, and set aside.

Wash out the whisk and the mixer bowl, and whisk the egg whites on medium until soft peaks form, 2 to 3 minutes. Fold the egg whites into the egg yolks and then fold in the flour. With a spatula, spread the batter evenly on the lined baking sheet. Make sure it's spread corner to corner, and bake until lightly golden and baked through, 10 to 12 minutes.

Meanwhile, dampen a kitchen towel large enough to cover the cake. Spread out the

towel on a cutting board and invert the cake onto it. Don't remove the parchment paper. Roll the cake into a log widthwise with the kitchen towel. The damp towel helps with the rolling. Set aside to completely cool to the touch, about 20 minutes.

Meanwhile, prepare the whipped cream. Place the cream, powdered sugar, and rose water in the chilled bowl of a stand mixer fitted with the whisk attachment. Whip on medium until soft peaks form, increase the speed to high, and whip until just set. Don't overmix, the whipped cream should be soft and spreadable. Store in the fridge until ready to use.

Set the cake roll on a board and unroll it. Carefully flip it around so the parchment side is facing up and the towel is on the bottom side. Gently peel back the parchment paper; it's okay if a thin layer of cake sticks to the parchment. Set aside about a quarter of the whipped cream and place back in the fridge. Spread the rest of the cream evenly over the cake, leaving a thin border.

Set aside a few strawberries as garnish and place the rest evenly over the whipped cream. With the help of the towel roll the cake into a log widthwise. Gently move the cake roll to a serving tray with the seam side down, and cover with plastic wrap placed directly on the log. Chill in the fridge for at least 1 hour or up to 24 hours.

To serve, remove the plastic wrap. Spread the remaining whipped cream on top of the cake, and top with a few strawberries. Scatter with crumbled dried rose petals, dust with powdered sugar, and garnish with slivered pistachios. Slice and serve.

MAKE AHEAD: The roulette can be made up to 1 day in advance, covered.

PREP AHEAD: The cream can be whipped and stored in the fridge in an airtight container up to 3 days in advance, but the scent of the rose water might dissipate a little.

Beh

Poached Quince

It takes some time, love, care, and patience to make a quince blush. But when you do, she rewards you like no other fruit. She's a chameleon of sorts. At first glance, she's tough, definitely astringent, and not very giving. But after a lazy bath in a slightly sweetened syrup she reveals her true self and all her glories. We love to eat and prepare quince in all manners. Gently poached, preserved, slowly cooked in savory stews, stuffed, and even raw, thinly sliced. It's also common to dry the seeds and make a gelatinous tea with them, claimed to cure a nasty cough.

Poached quince is one of our favorite winter sweet treats. Unlike traditional preparations, I prefer using less sugar, allowing the natural fragrance and taste of the quince to shine through. Sweeten to sate your taste buds. Serve simply, drizzled with its juices as an elegant dessert, as a topping for a creamy tart (page 328), on toast for breakfast, over yogurt as a snack, or with a dollop of fresh cream or mascarpone for something a little more decadent. Quince are in season by late fall and early winter, and they have become much more available at farmer's markets and some grocery stores.

MAKES ABOUT 4 CUPS

1 small lemon, halved

4 medium quince (about 2 pounds), peeled if the skin is very tough

½ cup sugar

Fill a large bowl with water, and squeeze half the lemon into it. Peel and slice the quince into about ¼- to ½-inch-slices. You'll have to put a little muscle behind this. Place the quince slices in the lemon water to keep the quince from turning brown. Make sure to completely cut out the tough core as it is very astringent. Place the seeds and peel in a cheesecloth. The peel and seeds are high in pectin, which will help thicken the quince syrup. Use if you like, but you can also skip this step.

In a heavy-bottomed pot, combine 3½ cups water and the sugar, and turn up the heat to medium-high. Stir to dissolve the sugar, and bring to a gentle boil. Drain the quince slices and add to the pot along with a squeeze of the rest of the lemon. Place the cheesecloth with the quince peel and seeds in a corner of the pot. If the water doesn't quite cover the quince slices, add a little more water. Reduce the heat to low, and wrap the lid in a kitchen towel or a couple of layers of paper towel to catch

Beh *(continued)*

the condensation, just like making rice. Make sure the kitchen towel or paper towels are secured up top so they don't catch fire! Place the lid firmly back on the pot.

The quince will soften and are ready after about 1½ hours. But if you really want to make them blush, and I suggest you do, simmer for about 3 hours. The longer they simmer, the rosier they get, and your house will smell like a Persian garden.

Remove the cheesecloth, and discard the peel and seeds. Gently place the quince slices in a container and pour the juices over the top. Set aside to cool. Cover and store in the fridge for up to 1 month, if they don't get eaten before then.

Quince and Labneh Tart

My mother's favorite refrain has always been "all you need to live is a handful of dates, nuts, and a small bowl of yogurt." To this day whenever I travel, or just step out of the house, I make sure to stash a little baggie of dates and nuts in my purse—just in case. Juicy, plump dates stuffed with nuts or yogurt are a quick and energizing snack or after-dinner treat. In homage to these "little whispers," the all-you-need ingredients are combined here and trans-formed into a rich and creamy dessert. Labneh is really thick yogurt with the consistency of whipped cream cheese. You can purchase labneh at Middle Eastern markets and some grocery stores, but it's very easy to make at home. You can top this tart with rosy poached quince (page 325) or with any poached fruit you like, or simply top with fresh summer ber-ries and a dusting of powdered sugar. Since I can't stash it in my purse, I like to serve Quince and Labneh Tart at home as an afternoon pick-me-up with a hot cup of tea.

SERVES 6 TO 8

TO MAKE YOUR OWN LABNEH

4 cups (one 32-ounce container) plain full-fat yogurt

Place a large fine-mesh strainer over a tall bowl. Line with a few layers of paper towel or cheesecloth. Place the yogurt in the lined strainer and cover with paper towels or cheesecloth. Place a small plate on top and place a large can (I use my neglected 5-pound hand weights) on top to weigh it down. Leave to strain in the fridge or at room temperature for 8 hours or up to 24 hours, until you have about 2 cups labneh.

Periodically check in on it and transfer the whey (the liquid in the bowl) to a jar so the bottom of the strainer never touches the whey. Labneh will keep in the fridge for more than a week.

MAKE AHEAD: The labneh can be prepared up to 1 week in advance.

FOR THE CRUST

1 cup raw almonds

1 cup walnut halves

1½ cups juicy plump dates (about 15), pitted and halved

2 teaspoons coconut oil

1 teaspoon vanilla extract

½ teaspoon ground cardamom

FOR THE FILLING

2 cups labneh, store-bought or homemade

3 tablespoons granulated sugar

2 teaspoons rose water, or 1 teaspoon orange blossom water

FOR THE TOPPING

Poached quince slices (page 325), about 25

1 tablespoon pistachios, chopped

Pomegranate seeds (optional)

OTHER SUGGESTIONS FOR TOPPING

Any poached fruit

Fresh summer berries

Sour Cherry Preserves (page 66)

Powdered sugar for dusting

Edible flowers for beauty

Lightly grease the bottom of an 8- or 9-inch springform cake pan. Line with parchment paper.

Place the nuts in a food processor, and pulse until the nuts are roughly chopped, but not powdered. Transfer to a bowl. Place the dates and the rest of the crust ingredients in the food processor. Process until you form a sticky paste. Add the nuts to the dates and pulse until you form a coarse mixture. The crust should come together and hold. Transfer to the prepared pan and spread the mixture evenly, packing it down with slightly wet hands or the back of a measuring cup. Place in the fridge while you prepare the filling.

Meanwhile, place all the filling ingredients in a bowl and combine well. The labneh should be nice and thick like cream cheese, so mixing will take a little effort. Evenly spread the filling on top of the crust, smoothing the top. Place in the fridge to set for 4 to 6 hours.

Arrange the poached quince slices on top of the labneh-filled tart. Garnish with chopped pistachios and pomegranate seeds (if using), and serve.

MAKE AHEAD: The tart can be made up to 3 days in advance but is best served within 24 hours as the crust might soften a little.

Chocolate Ferni

Chocolate Pudding

Ferni is a beloved rice flour pudding, also popular in various forms across the Middle East and India. Traditionally, it's prepared lightly sweetened with a hint of rose water, and served either warm or cold. Plain Ferni is every Persian mother's secret weapon in easing a sore throat. The smooth, creamy texture is said to coat and soothe the throat. This chocolate version doesn't have much to do with sore throats, but it certainly does lift everyone's spirits. Don't rush the process, though; keep stirring at a low heat for a smooth and light texture. Chocolate Ferni needs time to completely chill, which also makes it a fantastic make-ahead dessert for a party.

SERVES 6

¼ cup white rice flour

4 cups whole milk, divided

½ cup sugar

½ teaspoon ground cardamom (optional)

2 tablespoons unsweetened cocoa powder, sifted

3½ ounces bittersweet chocolate, finely chopped

1 teaspoon vanilla extract

TOPPINGS (OPTIONAL)

Fresh whipped cream

Chocolate shavings

Pistachio slivers

Raspberries

Strawberries

In a small bowl, whisk the rice flour and ½ cup of the milk until completely combined and not lumpy. Set aside. In a medium saucepan, combine the rest of the milk, the sugar, and the cardamom (if using) over medium-high heat. Stir or whisk frequently until small bubbles form on the surface and the sugar dissolves, about 5 minutes. Reduce the heat to medium-low and whisk in the rice flour mixture. Stir or whisk constantly for 10 minutes, and reduce the heat to low if necessary, making sure no clumps form and the pudding doesn't stick to the bottom of the pot or boil over.

Add the cocoa powder and the chopped chocolate. Stir well to combine. Keep stirring until the pudding thickens, coating the back of the spoon, 3 to 5 minutes. The pudding will thicken more as it cools, so you don't want it to get too thick as it cooks.

Immediately remove from the heat and stir in the vanilla. Quickly transfer to a large bowl or individual glasses or ramekins. Cover the surface of the pudding with plastic wrap so a skin doesn't form. Cool to room temperature and transfer to the fridge until well chilled, at least 6 hours. Serve as is or with any toppings you desire.

MAKE AHEAD: Ferni can be prepared 1 day in advance. Store it in the fridge.

Pistachio Sanbuseh

These light and flaky turnovers can be filled with savory meat or vegetable fillings (similar to a samosa), or they can be stuffed with a lightly sweetened filling. Here, raw pistachios are ground up and scented with cardamom and rose water. You need the rose water in the filling not only to perfume but also to help bind the pistachios. If you're not a fan of rose water, you can try orange blossom water (maybe a scant teaspoon, as it's stronger than rose water). Pistachio Sanbuseh are elegant enough to serve for dessert and easy enough to prepare and enjoy with an afternoon cup of tea.

MAKES 12 SANBUSEH

1 sheet puff pastry, thawed at room temperature

½ cup raw pistachios

¼ cup granulated sugar

1 teaspoon ground cardamom

1½ teaspoons rose water

Flour for dusting

Powdered sugar for dusting

Make sure the puff pastry thaws out only for the time recommended on the package, 30 to 40 minutes. If the pastry sits out too long it will be sticky and hard to work with.

Preheat the oven to 350°F with the oven rack in the center. Line a 12 x 18-inch baking sheet with parchment paper.

Grind the pistachios in a food processor or by hand with a knife. Place the ground pistachios in a small bowl and add the granulated sugar, cardamom, and rose water. Mix well.

Dust your workspace and rolling pin with flour. Roll out the puff pastry to about 9 x 12 inches or ⅛-inch thickness. Cut twelve 3-inch circles. Fill half of each circle with about 2 teaspoons of the pistachio mixture. Fold over the other half to form a half-moon shape. Seal the edges first with your fingers, and then crimp with a fork to ensure it's completely sealed. Make sure you get a good seal, otherwise the pistachio mixture will burst out, as it has been known to do for me. But even when it does, these sanbuseh are quite delectable. No stress.

Place the sanbuseh on the baking sheet with enough space in between each one so they have room to expand. Bake until golden on top, 18 to 20 minutes. Set aside to cool slightly, dust with powdered sugar, and serve with a cup of Turkish coffee (page 308) or tea.

MAKE AHEAD: Store in an airtight container on the counter for up to 1 day or in the fridge for up to 3 days.

PREP AHEAD: The pistachio mixture can be prepared up to 3 days in advance. Store in an airtight container in the fridge.

Orange Masghati

Think of masghati *as a cross between Jell-O and panna cotta. It's infinitely more refined than Jell-O, and it's not as wobbly as panna cotta. This Orange Masghati is a riff on the more traditional rose-scented one. Play around and use any fruit juice you like (pomegranate juice is also very popular). Masghati is traditionally prepared with wheat starch, commonly used in Persian kitchens as a thickener. Here, I've used cornstarch, which is easier to find than wheat starch, and it works just as well. The amount of sugar you use depends on your taste buds and how sweet the orange juice is. Make Orange Masghati a few hours in advance, and serve chilled out of the fridge with a drizzle of raspberry sauce.*

SERVES 6 TO 8

FOR THE MASGHATI

Butter for greasing the dish

3 cups no-pulp orange juice, divided

6 tablespoons cornstarch

3 tablespoons sugar (or to taste; optional)

Chopped raw pistachios (optional)

FOR THE RASPBERRY SAUCE

6 ounces raspberries

¼ cup sugar

⅓ cup hot water

Lightly butter a rimmed 1- to 2-inch-deep dish (a regular pie plate works well). Set aside.

In a small bowl, combine 1 cup of the orange juice with the cornstarch. Stir until completely smooth, without any lumps, and set aside. In a medium saucepan, combine the rest of the orange juice (2 cups) and the sugar (if using) over medium-high heat, and bring to a simmer to dissolve the sugar.

Give the cornstarch slurry a final stir to combine, and add it to the pot. Reduce the heat to medium and start stirring immediately. Continue stirring until it starts to thicken and set, about 5 minutes. Don't go anywhere during this process (the cornstarch sets quickly and can burn). You'll know the mixture is ready when it coats the back of a wooden spoon. You don't want it to get too thick as it will keep setting as it cools. Remove from the heat and immediately pour into the prepared dish and smooth over. Set

aside to cool at room temperature, and place in the fridge, uncovered, for 6 to 8 hours to fully set and chill.

Meanwhile, to make the sauce, set a few raspberries aside as garnish and place the rest along with the sugar and hot water in a blender. Blitz the raspberries until smooth. Transfer to a small bowl, and store in the fridge until ready to use.

To serve, you can either run a butter knife around the rim of the dish and invert the masghati onto a serving platter or serve directly from the dish. Serve cold, topped with pistachios, the reserved raspberries, and a light drizzle of the raspberry sauce.

MAKE AHEAD: Masghati is best prepared up to 1 day in advance. It will keep, covered, in the fridge up to 3 days.

Napoleon Cake

We have a small, old-school neighborhood bakery close to our house, the type that's quite rare in Los Angeles. Once in a while we like to stop by for an after-school treat. The glass cases display mouthwatering pastries and freshly made cakes, topped with cream and fresh fruits. Our little bakery pales in comparison to the elaborate pastry shops in Tehran, but it always reminds me of visits to those ghanadi—pastry shops—where we would pick up beautifully packaged boxes of sweet treats, like Napoleon Cake, as hostess gifts or to take home to share with family.

Napoleon Cake, related to the French pastry mille-feuille, is a classic layered puff pastry–and–pastry cream cake. You'll need to prepare a batch of pastry cream, which takes a little care and some good old-fashioned hand whisking. But it can all be done ahead of time. After that, layering the cream between sheets of flaky puff pastry takes no time at all. The whole thing can be assembled an hour or two ahead of time and served for a get-together or a party.

There doesn't seem to be a consensus as to why this cake is called Napoleon, but the theory that I found most appealing is that the cake has Russian roots and the crumbled pieces of puff pastry topping the cake represent the Russian snow that held back Napoleon's troops. Much like the Persian kitchen, symbolism abounds between every flake.

SERVES 8

2 tablespoons unsalted butter

½ cup granulated sugar

4 large egg yolks

¼ cup cornstarch

2 cups plus 2 tablespoons whole milk

1 teaspoon vanilla extract

2 sheets puff pastry, thawed at room temperature

Flour for dusting

2 tablespoons powdered sugar

Set up your workspace and have all the ingredients ready to go. Place the butter in a medium heatproof glass bowl that you will later use to store and chill the pastry cream. Set aside.

In a medium saucepan, whisk the granulated sugar, egg yolks, and cornstarch until smooth, and set aside.

In a small pot, heat the milk over medium heat, stirring often so the milk doesn't stick to the bottom of the pot, until it starts to foam, right under a boil, about 8 minutes. Reduce the heat to low, and place

Napoleon Cake *(continued)*

the egg-mixture pot beside you. Have a ladle and a whisk ready to go as you temper the eggs.

Slowly add a ladleful of the hot milk to the egg mixture as you whisk constantly and fervently so the eggs don't scramble. Keep adding about half of the hot milk, constantly whisking. If by any chance you curdle the eggs (it can happen), just pour the mixture through a strainer. Pour the rest of the milk into the egg-mixture pot, whisking away, and place the pot over medium heat. Keep whisking until the mixture thickens, and comes up just to a boil, about 5 minutes. It will feel like it will never thicken, but it will happen all of a sudden and very quickly. Just keep whisking away. As soon as it comes to a boil whisk for another 30 seconds or so to thicken, immediately remove from the heat, pour the mixture over the cold butter, and add the vanilla extract. Stir with a wooden spoon until the butter is mixed in and the cream is smooth. Set aside to cool for a couple of minutes, and then place a plastic wrap directly on the surface so the cream doesn't dry out and form a skin. Place in the fridge to chill completely, about 4 hours.

Preheat the oven to 350°F with the racks set in the upper third and lower third. Line two large baking sheets with parchment paper.

Make sure you only thaw out the puff pastry for the time recommended on the package, 30 to 40 minutes. If the pastry sits out too long it will be very hard to work with.

Flour your counter and rolling pin. Gently roll out each sheet to ⅛-inch thickness, about 12 x 16 inches. Place on the baking sheets and pierce all over with a fork. This is to keep them from puffing up, even though they'll still puff up a little. Bake for 25 to 30 minutes until golden. Leave to cool on the pan for a few minutes and then transfer to a cooling rack to cool completely.

To assemble, trim off about ½ inch of the edges of each pastry so they are even in size and uniform, about 8 x 10 inches. Crumble the trimmed pieces in a small bowl, toss with the powdered sugar, and set aside (you'll use this on top of the cake). Place one piece of pastry on a serving dish, spread half of the pastry cream on top and place the other piece of pastry on top, spread with the other half of pastry cream. Scatter the crumbled pieces of the puff pastry on top, like flakes of snow. Refrigerate for 1 hour and up to 24 hours. Cut and serve. It's easier to cut with a serrated knife on a board and then transfer back to the serving dish.

MAKE AHEAD: The pastry cream can be prepared up to 2 days in advance. Store in the fridge in an airtight container. The cake can be assembled up to 24 hours in advance.

Shir Berenj

Rice Pudding

Shir Berenj—Persian rice pudding—is at once down-to-earth, humble, elegant, and glamorous. Unlike most cloyingly sweet, gloopy rice puddings, this rice pudding is not sweetened at all, but served with a sweet toppings bar for everyone to sweeten as they like. The preparation requires some care and constant milk stirring, but the result is a decadent, creamy, rose-scented pudding that is worth every stir. The rose water here is key because it's the only essence perfuming and flavoring the pudding. You can serve this Shir Berenj as a dessert or for a special breakfast. For a striking presentation serve in individual clear glasses, so the pudding can shine like white snow, with sprinkles of green pistachios and maybe a few rose petals scattered on top and a drizzle of pure maple syrup.

SERVES 6

---

15 green cardamom pods

2½ cups whole milk

½ cup short-grain Japanese rice (sushi rice), rinsed and drained

1 tablespoon basmati rice, rinsed and drained

¼ teaspoon kosher salt

⅓ cup heavy whipping cream

¼ cup rose water, or to taste

TOPPINGS BAR SUGGESTIONS

Maple syrup

Honey

Sour Cherry Preserves (page 66)

Poached quince (page 325)

Orange blossom preserves (available at Middle Eastern markets)

Any fruit preserves of choice

Fresh berries

Grape molasses (available at Middle Eastern markets)

Date molasses (available at Middle Eastern markets)

Set out your serving bowls.

Use the flat side of your knife to bruise and lightly crack open the cardamom pods. Place the pods in a medium heavy-bottomed pot. Pour the milk into the pot and bring to a boil over high heat, 3 to 5 minutes. You'll have to keep a very close eye on the milk so it doesn't boil over, and constantly stir so it doesn't burn and stick to the bottom of the pot. As soon as the milk comes to a boil remove from the heat and strain into a bowl. Set aside and discard the cardamom pods.

Place the rice, salt, and 1½ cups water in a medium pot. Stir to combine, and bring to a boil over high heat. Reduce the heat to medium-low and cook, uncovered, stirring frequently, until the rice softens and absorbs most of the water, 8 to 10 minutes. The rice should have a creamy consistency, not too dry and not too wet. Place the bowl of strained milk next to you. Add 1 cup of the milk to the rice, stir until the milk comes up to a gentle boil and the mixture thickens to a texture similar to yogurt, about 5 minutes, then add another cup of milk, stirring as you go. Continue adding 1 cup at a time until you have added the rest of the milk and the mixture has slightly thickened. Add the cream and the rose water, give a quick stir to incorporate, and remove from the heat.

Have your serving bowls ready to go. Immediately divide the rice pudding among the serving bowls or transfer to one large bowl. Set aside to cool for a few minutes. Cover the surface of the rice pudding with plastic wrap so a skin doesn't form, and cool to room temperature. Transfer the bowls to the fridge, and chill well for at least 6 hours. Serve the rice pudding with any sweeteners or toppings you like.

MAKE AHEAD: The rice pudding can be prepared up to 2 days in advance, but the scent of the rose water might dissipate slightly. It's best if it's made the night before.

Persian Halva

Halva is one of the most traditional and symbolic Persian sweets. You can find halva— which means "sweet" in Arabic—throughout the Middle East in various iterations. In the West we might be more familiar with sesame seed halva. Persian halva is commonly prepared with gently toasted wheat flour and clarified butter, and drenched in a sweet rose and saffron syrup. Symbolically, Iranians make trays of beautifully decorated halva during religious ceremonies and funerals as a giving of alms. But, of course, it can be made anytime.

Preparing halva can't be rushed. You're going to be at the mercy of the initial slow toasting of the flour. This is what will determine the color and taste of your halva, so be patient. Just when you think the flour is never going to turn color and release its aroma, it does, and quickly. There is a delicate fine line between aromatic toasted flour and bitter, burned flour. This is an impressive rich treat that wows guests, and the best part is that you can prepare it ahead of time, worrying and fretting as you go, and then pretend like it was nothing at all when you serve it. I love having a batch of halva stashed in the back of the fridge to nibble on with my afternoon cup of tea.

SERVES 8

¾ cup sugar

⅓ cup rose water

½ teaspoon ground saffron

½ teaspoon ground cardamom

1 cup (120 g) unbleached all-purpose flour, sifted

⅔ cup clarified butter, melted

DECORATIVE TOPPINGS (OPTIONAL)

Slivered blanched almonds

Ground or slivered raw pistachios

Dried rose petals (see page 18)

In a small pot, bring the sugar and ¾ cup water to just a quick boil over medium-high heat, stirring to dissolve the sugar, 3 to 5 minutes. Remove from the heat. Add the rose water, saffron, and cardamom, and stir well to combine. This is your syrup. Set it close by.

Place the flour in a medium pot or pan over medium heat. Toast the flour, continuously stirring and nudging the flour this way and that, until it releases its aroma and turns golden or golden-auburn, depending on what color you prefer for the halva. Just don't burn it. This will take 20 to 25 minutes. So put on some music, lean one hip into the counter, and stir, stir, stir. Play with the heat, turn it down to medium-low, if necessary.

(continued)

Persian Halva *(continued)*

You'll start thinking the flour will never turn color, and you'll be tempted to crank up the heat—don't. Just when you're ready to lose hope you'll be hit with a nutty scent of toasted flour, maybe around the 18-minute mark. And then the flour will start to take on color, and quickly. When you're happy with the color of the flour quickly move ahead.

Drizzle in the clarified butter. Stir well to combine with the flour, until smooth with no clumps. Make sure your head isn't too close to the pan, taking in all the wonderful scents. Give yourself some distance, and add the syrup. It's going to hiss, sizzle, and spit, so be careful, but move with confidence. Quickly and rapidly stir until the halva thickens and comes together, 5 to 8 minutes. It will have the consistency of soft dough or a smooth paste. Keep stirring until you get there.

Now comes the fun part. Lift the pan off the heat, and roll the halva back and forth a few times, holding each side of the pot or pan. Rock and roll for a few minutes to form a dough-like crescent. This helps set the texture and tells you the halva is ready.

Spoon the halva onto a flat plate and smooth it out. You can decorate it as you like. Pinch the edges, like piecrust, or indent the edges and the top with a spoon into half-moons. Get as creative as you like with any of the toppings you like. Set aside to cool and serve, or cover with plastic and store in the fridge and serve chilled. Halva can be scooped with a spoon or a piece of lavash bread or cut into bite-sized pieces.

MAKE AHEAD: Halva is best prepared up to 3 days in advance and stored in the fridge. It will keep in the fridge up to 1 week.

Bastani-e Gol-o Bolbol

Flowers and Nightingales Ice Cream

On a particularly hot day in Los Angeles, I set out to make the ice cream of my childhood. The bright saffron, rose-scented, stretchy, and chewy bastani, with soft bites of frozen cream under tooth and sprinkled with green Iranian pistachios. Iran's national ice cream— Bastani-e Gol-o Bolbol—flowers and nightingales ice cream. In Persian poetry and literature, flowers and nightingales are symbolic messengers of love and the beloved.

This ice cream is also more commonly known as bastani-e Akbar Mashti, named after the first man to open an ice cream parlor in Tehran. I have adapted the ice cream base recipe from Jeni Britton Bauer of Jeni's Splendid Ice Creams. The result is a fabulous, silky ice cream base without any unpleasant ice crystals, which I often have an issue with. The cream cheese is the trick here to help keep the ice crystals from forming. But the taste of the cream cheese is hardly detectable, especially when blended with fragrant saffron and rose water. I encourage all who feel intimidated by homemade ice cream to give this lovers' ice cream a try.

Back in our Los Angeles kitchen, as the ice cream churned, then five-year-old Soleil exclaimed, apropos of nothing and to no one in particular, "I wonder who I'm going to marry?" Flowers and nightingales must have perched on her shoulders, whispering sweet nothings in her ear, spinning tales of love, saffron, roses, and sweet cream.

MAKES 1 PINT

2 cups whole milk, divided

4 teaspoons cornstarch

1¾ cups heavy cream, divided

⅔ cup sugar

¼ teaspoon kosher salt

¼ teaspoon ground saffron, dissolved in 3 tablespoons rose water

3 tablespoons cream cheese, at room temperature

Chopped raw pistachios (optional)

Before starting, set aside a large bowl which you will use for the ice bath and a medium bowl (that can fit in the larger bowl) for the ice cream mixture.

In a small bowl, stir together ¼ cup of the milk and the cornstarch until well combined. Set the slurry aside. In a medium pot, over medium-high heat, whisk together the remaining milk, 1¼ cups of the heavy cream, the sugar, and salt, and bring to a boil. This will take about 10 minutes. Whisk or stir often so the milk doesn't boil over or stick to the bottom of the pot. Don't go too far. When it comes to a boil, stir and cook for

Bastani-e Gol-o Bolbol *(continued)*

4 minutes longer. Stir in the cornstarch slurry, return to a boil, and cook, stirring, until thickened, 2 to 4 minutes. Remove from the heat, and stir in the saffron rose water.

Place the cream cheese in the medium bowl you had set aside, pour in ¼ cup of the hot milk mixture, and whisk until smooth. Try to get it as smooth as possible. Whisk in the remaining milk mixture, until smooth and no lumps remain. Prepare your ice bath. Fill the large bowl halfway with cold water and throw in some ice cubes. Place the bowl with the ice cream base inside the ice bath and let cool until completely chilled. Alternatively, you can transfer the mixture to the fridge until well chilled.

In the meantime, pour a thin layer of the remaining heavy cream across a small freezer-safe tray or plate. Place in the freezer until frozen.

Pour the chilled base into an ice cream maker, and process according to the manufacturer's instructions. Remove the frozen cream, break off into small pieces, and add it to the ice cream in the final minute of churning. Transfer the ice cream to a container, place a piece of parchment directly on top, cover, and freeze until set, about 4 hours. Take the ice cream out of the freezer 5 minutes before scooping. Top with pistachios, if desired.

MAKE AHEAD: The ice cream can be prepared up to 3 days in advance.

EPILOGUE

UNTIL WE MEET AGAIN

It concludes with a splash of water. As it always will.

Our summer vacations in Vancouver inevitably come to a close with Drew, the girls, and me loading suitcases into our rental car. They are stuffed with various fresh baked breads (*barbari, sangak*) from the local Persian bakery, paper bags brimming with dried mulberries—*toot*—pistachios, almonds, a securely closed orange pill bottle or two filled with newly ground saffron, *kotlet* and pickle sandwiches for the plane ride home, and sturdy containers, double and triple sealed, filled with home-made *khoresh*. Never mind that we're returning to Los Angeles, home to the largest Iranian community outside of Iran, with plenty of its own Persian markets teeming with all these goods.

Only a year ago Maman would have walked us out, a pitcher of water in hand, as Baba and my stepmother, Kumi, pulled up, ready to follow (escort) us to the airport. Even in these days of rental cars and independence, Baba would always show up at the airport to properly greet us or bid us adieu. But it has gotten harder for Maman to make her way downstairs, and Baba is no longer able to make the drive.

Instead, as we pull away, Maman stands at her balcony, a tall glass of water in hand. As we roll down our windows, the girls frantically wave good-bye, and from the rear window we watch as Maman splashes the water behind us. No matter how secular and pragmatic a household, there are certain rituals that are ingrained deep, that bring solace. For Maman it's the splashing of water, and for Baba, it's the airport escort. In Persian tradition, splashing water behind travelers symbolizes safe travels and the hope of meeting again soon.

The first couple of splashes come at us in quick, gushing waves, but as we slowly turn the corner we lose sight of Maman, and the last remaining drops trickle down the rear window, leaving a flowing river behind us. These gentle streams and rivers have carried us across three continents and over three decades, just as the scent of saffron steamed rice has pulled us back home. Wherever that may be.

On our way to the airport, Baba calls to make sure that we're on time. He makes us promise to call twice, once at boarding and once when we land. A few moments later my brother, Ramin, calls from Toronto, checking in to see if Maman splashed the water, if Baba called, and what we're planning on making for dinner.

A life spent departing, arriving, and contemplating dinner.

And so I leave you with rivers and streams, and the hope that you will find your way back to these pages when the conversation inevitably turns to dinner—as it always does.

Until we meet again.

APPENDIX

Pucker Up Ingredients

DRIED LIMES—*LIMOO OMANI* These hard, shriveled-up, somewhat alien-looking dried limes deliver a unique Persian burst of flavor and fragrance to stews, Aabgoosht, and even tea. To use limoo Omani give them a rinse, dry them very well, and set them on a cutting board. Using the tip of a sharp paring knife or a fork, very carefully pierce them in a couple of spots. As the limoo Omani cook they will soften and release their juices. You can help them along by squeezing them a couple of times with a wooden spoon against the side of the pot, releasing their juices and flavor. But don't squeeze so much that they burst, as the seeds can be bitter and the color of your dish might turn more brown. You can discard them once the dish is served, but some people (like me) enjoy eating them along with the food. I don't recommend eating the seeds though. If you plan on making Khoresh Gheymeh (page 165), Khoresh Ghormeh Sabzi (page 154), Aabgoosht (page 92) or Soup-e Jo ba Adas (page 84) I highly recommend seeking out limoo Omani which can be found at Iranian or Middle Eastern stores and online.

FERMENTED YOGURT—*KASHK* Kashk is often labeled as "whey." However, it is not whey, as we associate whey with the yellowish liquid left over from straining yogurt. Iranian kashk is often made from cooked-down and concentrated yogurt. It has an extremely rich and intense flavor, much like a pungent aged cheese like Parmesan. Kashk can be added to *aash*, eggs, and dips for a rich depth of flavor. Much like the addition of a Parmesan rind to a soup, kashk packs plenty of flavor to any dish it is added to. You can purchase dried balls of kashk, which need to be rehydrated in water, or you can purchase thick liquid kashk in jars from an Iranian or Middle Eastern market. The Sadaf brand is a good choice. I prefer using liquid kashk and can eat the stuff by the spoonful, which is not surprising, as it is part of the yogurt family.

LEMONS AND LIMES—*LIMOO, LIMOO TORSH* A Persian kitchen is always well-stocked with plenty of lemons and limes on hand. They are consistently used to flavor and brighten

up stews, soups, dips, marinades, salads, and drinks, and they're drizzled on granita-like desserts to balance the sugars. I think of lemons as the Band-Aid of cooking. When all else fails, add a squeeze of lemon to just about anything to rescue most cooking mishaps. Fresh lemon and lime juice (not the stuff stored in plastic bottles) can be used as a substitute for most of the acids used in this book.

POMEGRANATE MOLASSES/CONCENTRATE—*ROBB-E ANAR* Pomegranate molasses has become much more popular and available in the West, which is good news for all lovers of Persian food, in particular northern Iranian cuisine where pomegranate molasses is frequently used in stews, soups, dips, and marinades. Pomegranate molasses is simply reduced pomegranate juice, often with a little added sugar. Pomegranate concentrate has no added sugar. Try incorporating a little in your salad dressing, or drizzle it as is on roasted vegetables. Bottles of pomegranate molasses can vary quite distinctly in flavor. Some are more sweet, some more sour, and some slightly bitter. The dishes in this book rely on the more sour variety, but I suggest trying out a couple of different brands to see which one appeals to your taste buds. Look for pomegranate molasses at most grocery stores, specialty stores, Iranian or Middle Eastern stores, and online. I currently like to use Sadaf sour pomegranate molasses with a touch of Cortas brand mixed in.

SOUR GREEN GRAPES—*GHOOREH* These are the sour green grapes that verjuice is made from. My kids call them sour pops. Sour green grapes have a very short season, a few weeks in midsummer, so Iranians flock to the market to stock up on these mouth-puckering little grapes. Sour green grapes are not for eating out of hand; instead they are added to stews, *aash*, and sauces for acidity and a bright pop of flavor. As they cook down, they soften, releasing their flavor and juices, and can be eaten with the finished dish. If you happen to come across fresh sour green grapes, remove them from the stem, soak them in water to remove dust and grit, rinse them, and dry them completely. Use them fresh or freeze them in resealable plastic bags to use all year round. Sour green grapes can also be purchased pickled in jars. Rinse these with fresh water as they're typically quite salty from the brine. Add ghooreh to any stew, soup, or sauce for an unexpected sour pop.

SOUR GREEN PLUMS—*GOJEH SABZ* Sour green plums are unripened plums, and we love to eat them out of hand with a sprinkle of salt. But they are also used to cook whole in stews, such as Khoresh Na'na Jafari (page 152) and *aash*. The harder and sourer, the better they are for cooking. Be mindful when serving and eating, as they have pits. Sour green plums are available for a brief whisper of a moment in the spring; find them online and in Iranian, Middle Eastern, and Mediterranean markets. I've also been spying them at farmers' markets. If you see them, grab a bag. And if you don't finish the entire bag by the time you get home, throw some in a fresh and flavorful stew.

TAMARIND—*TAMBREH HENDI* Tamarind pulp, made from the fruit of the tamarind tree, appears typically in the cuisine of the southern region of Iran. Tamarind packs quite a sour punch so it's usually mixed with a sweetener like sugar or honey for balance. It can be used in stews and soups and it also makes a refreshing chilled drink, Sharbat-e Tambreh Hendi (page 304), much like the popular Mexican *agua fresca de tamarindo*. You can purchase tamarind as a solid block, which needs to be soaked and then pushed through a sieve to separate the pulp from the seeds and fiber. This can be a little bit of work so I prefer to use tamarind concentrate, which can be found at most grocery stores in the international foods aisle, online, or in Middle Eastern, Indian, and Mexican markets. Just be sure to use a jar that only lists tamarind in its ingredients list, as some can be packed with preservatives, salt, and such. My current favorite brand is Neera's.

TOMATO PASTE—*ROBB-E GOJEH FARANGI* Tomato paste is right up there with lemons, limes, and yogurt as an indispensable ingredient in the Persian pantry. It delivers the requisite acidity, depth of flavor, body, and color to any number of stews, *aash*, and sauces. Just like any other ingredient, not all tomato pastes are created equal. Try different brands, and find one that has a deep and rich flavor. You can add tomato paste directly to a dish or first dilute it in hot water. I store leftover tomato paste from a jar or can in a small resealable plastic bag, flattening it out into a thick block, freezing, and breaking off chunks as needed.

VERJUICE OR VERJUS—*AAB GHOOREH* Verjuice is the juice of unripe sour green grapes. It is milder and more delicate in tanginess and acidity than white wine vinegar, and it is commonly used to lift and brighten Persian stews, *aash*, and dips. You can purchase jars online or from Iranian, Middle Eastern, Mediterranean, or specialty markets. Use verjuice as you would lemon juice in sauces or dressings for a delicate burst of flavor.

VINEGAR—*SERKEH* Red wine, white wine, and apple cider vinegars are the workhorses in salad dressings, and they are used as a finishing touch and flavor enhancer in *aash*, dips, cooling drinks, and as a base for *torshi*—Persian-style pickles. I also like to drizzle the more syrupy-sweet balsamic vinegar on Aash-e Shooli (page 87).

YOGURT—*MAAST* Yogurt at the Persian table is nonnegotiable. A tub of plain, cooling, creamy yogurt is always present, enjoyed on the side with the rice and stew dishes to cut through the richness and aid in digestion. Persian kitchen folklore touts yogurt as the healer of almost anything. Yogurt is consistently used as a base for a myriad of dips, dolloped on *aash* for depth of flavor and a silky finish, stirred into eggs, used as a tenderizer in marinades, and is the star ingredient in Aash-e Dogha (page 76).

A Field of Greens Ingredients

BASIL—*REYHAN* Persian basil is the sweet, intoxicatingly fragrant, smaller-leafed variety, also known as lemon basil. Persian basil is most often used fresh and raw as part of a Sabzi Khordan platter (page 32), or it is tucked in a sandwich. Look for Persian (lemon) basil in Iranian and Asian markets, or at farmers' markets.

CILANTRO AND GROUND CORIANDER—*GASHNEEZ* Cilantro is abundantly used in stews, *aash*, and dips. And the bright citrus flavor of ground coriander (the seed of the cilantro plant) can be added to soups, stews, and spice mixes.

DILL (FRESH AND DRIED)—*SHEVEED* Both fresh and dried dill are staples in my spice cupboard and crisper, and they are used interchangeably in dips and main dishes.

FENUGREEK—*SHANBALILEH* Fenugreek is an herb used commonly in Persian and Indian cooking. Fresh fenugreek is harder to come by, but can be found at Indian markets and Middle Eastern markets. Dried fenugreek is more commonly available and used in Persian kitchens. It is quite bitter on its own but used in small quantities, it imparts a distinct bitter-sweet flavor, especially in Khoresh Ghormeh Sabzi (page 154).

GREEN ONIONS—*PIAZCHEH* Green onions are abundantly used by the bunch, and they appear either raw in a Sabzi Khordan platter (page 32) or cooked in *aash* or stews. Take care not to chop green onions to a mush in the food processor as they can turn bitter.

MINT—*NA'NA* Of all the fresh and dried green herbs, my favorite and most used is dried mint. Dried mint is not necessarily a direct substitute for the fresh variety, as it has a deeper and bolder flavor and fragrance. I love sprinkling dried mint on all sorts of yogurt-based dips, fried onions, and to a variety of stews and *aash*. Rub dried mint between your fingers to release its perfume and flavor. It is also believed that mint aids in the digestion of harder-to-digest ingredients such as beans, so you'll see a little mint added to most bean-based aash. Fresh mint (regular mint/spearmint, not peppermint) is used in a Sabzi Khordan platter (page 32) and also cooked in stews. Keep in mind that mint, both fresh and dried, can quickly burn and turn bitter.

PARSLEY—*JAFARI* Parsley, so often relegated to a sad, overlooked side garnish in Western cuisine, is enthusiastically embraced and loved by Iranian cooks. Some claim curly parsley to be juicier, with a fresher, brighter flavor, while some consider the more fashionable flat-leaf parsley more flavorful. In the true spirit of Iranian cooking I recommend using what you have on hand, but give curly parsley a second chance!

SUMMER SAVORY—*MARZEH* Summer savory adds an earthy sharp note to the meatball mix for Koofteh Tabrizi (page 282) or the stuffing for Dolmeh Barg (page 265). It is sweeter and milder in flavor than winter savory. Fresh summer savory can be found during the summer months at Iranian markets and occasionally at farmers' markets. Dried summer savory is available year-round at most supermarkets.

TARRAGON—*TARKHOON* Tarragon adds a lively, sharp, and assertive note to a shallot dip like Maast-o Musir (page 44) or an eggplant frittata like Varagheh (page 204). It's one of my favorites to have on hand to liven up a dish.

Spice Cupboard Ingredients

ALLSPICE Allspice is not a traditional Persian spice. But its fragrant scent and flavor, with hints of cloves, cinnamon, and nutmeg, are welcome additions to any number of Iranian stews, meat mixes, and pickles. Contrary to its name, allspice is not a combination of various spices, but the dried berry of a tree in the myrtle family (botanical name *Pimenta dioica*). I like to use ground allspice in stews, sauces, and meat mixtures, and allspice berries as part of my Advieh Torshi spice mix (page 68).

CARDAMOM (GREEN)—*HEL* The scent of cardamom fills me with warmth and comfort. Another fragrant and warming spice, cardamom is used equally in savory and sweet dishes. I mostly use ground cardamom for the recipes in this book, and I add whole pods to perfume a cup of tea or use them in Shir Berenj—Persian Rice Pudding (page 338).

CINNAMON—*DARCHEEN* We most often associate cinnamon with sweet dishes, but in Persian food, ground cinnamon is most frequently used in savory foods for its warmth and sweet perfume. Like turmeric, cinnamon is a go-to flavoring in the Iranian spice cupboard.

CUMIN—*ZEEREH* I use warming and fragrant ground cumin to flavor stews, soups, and mixed rice dishes. You can also scatter cumin seeds in between layers of rice while steaming to elevate a simple platter of rice.

NIGELLA SEEDS—*SIAH DANEH* Siah daneh is often mislabeled as "caraway seeds," in fact, it is the nigella seed. Siah daneh is sprinkled on flatbreads such as Naan-e Barbari—Barbari Bread (page 180) and is most often used as part of the spice mix in Advieh Torshi (page 68).

PERSIAN HOGWEED—*GOLPAR* Golpar is often mislabeled as "angelica." Its botanical name is *Heracleum persicum*, and it is sometimes referred to as Persian hogweed, which sounds like a magical herb from a children's fantasy book. We'll just stick to calling it golpar, which translates to "flower feather." Golpar is a plant native to the mountainous regions of Iran. Its seeds are ground to a powder and used frequently in stews, soups, and pickles, and sprinkled on fava beans, pomegranates, and other fruits, along with a sprinkling of salt. A bowl of pomegranate seeds sprinkled with golpar is one of my favorite snacks to curl up with in the wintertime. Golpar has a very distinct, sharp scent, and a deep citrusy taste reminiscent of coriander seeds. Currently, golpar can only be found in Iranian markets and thankfully online. Symbolically, golpar is said to ward off the evil eye.

SUMAC—*SOMAGH* Crimson in color, bright and tart in taste, sumac, ground from the sumac berry, adds a fresh and sharp note when sprinkled on meats, seafood, and vegetables. At the *haft seen* table (the decorative Nowruz—Persian New Year—table) sumac symbolizes the color of sunrise—a new day.

TURMERIC—*ZARDCHOOBEH* Ground turmeric is the workhorse of spices when it comes to Persian food. It is used in almost all savory dishes to impart a deep, musky flavor and a bright yellow hue. Fresh turmeric can also be used. In our kitchen, we mostly use the more accessible dried powder. Recently turmeric and its healing properties have gained superstar status, but it should be mentioned that like all spices, a little goes a long way. Too much turmeric can turn a stew or *aash* bitter and unpalatable.

Pantry Staples

ALMOND FLOUR—*ARDEH BADAM* Almond flour, finely ground from skinned (blanched) raw almonds, is used in baked goods. Make sure you purchase almond flour and not almond meal, which is made from almonds ground with their skins on and is coarser in texture. Almond flour is available at most grocery stores and online.

BARBERRIES—*ZERESHK* My daughter Luna calls barberries "little red balloons." They are tiny, oval, crimson, dried berries with a stem, and they grow on shrubs. These little red balloons add a lovely sharp, tart flavor scattered between ivory grains of rice or mixed with dried fruits as a stuffing for meatballs. They are one of my favorite ingredients in the Persian kitchen both for their burst of flavor and pop of color. Barberries can also be juiced and served as a *sharbat* (a refreshing Iranian drink), and they are also turned into jams. Barberries, like memories, first need to be sorted through. Scatter them on a plate as you would dried legumes, and with a discerning eye pick out the older, shriveled, and darker-looking ones. Hang on to the bright crimson ones. If you come across a small stone, pebble, or something of the sort, give those the boot as well. While you're at it remove the little stems, too. Next give the zereshk a bath. Place them in a bowl and fill with cold water. Let them sit and soak for about fifteen minutes, as the ruby-red jewels rehydrate, plump up, and rise to the top while the sand settles to the bottom. Reach in and gently lift up the barberries (you can use your hands or a small mesh strainer for this) without disturbing the sand that has settled on the bottom. Place the barberries in a strainer, give a quick rinse, and set aside to drain. Barberries burn very quickly and turn bitter so they only need a very quick sauté in butter, maybe with a little sprinkling of sugar to balance their tart bite, over low heat. Barberries can be found online and at Iranian and Middle Eastern grocers. But I predict we will be seeing ruby-red zereshk popping up at more conventional stores very soon.

BARLEY, BULGUR, AND FARRO—*JO, BALGHOOR* A variety of wheat grains are commonly used in soups and *aash* to thicken, flavor, and add body. Typically barley (which is part of the grass family) and bulgur wheat are used. I also love Italian farro. You can purchase hulled, semi-pearled, and pearled barley. Hulled barley is barley in its whole-grain form, which is chewier and requires soaking and a longer cooking time. Semi-pearled barley and pearled barley don't require soaking and cook faster. Choose what works best for you. Bulgur is a cracked wheat that has been parboiled and dried. Bulgur wheat has a nutty flavor and comes in different grinds or sizes: fine, medium, coarse, and extra coarse. For flavoring, texture, and thickening aash I use either a medium or coarse grind. Farro is a grain favored in Italian kitchens for its chewy texture and nutty flavor. I sub in farro for bulgur in aash and prepare it like a rice dish in my Cabbage Farro (page 132). Farro is usually sold pearled and doesn't require soaking. Barley, bulgur, and farro can be found online and at most grocery stores, Middle Eastern markets, and Mediterranean markets.

BUTTER—*KAREH* I use unsalted butter for all the recipes in this book. I also like to use clarified butter for some of the sweets and for making *tahdig*. It's very simple to clarify butter and it keeps in the fridge or the freezer for months, so it's well worth making a big batch. You can also use ghee, which is butter that has been clarified for a longer time, until the solids brown. Ghee has a stronger, richer, nuttier taste. I prefer the more delicate taste of clarified butter. Use whichever you prefer.

DRIED FRUITS—*MIVEH KHOSHK* In the spirit of preserving the bounty of spring and summer, dried fruits, like nuts, occupy valuable real estate in a Persian pantry. We love to mix them with dried nuts and snack on a variety of dried fruits, such as apricots, prunes, peaches, and apples, just to name a few. Dried fruits are also frequently used in stews, *aash*, rice dishes, and meatball stuffing for texture, a blend of the sweet and sour, and a hint of summer. One of our favorites, and a prized school-lunch snack, is dried mulberries. These sweet, soft treats resemble small blackberries in shape and are called *toot* in Persian. Dried mulberries are becoming more widely available at specialty stores and can always be found at Iranian markets and online. Give the package a squeeze and make sure the mulberries are nice and soft.

LEGUMES—*HOBOOBAT* Beans of all shapes and colors are used in the Persian kitchen to add texture and flavor and to fill out stews, soups, *aash*, and dips. Beans cooked from scratch are tastier than the canned variety and their cooking water (broth) provides plenty of flavor and body. Beans are so frequently used in Persian cooking that it is more economical to purchase them dried. But if pressed for time, canned beans (drained and rinsed) can be substituted. Most of the recipes in this book use dried beans and amounts of water and cooking times are specific to dried. Adjust the liquid if using canned. When cooking beans from scratch, you want to cook them long enough so they soften and completely cook through without falling apart. In some instances, I like to parcook the beans separately and add them to the dish halfway through so I can control their cooking time and texture. I store my dried beans in glass jars sprinkled with a little salt to keep out humidity and pesky bugs. Pick through the beans and remove any small stones and such before soaking or cooking. Lately, there has been a debate questioning the merits of soaking dried beans. Personally, I still prefer to soak most dried beans. I have tried cooking dried beans without soaking and was disappointed, as it took much longer and caused digestive issues—a major concern in the Persian kitchen. Throw out any older beans that rise to the top while soaking. If you, like me, have the best intentions in mind but are not always on top of everything and forget to soak your beans you can also try the quick-cheat soak: cover beans with boiling water and soak for one to two hours.

NUTS—*AJEEL* Nuts of all varieties are a cornerstone of Iranian life. In Iran you will find dedicated nut stores, with beautifully packaged mixed nuts in boxes or sold in bulk. They are eaten raw or roasted depending on the occasion. Raw, unsalted nuts, such as almonds and pistachios, are also mixed in or used to garnish rice dishes and stews. It is very common to find a bowl of mixed nuts always present at a Persian home.

OLIVE OIL—*ROGHAN ZEYTOON* The oil of choice in my pantry and throughout this book is extra-virgin olive oil. It's cozied up right next to the saltcellar and my saffron jar. I don't spend a fortune on fancy bottles for everyday cooking but will splurge a little more on a small bottle to use for drizzling on finished dishes and in dressings.

RICE—*BERENJ* Rice is the crown jewel of Persian food. The rice paddies of northern Iran produce the country's staple grain. Iranian rice is distinguished by its long grains and fragrance. Iranian rice is not readily available in the West, but a good-quality Indian basmati rice is a great substitute. I use both white basmati rice and brown basmati rice depending on the collective family mood and the particular dish. For soups, *aash*, and Koofteh Tabrizi (page 282) I like to use jasmine rice. The starches of rice add flavor and thicken soups and aash and help bind *koofteh*. Look for good-quality and fragrant basmati rice online and at Iranian, Middle Eastern, and Indian markets.

RICE FLOUR—*ARDEH BERENJ* Rice flour is commonly used in Persian cuisine to thicken soups or stews, as a pudding, and in baked goods. Rice flour is available online, at most grocery stores, and Iranian and Middle Eastern markets.

ROSE WATER AND ORANGE BLOSSOM WATER—*GOLAAB, ARAGH-E BAHAR NARENJ*
Flower waters (essences) are used as frequently in Persian baked goods as vanilla extract is used in the West. Floral waters are also used to scent and flavor drinks—*sharbat*—teas, and savory dishes. Intensely fragrant and potent, both rose water and orange blossom water should be used with a delicate touch. Flower waters should never be cooked at high heat as they will burn, turning bitter, and their aroma will dissipate. Add flower waters to cooked foods right at the very end, give a quick stir, and take off the heat. Rose water is made from distilling the steam of rose petals simmered in water. Orange blossom water is distilled from orange blossoms, the flowers of the Seville orange. Rose water, the symbol of love, is also used medicinally and left out in small decanters to purify the air. Rose water and orange blossom water can be purchased online and from most grocery stores, and from Iranian, Middle Eastern, and Mediterranean markets. Make sure you purchase food-grade floral waters, and when you twist open the top you should be swept away by the scent of love and a blooming Persian garden. If not, it's time to change brands, as some brands dilute (kill) the floral essence with the addition of too much water. Currently my preferred brand is Cortas. Flower waters should be stored in the fridge once opened.

PICKLES—*TORSHI* In keeping with the Iranian love affair with all things tangy, the Persian pantry boasts a plethora of pickled goods, ready to be served alongside just about any meal. Ranging from tangy pickled cucumbers to sweet, melt-in-your-mouth garlic—*seer torshi*—that has been pickled for up to ten years! In this book, I offer a homemade recipe for Torshi Liteh—Eggplant and Herb Pickles (page 68). It's also well worth perusing the shelves of Iranian, Middle Eastern, and Mediterranean markets, and the international food aisle of your local grocery store and looking online to add some new jars of pickled goods to brighten up your daily meals.

Online Sources for Iranian Ingredients

Amazon.com	Ofdusa.com	Mountainroseherbs.com
Sadaf.com	Kalamala.com	Sahadis.com
Persianbasket.com	Kalustyans.com	

فروشگاه تهران

1417

TEHRAN MARKET

PARKING FOR
TEHRAN
MARKET
ONLY
ALL OTHERS WILL BE
TOWED AT OWNERS
EXPENSE
YOU MAY BE CITED

PARKING FOR
TEHRAN
MARKET
ONLY
ALL OTHERS WILL BE
TOWED AT OWNERS
EXPENSE
YOU MAY BE CITED

ACKNOWLEDGMENTS

It takes a village to gently simmer, stir, and bring a book to life. I am forever grateful for and indebted to my village that spans seas and oceans. This book exists solely because of your love, support, and encouragement. Thank you all from the bottom of my heart and the bottom of my pot.

To Steve Troha and Dado Derviskadic, my superstar secret agents. None of this would have happened were it not for your patient persistence, invaluable guidance, and warm friendship. Thank you for holding my hand every step of the way, and for offering a shoulder and a laugh when I needed it the most.

To the entire team at Flatiron Books and Macmillan, for believing in these stories and recipes from day one. To my editor, Kara Rota, for your immeasurable wisdom and calm and positive perspective. I couldn't have asked for a more thoughtful and gracious partner on this journey. To Will Schwalbe, for all your kind words, astute foresight, and support. To Bryn Clark, for enduring my repeated technical questions and patiently guiding me through it. Sincere thanks to Michelle McMillian, designer Rita Sowins, production editor Emily Walters, copyeditor Jenna Nelson, Kimberly Escobar, Nancy Trypuc, and Molly Fonseca.

To Eric Wolfinger, for shining your light and magic on every single frame of this book with charm and ease. You instinctively knew what I was looking for before I did and you flip a mean *tahdig*! Also, thank you for putting together such an amazing creative team: To the inspired and beautiful food styling of Valerie Aikman Smith, and her lovely assistant Sandra Tripicchio. Thank you both for your talent and tireless efforts. To Alma Espinola, for your keen eye and relentless attention to detail in picking out just the right props. My afternoon teatime is not the same without you! To Connor Bruce, for covering all bases with a smile.

To my mentor and wickedly wise and funny friend, Cheryl Sternman Rule. Thank you for patiently listening and counseling me through every step of this incredible book-writing journey. To lovely Maureen Abood, for all your generosity and helpful advice. To the always inspiring Aglaia Kremezi, for your continued support and kind words.

To Chefs Hoss Zare and Hanif Sadr, for sharing your talent and passion. To Fariba

Nafissi, for all your lovely words from the early days of my blog and for inviting me into your kitchen and sharing your art and your *gata* bread with me.

A heartfelt thanks to all the readers of my blog. And to our Persian food bloggers group, I'm so happy to have found such a supportive community.

To all my dear friends who gently but assertively encouraged me to bring these recipes and stories out of the recesses of my mind and onto the page: Vajdon Sohaili, Krista Tucker, Amanda Wilkins, Thom Vernon, and Rozana Alam. And to Oliver Jones, for reading endless drafts and for your smart and poignant notes and observations.

To my L.A.-based family, for having my back and constantly checking in, and feeding me with encouragement and provisions when I was out of words and supplies: Lisa Clifton, Heather Shannon, Keith Dietz, Kahlil Sabbagh, Ginger Smith, Chris Flanders, Oscar Romero, and Allison Wood. With a very special thank-you to Martha Romero for your artistry and for putting me together for this book.

To my lifelong Vancouver friends who have picked me up through the lows and been my biggest cheerleaders through the highs: Jennifer McLean, who can turn my day around with a single text; Paul Norman, Kendall Cross, Hans Bergstrom, Sophie Yendole, Cam Cronin, Peter Eastwood, Gail Johnson, Erin Jeffery, Martin Lowe, Kim Mankey, and Rhys Lloyd. You all have my heart.

A huge thank-you to all my family and friends who relentlessly recipe tested and sent back detailed notes and photographs. You all have my infinite gratitude.

My deepest gratitude to all the moms and dads who had my girls over countless times just so I could get a few more hours to write: Sarah Whitney, Oliver Jones, Amy Washburn, Jenifer Kinnear, and Martha and Oscar Romero.

To Manu Chao for seeing me through the cooking, Tom Waits for seeing me through the writing, and NPR and KCRW for seeing me through the madness.

To Tehran Market in Santa Monica, for keeping my pantry and spice cupboard well supplied.

To Mrs. Kiaii, for inspiring so many of the Gilaki recipes; your *fesenjan* is insurmountable. To Mercedeh Kiaii, for your love and friendship. And to my late childhood friend Sepideh Kiaii, who shared my love for gathering around the *sofreh* with great food, music, friends, and family. I miss you.

To my gracious and elegant friend Shiva, who is like a sister to me and one of the best cooks I know. Thank you for sharing your *shir berenj* recipe with me.

To the best in-laws I could ever ask for, who have wholeheartedly embraced a love for *tahdig* and Persian food. To the New Hampshire clan: Steve, Cindy, Jane, and Mike. To my lovely sister-in-law Sarah. To my always charming and supportive father-in-law, Dr. Bob. To my amazing mother-in-law, Susan, for patiently listening to these stories over and over again at the eleventh hour and giving me the final push and encouragement to finish it.

To my family, near and far, all of whom graciously shared their recipes, stories, and memories. This book is for you. To my Deravian cousins: Fahimeh, Fattaneh, Shouka, and Laleh. To my Taha family: Zarin, Farin, and Roohi Jan. To my Daee, thank you for letting me cook for you and test recipes on you those early years in L.A. And to my late aunt Dixie—my biggest cheerleader, you are dearly missed.

To my nephew Jordan, for loving my fesenjan. To my beautiful sister-in-law Teresa, for always offering to read through a draft, and keeping me nourished with your *brodo*.

To my brother, Ramin, for holding my hand through thick and thin, from Tehran to Rome and beyond. Thank you for always picking up the phone and coming to my rescue, big and small. You inspire me every day.

To my stepmother, Kumi, you have always been tenacious in your support and belief in me, and your strength and positivity are a constant inspiration. Thank you for all your love.

To Baba, your love is limitless and your generosity vast. Thank you for always having a song ready at the dinner table and for keeping us laughing through it all. *Ti amo da morire.*

To Maman, there would be no book were it not for you. Our daily phone conversations, reading each and every draft, pushing me to never compromise. Thank you for the poetry, the music, and all the platters of *loobia polo* that have filled my heart with love.

To my girls, Luna and Soleil. For constantly reminding me that I could do it, and for the endless supply of hugs, kisses, snacks, and drinks. I love you both immensely. Beyond the universe and back.

And finally, to Drew. You never once wavered in your belief in me or this book, even when I did. You sacrificed weekends, anniversaries, and birthdays just so I could get in a few more words. Thank you for loving Persian food maybe even more than I do. This book wouldn't exist without you. Thank you for holding me up.

INDEX

"In her debut cookbook, *Bottom of the Pot*, Naz Deravian brings us right to her table, and to all the tables that have informed hers. Every bit of writing and each recipe is a poem, each photograph so tempting. I am so taken by this book and am reminded of what made me fall in love with cookbooks in the first place: they teach us about the world outside our own walls, introduce us to people we might not otherwise know, and invite us to make new memories and traditions in our own kitchens. In this way, cookbooks are the most hospitable political tool I know. They don't build walls; they elongate tables. Thank you, Naz, for this beautiful book, which I already cherish."

—JULIA TURSHEN, author of *Now & Again*, *Feed the Resistance*, and *Small Victories*

"Like Madhur Jaffrey and Marcella Hazan before her, Naz Deravian will introduce the pleasures and secrets of her mother culture's cooking to a broad audience that has no idea what it's been missing. America will not only fall in love with Persian cooking; it'll fall in love with Naz."

—SAMIN NOSRAT, author of *Salt, Fat, Acid, Heat*

"Colors, aromas, and stories seduce and transport the reader to a world of food that is simply irresistible! Naz Deravian, a passionate home cook, created this brilliant collection of easy-to-follow recipes from her native Persian cuisine—the mother of urban Eastern Mediterranean cooking. The author's personality permeates the book as she complements the recipes with family narratives and traditional tales. She describes appetizers as 'music and poetry,' soups as 'heart,' and *khoresh*—the long-simmered, jamlike stews—as 'the soul.' Rice dishes, with their crunchy *tahdig*, are the 'jewels' of Persian cooking, and the ever-present *naan* (breads) are, of course, 'life;' *kookoo*—my favorite frittata-like, egg-and-vegetable dishes—are 'the light.' And we mustn't forget 'love,' the well-chosen, simple desserts. With easy to find ingredients and wonderful spice and herb combinations every dish becomes a new adventure: 'Follow the recipe for the first time,' the author advises, 'then relax, throw it all away, play, and, make it your own.' The book's beautiful pictures and clear instructions on what to precook and how to store—most dishes are better the next day—or freeze, inspire everybody to get into the kitchen and re-create these tantalizing, age-old savory and sweet dishes."

—AGLAIA KREMEZI, author of *Mediterranean Vegetarian Feasts*

"With seductive, 'Must make it now!' recipes and gorgeous lyrical prose, Naz beautifully captures the saffron-scented allure of Persian cooking, creating a rich, multilayered evocation of an entire culture at table. Whether you want to master the delicate fragrant Persian pilafs or just savor the heartrending family stories of exile and longing, every page of *Bottom of the Pot* is full of rewards. This is one of those rare books that both captures the culinary zeitgeist and transports you to an exotic world you don't want to leave."

—ANYA VON BREMZEN, author of *Mastering the Art of Soviet Cooking* and *Paladares*

"An easy access to a sophisticated cuisine. Delicious homemade gourmet food. Just follow the instructions, uncork the wine, and get ready for a royal feast."

—SHOHREH AGHDASHLOO, Emmy Award winner

"In *Bottom of the Pot*, Naz Deravian has crafted a superb cookbook that combines cultural and family history with mouthwatering recipes to create a full and rich portrait of Persian cuisine. Personal memories weaved into each made-from-scratch Persian dish evoke a strong sense of place and bring alive the senses. This is a must-have cookbook that breaks down barriers by introducing readers to a colorful and vibrant cuisine and gives well-crafted advice to those already familiar with this beautiful tapestry of dishes. More than just a cookbook, its stories and recipes nourish and soothe, celebrate and unite. I will be giving *Bottom of the Pot* to my friends and family for years to come!"

—MARJAN KAMALI, author of *Together Tea*

"This beautiful book tells the story of the Iranian diaspora through recipes ranging from breathtaking feats of culinary mastery to humble, everyday family meals. What an absolute pleasure to join Deravian on this sweet and tender journey; her warmth and Persian hospitality shine through the page, inviting you in like family to her dinner table."

—LOUISA SHAFIA, author of *The New Persian Kitchen* and *Lucid Food*

"From cover to cover of her beautiful book, Naz invites us into the intoxicating embrace of Persian American cooking. Her stories are as charming and welcoming as her recipes, gently wafting into our own kitchens with the promise of aromatic flavors we can't wait to experience. The procession of ingredients—from saffron and fresh herbs to rose petals and cool yogurt—is dazzling, and I feel completely at ease under Naz's guiding hand to explore them all. The bottom of my own pot will happily never be the same!"

—MAUREEN ABOOD, author of *Rose Water & Orange Blossoms*

"For Persians anytime (ancient and modern) and anywhere (east and west), food is the *music of love*, in every pot, top to bottom, where Naz Deravian sings its rhythms in every rice kernel, pomegranate seed, and rose petal. Breathe deep and sing along."

—BETTY FUSSELL, author of *Eat, Live, Love, Die*

"This book is written with love and filled with beautiful recipes that will take you straight to the heart of Naz's Persian kitchen."

—MEERA SODHA, author of *Made in India* and *Fresh India*